Fet

THE AFRICAN

AMERICAN

BARDIC POET

FROM SLAVERY

TO CIVIL RIGHTS

Fettered
Genius

Keith D. Leonard

University of Virginia Press
CHARLOTTESVILLE AND LONDON

University of Virginia Press
© 2006 by the Rector and Visitors of the University of Virginia
All rights reserved
Printed in the United States of America on acid-free paper
First published 2006

9 8 7 6 5 4 3 2 1

Library of Congress Cataloging-in-Publication Data

Leonard, Keith D., 1969–
    Fettered genius : the African American bardic poet from slavery to civil rights /
Keith D. Leonard.
        p.   cm.
    Includes bibliographical references and index.
    ISBN 0-8139-2505-3 (acid-free paper) — ISBN 0-8139-2506-1 (pbk. : acid-free
paper)
    1. American poetry—African American authors—History and criticism.
2. African Americans—Intellectual life. 3. Civil rights movements in literature.
4. Antislavery movements in literature. 5. Bards and bardism in literature.
6. African Americans in literature. 7. Race relations in literature. 8. Slavery in
literature. 9. Racism in literature. 10. Race in literature. I. Title.
PS310.N4L6 2006
811.009'896073—dc22

                                                        2005014853

Contents

This conversation about the political meaning of African American aesthetic practice started long before I even thought about being a professional academic. I am honored to be joining Houston Baker, Henry Louis Gates Jr., Hazel Carby, Paul Gilroy, bell hooks, Cornel West, Fahamisha Patricia Brown, Aldon Lynn Nielsen, Lorenzo Thomas, and Meta DuWa Jones in understanding and validating the African American expressive tradition.

And it all began with Edward and Ernestine Leonard, without whom I would quite literally be nothing. I attribute all that is of value in this book to the commitment to doing the best work possible and to the ethics of fairness, acceptance, and sympathy that I learned from them. Earl, Kevin, Andrea: growing up with you let me know what it meant to stand on my own two feet. Thanks for always pushing me. Thanks to Christian Pitter for so many of those conversations that helped me to clarify my thinking. And thanks for the wonderful last sentence. To Meta Jones, thanks for your inspiring energy, stunning intellect, and our mutually supportive work in the study of African American poetry. And I would like to give a big tip to the servers at Tryst Café in Washington, DC, for their nourishing contributions to this project.

Finally, I would like to acknowledge the following people and institutions for allowing me to use the material quoted in this book. Thanks to Maia Patillo and Melvin B. Tolson Jr. for their permission to reprint excerpts from the poetry of Robert Hayden and Melvin B. Tolson, respectively. Selections from *The Poems of Phillis Wheatley,* edited and with an introduction by Julian D. Mason Jr., copyright © 1966 by the University of North Carolina Press, renewed 1989, used by permission of the publisher. Selections from *The Black Bard of North Carolina: George Moses Horton and His Poetry,* edited by Joan Sherman, copyright © 1997 by the University of North Carolina Press, used by permission of the publisher. Selections from *Lyrics of Lowly Life* by Paul Laurence Dunbar, copyright © 1984 Citadel Press, all rights reserved, reprinted by arrangement with Kensington Publishing Corp., www.kensingtonbooks.com. Excerpt from "Preface" by James Weldon Johnson in *The Book of American Negro Poetry,* copyright © 1931, 1922 by Harcourt, Inc., and renewed 1959, 1950 by Mrs. Grace Nail Johnson. Excerpts from "Heritage" and "Yet Do I Marvel" by Countee Cullen reprinted by permission of GRM Associates, agents of the estate of Ida M. Cullen, from the book *Color* by Countee Cullen, copyright © 1925 by Harper and Brothers, copyright renewed 1953 by Ida M. Cullen. Excerpts from "If We Must Die" and "To the White Fiends" by Claude McKay used courtesy of the Literary Representative for the Works of Claude McKay, Schomburg Center for Research in Black Culture, The New York Public Library, Astor, Lenox and Tilden Foundations. Selections from *Selected Poems* by Sterling Brown reprinted by permission of John L. Dennis. Selections from *The Collected Poems of Langston Hughes* by Langston Hughes, copyright © 1994 by The Estate of Langston Hughes, used by permission of Alfred A. Knopf, a division of Random House, Inc. (Permission for the United Kingdom and the Commonwealth granted by Harold Ober Associates.) Excerpts from "Stillicho Spikes" and "The Underdog" reprinted from *A Gallery of Harlem Portraits* by Melvin B. Tolson, edited by Robert Farnsworth, by permission of the University of Missouri Press, copyright © 1979 by the Curators of the University of Missouri. "A Ballad of Remembrance" copyright © by Robert Hayden; "Richard Hunt's 'Arachne'" and "The Night-Blooming Cereus" copyright © 1972 by Robert Hayden; "The Peacock Room," "For a Young Artist," "Two Egyptian Portrait Masks," "El-Hajj Malik El-Shabazz," "Words in the Mourning Time," and "Middle Passage" copyright © 1962, 1966 by Robert Hayden, from *Collected Poems of Robert Hayden* by Robert Hayden, edited by Frederick Glaysher, copyright © 1985 by Emma Hayden; used by permission of Liveright Publishing Corporation. "To Mary Church Terrell—Lecturer" and "The Heart of a Woman" from the *Selected Works of Georgia Douglass Johnson* by Georgia Douglass Johnson, copyright © 1997 by G. K. Hall, reprinted by permission of The Gale Group. All Brooks selections reprinted by consent of Brooks Permissions.

Fettered Genius

Introduction

Yet do I marvel at this curious thing:
To make a poet black, and bid him sing!

—Countee Cullen, "Yet Do I Marvel"

y first encounter with the remarkable political agency of what I am calling the African American poet's "fettered genius" was in my junior year of college. That year, in an African American poetry course, I read a review of Pulitzer Prize–winning poet Gwendolyn Brooks that broke my heart. In a review called "Pity the Giant," excerpts of which were included on the back cover of Brooks's *Selected Poems* (1963), critic Harvey Curtis Webster claimed that, since Brooks had mastered the poetic conventions of the British tradition and had applied them to African American experience and culture, her central genius was constituted by the fact that, while she "accept[s] Negroness as prizeable differentiation and a dilemma," she also "refuses to let Negroness limit her humanity." I still remember the sinking feeling of rage and confusion that I felt when I realized that Webster's review was being used to market Brooks's book, as if his terms were unmitigated praise. To be fair, Webster did not mean to suggest that being black was a limitation to being human. Instead, he meant to identify and celebrate a true distinction of Brooks's genius: her capacity to articulate through the representation of social and cultural difference the shared values, ideals, and experiences usually defined as "human" or "universal" in literature. He thus meant to characterize the paradoxical use and affirmation of ethnic culture as the means to reject racist conceptions of absolute biological difference and inferiority. And he meant to suggest that her virtuoso use of traditional poetic forms worked better than the didacticism and complaint of other African American poets for expressing this broad-minded vision of shared humanity. Had he said this, he would

have been absolutely right. But what he said was that "Negroness" *limited* humanity, a racist implication indeed. And this implication that black people who claimed their heritage were somehow not fully human distracted me from the genuine literary insights Webster had to offer. The review still breaks my heart.

But, oddly enough, critics since Webster—even those of African American descent—have not done much better in dealing with the complexities of the relationship in traditional poetic form between African American ethnic difference and shared humanity. For example, Houston Baker is only partly right in his provocative conception of Brooks's artistry as "white style and black content—two warring ideals in one dark body" ("Achievement of Gwendolyn Brooks," 21). Clearly, Brooks's verse does operate more from this tension between African American and Anglo-American traditions than from Webster's premise that blackness limits humanity. As Baker suggests, Brooks's virtuosity "exceeds" the "white framework" associated with her choice of traditional poetic forms and conventions because she uses those "white" forms to illuminate ethnic culture. Thus, her work is not as alienated from black culture as Webster and some African American critics have suggested, nor is it hermetic in its affirmation of ethnicity. As Baker concludes, Brooks's work inhabits a space between cultural worlds that prevents her from being fully appreciated in either. But even as he recognizes this aesthetically productive and politically provocative middle ground, Baker still accepts the premise that the forms of the Anglo-American tradition are almost exclusively the cultural province of white people and that all a black person can do with those forms is to insert black cultural content. Neither the form nor the content changes; they can only conflict. As Baker put it in *Modernism and the Harlem Renaissance,* such forms are mastered "masks" with which black people cover their true selves in order to protect themselves and to manipulate white people. Scholars other than Baker have identified this middle ground, but, as in Baker's case, that space often disappears from their theories in favor of implicitly or explicitly affirming black folk culture as the only true source of African American identity. Though not nearly as troubling as Webster's opposition, Baker's flawed dialectic fails to capture how fully Brooks's verse— and that of the major African American formalists like her—rewrote both "white" and "black" frameworks. In effect, then, many contemporary critics, like Baker, have in the interest of antiracist ethnic self-definition reinforced the logic of Webster's review.

And this logic continues to disturb me, because it is more than an isolated matter of semantics or a simple issue of ineffective close reading. It is not that people are using politically incorrect language or overlooking facets of the poem, in other words. Rather, the fundamental logic of these dueling oppositions is a symptom of the subtly overwhelming power of divisive racial ideologies that consistently and in myriad ways reiterate the notion that ethnic difference is absolute. Those ideologies therefore prevent us from appreciating fully how African American poets adapted traditional poetics and ethnic culture to one another in ways that rejected those oppressive ideologies and their binary logic, a practice that constitutes the central beauty of this verse. Whether in Baker's brilliant and influential affirmation or in Webster's distorting lens of the allegedly universal, this long-standing opposition validates Harlem Renaissance poet Countee Cullen's apt conclusion in his 1925 poem "Yet Do I Marvel" that the marvel of the African American poet—especially the poet of traditional tastes such as Cullen—was the fact that he or she was able to write at all. On the one hand, from the time of slavery until the Civil Rights Movement, most African Americans were deprived by a slaveholding and then a segregationist society of the material resources necessary for sustenance, let alone for writing and publishing poetry. Those privileged enough to have those resources—education, leisure time, money for pencils and paper—were expected to protest these conditions, though such protests were not necessarily artistic. They were therefore not considered to be part of the representation of the human. Moreover, such privileged poets were obliged to use the techniques of the Anglo-American literary tradition in order to have their art, and therefore their complaints, taken seriously. But that tradition usually posited African or African American identity as the antithesis to a cultured human identity, effectively incorporating the oppositions of race politics into the binary logic of Western rationalism and empiricism in ways that made "black" people analogous to the evils associated with the color "black." This association was reinforced by cultural practices such as blackface minstrelsy, literary characters such as Robinson Crusoe's Friday, and storylines such as in the novel *Heart of Darkness,* which involves a white man, allegedly an "Everyman," confronting and conquering the worst parts of himself by encountering and conquering symbolic black people. This "cultural strangulation," as Addison Gayle called it, makes this necessary use of traditional poetics a dicey proposition for the African American poet. As Henry Louis Gates put it, how can African Americans posit a "full and sufficient self in a language in which blackness is a sign of absence" (*Signifying Monkey* 169)? Protest could compromise artistic self-definition, and poetic mastery could be construed as cultural self-erasure or a political sellout. Either way, blackness, defined as a political problem rather than a cultural self, does seem opposed to humanity, defined as common experiences and ideals. Many critics then and since have therefore concluded, as Cullen seemed to, that a racially self-affirmed and traditionally artistic "black poet" is a contradiction in terms.

In this book, I pursue a way out of this problem by following Baker's lead into the cultural middle ground of this verse, the liminal cultural space that defies these empowered ideologies. The "black poet" is not a contradiction in terms. The triumph of the African American formalist poetic tradition is the fact that African American poets from slavery to Civil Rights did indeed resolve the oppositions of this binary logic of race politics in their best poems by combining the aesthetic power and social validity of traditional formalist artistry with the complexities of African American experience, culture, and heritage to produce a full and sufficient African American artistic and cultural self. Their art allowed them to inhabit and enact this middle ground, and it did so by transforming the artistic construct and social role of poetic genius—the allegedly nonracial terms of achievement implicit in Webster's acclaim for Brooks's virtuosity—into an ideal version of that ethnic self. Instead of wholeheartedly accepting mainstream literary terms at the expense of his or her own cultural identity, the African American traditionalist poet effectively made traditional literary culture and racial identity into extricable aspects of one another in formalist poetic achievement. Instead of protesting at the expense of artistry, these poets made artistry itself into protest. Formalists such as Cullen lent traditional artistic credence to the representation of an affirming racial identity in art—something often dismissed as "propaganda" in the early years of the tradition—by making it "classical." At the same time, their poetry posited the traditional Western poet's pursuit of individual artistic distinction as a microcosm of the African American communal pursuit of cultural self-determination. This dialectical process affirmed a hybrid African American self as the cultural means by which the poet could transform racial difference into the paradoxical embodiment of shared humanity. This construction of the poetic self resisted the worst implications of cultural strangulation by synthesizing allegedly opposed aspects of American culture—the European and the African diasporic culture—into one aesthetically coherent self. While I acknowledge the difficulties of self-definition that cause Cullen and most critics such anxiety, I conclude that, rather than being entirely strangled, the African American self was constructed and subtly affirmed by traditional poetic artistry. Therefore, formalist poetics enacted an underappreciated cultural agency, a subversive rewriting of mainstream culture through assimilation of that culture.

In the following pages, I characterize the historical conditions and artistic practices that produced this often ambivalent "fettered genius" as it changed over time and as it attributed to African American formalist verse its misunderstood antiracist agency of cultural self-definition. This literary-historical perspective refutes the logic of Webster's review and some of the most fundamental pieties of African American literary study, including the almost exclusive emphasis on the vernacular and the models of political meaning predicated strictly on direct opposition. I trace this practice from eighteenth-century slave poet Phillis Wheatley's use of neoclassical poetics to write herself quite literally into citizenship to nineteenth-century dialect poet Paul Laurence Dunbar's use of romantic genius to expand and articulate a poetics of racial uplift that made African American self-definition heroic. This commitment to individuality and achievement evolved into the emerging commitment to formal innovation as self-conscious ethnic self-definition among the diverse poets of the Harlem Renaissance and then into the full fruition of this formalist practice in the formally innovative work of mid-twentieth-century poets Gwendolyn Brooks, Robert Hayden, and Melvin B. Tolson. In this evolution, each of these moments in African American literary culture added a facet to the antiracist social functioning of fettered genius, from cultural assimilation as resistance to romantic genius as ethnic affirmation and from that validation of individual selfhood to existential self-definition as communal cultural self-determination. Throughout this history, these poets represented the internal lives and individuality of African American people as spaces of cultural crossover and sites of conflict. African American cultural self-definition created a paradoxical blending of cultures that provisionally rewrote the oppressive discourses of the oppressive mainstream culture it assimilated. In each case, the poetic persona exemplified the idea that the relationship between consciousness and cultural form was an analogy for the relationship between the human and the ethnic. These terms clarify more fully than existing theories of African American literary culture how this body of formalist poetry constitutes a component of a larger ethnic expressive tradition. So while there are substantive limitations on this mode of formalist poetic agency, I insist that there is a subversive character to poetic mastery that makes it an act of self-defining resistance and that implies alternative terms for understanding the African American ethnic self in art.

This paradoxical ethnic self-definition through cultural assimilation and the poets who pursued it constitute what I call "fettered genius." The term refers to the ideal of distinctive creativity and the social and cultural forces by which that ideal gets constructed and then attributed to a given poet. It also emphasizes the intellectual fetters that traditional racial ideology locks onto our conception of African American artistry. Turning to a postcolonial framework rather than the traditional oppositional terms of identity politics in African American cultural studies, I demonstrate through this metaphor how the interaction of cultural discourses—including traditional aesthetics and African American experience—interact on the body of the African American poet and her poetic persona to produce antiracist meaning. The fetters on African American poetic genius were constituted both by the social and cultural forces that made traditional formalism potentially the strangulation that worried Cullen and by the reading strategies then and since that have been so beholden to this binary thinking of race politics. The genius these fetters created, and the genius that resisted or subverted them, was derived from the fundamental notion that the imaginative gifts of the poet and the person who exhibits them are simultaneously distinctive from the common run of humanity and exemplary of that humanity. In these terms, the recognized and celebrated achievements of African American formalist poets was constituted by an intersection of discourses of commonality and difference that challenged both kinds of fetters (Schopenhauer 3). In this context, the African American formalist's claim to this creativity and achievement through mastery of traditional poetics was in fact understood to be both the highest expression of a common human capacity and the fullest cultural realization of his or her excluded and marginalized ethnic community. That social and aesthetic space thereby brought the alleged universals of traditional literary thought into conflict with the assumptions about absolute difference that were central both to white supremacy and to the ethnic affirmation justifiably offered in response. While fettering African American poetry to Eurocentric literary standards, conventional poetic achievement also validated African American identity, making those fetters a contradictory part of a full and sufficient African American self. The construction of this culturally synthesizing and ethnically affirming poetic genius constitutes the central artistic continuity and the defining political significance of the African American formalist poetic tradition.

I offer this conception of the historically changing, antiracist meaning of these literary masteries in order to provide a necessary and complementary alternative to the wonderfully insightful scholarship based on affirming the vernacular in African American literature, work which offers but limited insight into the role and value of traditional literary genius for African American formalists. It obscures the simple premise that "Negroness" *is* humanity. This alternative is necessary because most theorists of African American culture operate under the mandate that Fahamisha Patricia Brown made explicit in *Performing the Word: African American Poetry as Vernacular Practice:* "Although I concede an essential hybridity of African American culture, in this work I explore the specificity of that culture" (4–5). Paul Gilroy characterizes very well the problem with the exclusive emphasis on the specificity of a culture rather than its hybridity:

> Regardless of their affiliation to the right, left or centre, groups have fallen back on the idea of cultural nationalism, on the overintegrated conceptions of culture which present immutable, ethnic differences as an absolute break in the histories and experiences of "black" and "white" people. Against this choice stands another, more difficult option: the theorisation of creolisation, metissage, mestizaje, and hybridity. From the viewpoint of ethnic absolutism, this would be a litany of pollution and impurity. These terms are rather unsatisfactory ways of naming the processes of cultural mutation and restless (dis)continuity that exceed racial discourse and avoid capture by its agents. (2)

This kind of absolutism subtly dominates the study of African American poetry. For example, in his magisterial *Drumvoices: The Mission of African American Poetry,* Eugene Redmond is right to assert that any understanding of African American poetry must start in the richness of the African cultures and the African American folk practices by which African Americans have responded to the situation of exclusion and deprivation in the United States. But Redmond treats the use of formalist culture as the attenuation of the African American self rather than as its hybrid reconstruction or adaptation. Similarly, Stephen Henderson declares in *Understanding the New Black Poetry: Black Speech and Black Music as Poetic Reference* that the defining characteristic of African American poetry lies almost exclusively in a given poem's references to black speech and black music, implying that formalist poetics is not "black." Only Aldon Nielsen, in his recent *Black Chant: The Languages of African American Postmodernism,* recognizes that the formal character of literature and the African American oral voice are not closed and opposed systems of meaning; but since he focuses on the almost entirely neglected African

American avant garde, his work understandably does not illuminate traditional formalism. In the end, studies of African American poetics depend too much upon identifying the political consciousness of individual poets in terms of how fully they embrace African American vernacular culture. This approach does a disservice both to individual poets and, more important, to the nature of aesthetic meaning.

Not only does my alternative mode of analysis break down these false boundaries of authenticity, it also provides better terms for appreciating how the sheer artistry of formalist poets constitutes the means by which this verse revises the social discourses that oppose blackness to humanity. First of all, the concept of fettered genius acknowledges that traditional poetics has as much to do with the construction of racial selfhood—even through assimilation—as does vernacular poetics, especially since the most successful African American poets of these eras combine the two, allowing us to redefine the relationship between aesthetic meaning and political meaning in the representation of African American identity in verse. Understanding the folk roots of African American poetry is crucial, then, but should not be our exclusive focus, and the analysis of traditional poetics should proceed as a means to conceptualize the hybrid nature of the African American cultural self and the sometimes unfortunate mutations it experiences in the face of oppression, including the attempt by blacks to erase difference. Seen as one grand instance in the historical processes of cultural mutation that Gilroy rightly privileges, African American poetic formalism becomes a component of the ongoing and generally affirming practice of cultural adaptation in its antiracist agency of self-definition by which African Americans have survived in the United States. In these terms, traditional poetic form is not merely the direct expression of the oppressive ideology of racist Western cultural norms. Rather, such forms consist of a set of strategies that garner their meaning from the individual uses of individual poets. They can articulate affirming ideals of ethnic selfhood analogous to those expressed by vernacular poets. The difference is in the degree.

The second advantage of this idea of the contradictory antiracist implications of poetic genius, therefore, is a subtler and more appropriate definition of how the formalist tradition and its complex aesthetic effects garners the capacity to challenge inimical discourses of difference. Instead of thinking of the political agency of African American poetry exclusively in terms of protest or explicit ethnic affirmation, as most scholars do, I think of it in terms of how the process of constructing meaning transforms the terms by which that meaning gets constructed. What I have in mind here is analogous to Judith Butler's use of poststructuralist thought to redefine *agency* in the construction of gender identity: "The shift from an *epistemological* account of identity [in which the perspective of the subject is paramount, an idea central to African American literary studies] to one which locates the problematic within practices of signification permits an analysis that takes the epistemological mode itself as one possible and contingent signifying practice. Further, the question of *agency* is reformulated as a question of how signification and resignification work [original emphasis]" (143). Like Butler, I understand agency in "self"-defining cultural production (as in African American formalist poetry) to emerge from processes of signification in language and, more broadly, social construction in culture and history, in which the "I" is inextricably situated and ineluctably in process. And it is this process of producing discursive meaning through active practices of language that constitutes the existence of the self and its capacity to transform the institutional terms that limit its cultural space. I concur with her that, even in the expressive tradition of African American people, "what is signified as an identity is not signified as a given point in time after which it is simply there as an inert piece of entitative language" (145). In fact, I would argue that this conventional idea of static identity is part of the problem, an ideal in African American literary thought that is a consequence of white supremacy more than resistance to it. Not an unchanging, authentic entity, in other words, the poetic and racial identity of the African American formalist poet—like all identity—is signified in each instance of poetic expression and reception and is the product of the contentions in culture that produce that unstable but no-less-real ethnic self. While the poets did not explicitly theorize these notions, their verse enacted it.

This conception and reality of the self in process provides a greater sense of how African American formalist poetics resists white supremacy, both for the poets in their time and for us as critics in our own. Seen as the space of contention enacted by the combined effects of cultural signification that construct the "I" rather than as an authentic preexisting entity, the African American artistic self becomes a complex process of signification that resists any given attempt to fix it and always exceeds or contravenes those attempts, whether racist or essentialist. Analogous to Gates's influential conceptualization of a distinctive African American mode of "signifyin(g)," this version of agency likewise revises standard English conventions with a "black difference," but it is not unique to black people. Instead, African American formalist poetry is a particular historical engagement in this meaning-making function of all language practice, all signifying, enacting the signification of alternative notions of self in and through the racist significations in which it is ensconced. I therefore take to heart Werner Sollors's assertion that "it is not a priori cultural *difference* that makes ethnicity," because ethnicity "is not a thing but a process" (xvi, xv). This interaction of discourses created by the self-constituting of African American ethnicity in general and poetic genius in particular clarifies how cultural mutation is not exclusively cultural assimilation, nor is it at all a political sellout for poet or critic. Assimilation becomes a challenge to certain components of racist ideology, as is well known, but when seen in this mode of "signifyin(g)," the African American self and the use of traditional poetics need not operate under the assumption that Anglo-American culture is superior to and other than African American identity. The fixed oppositions of racism become the complex dynamics of cultural self-knowing, revising the social boundaries of race as biology by attributing difference to cultural heritage. This practice acknowledges how culture and language always resist or subvert those artificially fixed boundaries of race.

In other words, since societies are no more fixed in their constitution than the African American self, African American formalist poetics can function through the fetters of traditional literary culture to construct a poetic genius that not only validates racial experience in conventional terms but also uses those fetters of potentially racist literary standards to resist the limiting discourses of racial ideology. As Stuart Hall observes, the ideological structure of society is as hybrid as this self, constituted as it is by "the web of meanings and discourses, the strings of connotation and their means of representation, within which social practices, consciousness, identities and subjectivities are placed" (Grossberg and Slack 89), becoming subject to what Hall calls "ideological struggle": "A particular ideological chain becomes a site of struggle, not only when people try to displace, rupture or contest it by supplanting it with some wholly new alternative set of terms [as in traditional ideas of Marxist or antiracist activism], but also when they interrupt the ideological field and try to transform its meaning by changing or re-articulating its associations, for example from the negative to the positive" (112). For Hall, the most salient examples of such ideological struggle are the shifting implications of racial terms like "colored," which in his native Jamaica connoted an admirable class status but which was a slur in Britain; or the way in which "black" was reclaimed by militant activists from a slur to become a rallying cry for revolution in the late 1960s in the United States (113). All manner of African American cultural practices function this way, as in the ongoing challenge to popular-culture media to represent blacks more positively or in the celebration of respected African Americans in magazines like *Crisis, Opportunity, Jet, Ebony,* and *Essence.* It is the defining process of racial meaning in African American formalist poetics, especially since being good at one's social role is one of the ways in which African Americans "rearticulate" these terms of their culture. After all, the most powerful social import of artistry is revised meaning, and one of the most substantive ways for the artist to produce alternative meaning is to produce an accomplished work of art, especially when accomplishment must be defined on the boundaries between two cultural traditions with potentially opposed systems of value.

In identifying these African American formalists' embrace of hybridity and the consequently alternative notion of agency, I am not seeking to privilege formal poetics over folk culture, nor am I therefore giving up in any way on the idea of a distinctive African American cultural self or tradition. Rather, I am seeking to suggest ways in which readers of this literature can get outside of these binary hierarchies of racial ideology in the West in general and the United States in particular to embrace the full range of affirming (even if fettered) African American poetic expression. New visions of social unity and new strategies of antiracist resistance or cultural subversion are available if we think outside of these limits of traditional racial discourse. That is why I turn to postcolonial thought to characterize how these ideals inform African American formalist poetics. I concur with Homi K. Bhabba that "the social articulation of difference, from the minority perspective, is a complex, ongoing negotiation that seeks to authorize cultural hybridities that emerge in moments of historical transformation. The 'right' to signify from the periphery of authorized power and privilege does not depend on the persistence of tradition; it is resourced by the power of tradition to be reinscribed through the conditions of contingency and contradictoriness that attend the lives of those who are 'in the minority'" (2). In other words, the hybrid self of African American poetic genius is one complex cultural mode of authorization for the reality of the hybrid African American cultural self, an identity that always has been and likely always will be invested not just in its persistent vernacular tradition but also in its dominant, colonizing culture. This investment is a compromise but it is also self-assertion, a cultural crossover in which two allegedly pure and opposed cultural traditions are transformed. Unless scholars come to embrace the idea—which most already recognize—that African American vernacular culture is neither the only African American culture nor the exclusive truth of that culture, we will continue to do a disservice to aspects of that culture, even to the extent of excluding it. And we will miss how fully the agency of much African American literary culture, including much of its vernacular poetics, garners its agency from this hybrid self-constitution of linguistic and cultural signification.

With these subtle revisions of approaches to African American poetry in mind, I can locate with meaningful accuracy how much of the genuine antiracist meaning of African American formalist poetics was located in the pursuit of traditional achievement and the cult of personality that surrounds the construction of the achieved artist. The emphasis on individuality in this pursuit informs a retrospective awareness that this individuality was always implicated in the history of its own making. I call these fettered geniuses *bardic poets,* then, because, even in their occasional resistance to political obligation, they functioned as spokespeople for the race that articulated its cultural self through their resistance to social exclusion and to aesthetic limitation. I do not call them bards outright, because in common critical parlance that term has come to mean a vernacular spokesperson in the mode of Langston Hughes, an explicit, self-conscious voice of the people that, in the formalist tradition, is often muted in favor of individual distinction. Rather than redefine the meaning of bard altogether, then, I suggest that the African American formalists inhabit that same role by being celebrated as accomplished traditional poets, becoming like bards in their attempts to become great poets in the most traditional terms. This idea of the bard is more persuasive for understanding these poets than the analogies to the minister or the blues musician so popular in literary scholarship about the African American poet. William Shakespeare's iconic status as "The Bard" better evokes the ideal relationship between artistic achievement and representative cultural meaning that creates the ideological struggle characteristic of the artistry and agency of the African American formalist poet. No African American poet achieved Shakespeare's exalted status, but most in the formalist tradition sought such status, and their pursuit of it was predicated on a poetic self that was purported to embody both the distinctive values of black people and the values black people share with the nation. Just as nineteenth-century Celtic and British antiquaries found the original Celtic bards and court poets to be retrospective sources of ethnic heritage, as Katie Trumpener argued in *Bardic Nationalism,* I find African American bardic poets to be a locus of both an indigenous and a colonial culture. To borrow terms from Ceri Lewis, African American bardic poets functioned in their culture as if they held "an official position by virtue of [their] training, [their] learning [and their] knowledge of the history and traditions of his country," through which they "helped effectively to unite tribal units and their rulers" (12). African American bards fulfilled these roles. Wheatley wrote numerous occasional poems, while Paul Laurence Dunbar and many Harlem Renaissance poets had white patrons. Official "bardic" positions included poetry consultant for the Library of Congress (Robert Hayden), reviewer and teacher of poetry workshops (Gwendolyn Brooks), and poet laureate to Liberia (Tolson). In such positions, as Trumpener argues, African American poets, like the Celtic bards, found themselves greeted as inadequate, imitative poets by the imperial culture while being co-opted by that culture, even as they were greeted in their own communities simultaneously as politically compromised lackeys and as founts of an anticolonial culture. This liminal space is constituted by the moment of cultural crossover in poetic mastery, making the hybrid African American self one of the primary implications of that mastery.

As such, the best way to appreciate the inextricable artistry and politics of African American formalist poetics is to recognize how the construction of a full and sufficient African American self was enacted on this shifting ground between cultural traditions embodied in the union of formalist poetics with racial experience, mainstream public reception with African American culture, traditional literary values with a distinctive heritage of ethnic cultural ideals and practices, all enacted on the "body" of signification that is poetic genius. While these formalist poets seldom consciously defined themselves in this role, the way they were constructed and even fettered in society—which depended upon how they constructed themselves in their verse—enacted the ideological struggle necessary for the constitution of an empowering ethnic self and for the antiracist agency that inhabited that constitution. Thus, Tolson's little-known poem "The Bard of Addis Ababa" (1944) exemplifies the central practices and effects of the African American bardic tradition, as I like to call it. In the poem, Tolson's ideal bard is an Ethiopian who criticized the Fascist invasion of that country in the Second World War. Since, as Lorenzo Thomas put it, "for Africans and African Americans, the Italian invasion of Ethiopia was as shocking a challenge [to ideals of justice and democracy] as Guernica was to the rest of the world," Tolson aligns his ideal bard with the largely laudable motivations of the Allies in the war (125). Tolson's bard offers explicit protests, as "the battle-cry of his ballads" and his "chants of men fleshed in epics" have the capacity to "Stir the palace and the marketplace."[1] In the second section of the poem, the imaginary bard's verse conforms to the traditional oppositional logic of race politics: "Rise up, ye warriors, do or die! / It's tooth for tooth and eye for eye!" (lines 55–56). Tolson's bard then prophesies,

> The Fascist jackals shall die on the dunes,
>   From Gambela to Danakil,
> And the rain and the sun shall rot their thighs
>   From Gojjam to Bodobo Hill.
>   (lines 61–64)

Here the bard's leadership is political complaint, protest, and a call to action. Here the bard's expression most fully resembles the conceptions of political and cultural leadership so central to vernacular theories of African American poetry.

But that call to action is not as important for Tolson's bard in particular—and for the historical African American bardic poet in general—as the poet's capacity to embody quite literally the multicultural values of the society, values that the bard posits as an alternative to the reality of oppression. Described as "A blooded Amharic scholar / With the lore of six thousand years" (lines 31–32), Tolson's bard garners his authority from his knowledge of Amharic, the six-thousand-year-old Ethiopian language, and, presumably, of the nation's history as well. Here Tolson rejects the notion that Africans have no history. More important, though, the bard balances East and West in his person, as "A Chinese dagger in his girdle / Ranks a pistol of English peers" (lines 35–36). This dialectical cultural balance implies wisdom and fairness, making the bard an embodiment of justice. As the poem explains, rather than being beholden to a court—especially since that court is an invader or colonizer—the bard as Tolson imagines him is his own court, as "debtors appeal to *him* for release [emphasis added]." This balanced, fair-minded self—"A hero of *grazmatch* and vendor / Of *hakim* and beggar and wag [original emphasis]" (lines 29–30)—can thereby manipulate traditional artistry for the sake of racial justice so that even his poetics participate in this cultural crossover. Epics and ballads are, after all, terms of Western poetics attributed by Tolson to this African poet, evoking the Eurocentric formalism of Tolson's own verse while also recalling the origins of these forms in a worldwide oral culture. Like African *griots*, who are the voices of their societies, and like Shakespeare, who mastered Western poetics, Tolson's secular prophet leads by "fleshing" multicultural heroes in verse and envisioning alternative social possibilities of intercultural communion, "the Palaver House to be," which he enacts in his personal reputation.

In essence, the bard's self arguably rearticulates race at least as much as his protests do. And Tolson implicitly claims to be that bard, since he included the poem in his 1944 volume *Rendezvous with America,* an allusion to Walt Whitman through which Tolson claims Whitman's ideal of the poet as democratic leader. Associating his World War II poetic leadership with that of the Civil War's "Great Gray Bard," Tolson claims his own balance of East and West for the sake of an African heritage and an ideal of justice. He also claims Whitman's sense of being an almost literal embodiment of his ideals. Reviews of the volume confirmed the effect of this association of Tolson with Whitman, and therefore with an American tradition of poetic activism through a song of the poet's self. This poetic self becomes an antiracist self through all of these associations, not just the commitment to the freedom of Ethiopia. But this fullness is only visible if readers consider the construction of the poetic self as a version of postmodern self-constitution.

The bulk of the African American formalist poetic tradition demands to be read as Tolson's poem does, through an awareness of the cultural overlap produced by such mastery; and that is the central process of cultural self-definition theorized by postcolonial studies. Such awareness necessitates that readers of this verse supplement and even supplant the traditional terms of race politics in literary analysis with the combination of traditional literary history and ideological analysis, characterizing how artistic forms and techniques are components of culture, whose implications shift and conflict in the formal and thematic structure of a given poem and in the larger society. In other words, poetic forms have traditional meaning but not stable meaning, and they derive their most significant meanings through their *use,* as in Tolson's overlapping uses of epic, ballad, and *griot* traditions to define his bard. Thus, Houston Baker is only partly right in his provocative formulation of African American formalist poetry as "white style and black content—two warring ideals in one dark body," because any given binary or dialectic in a given poem is complicated by several others and is always provisionally resolved within itself and in relationship to those others in a formal whole ("Achievement of Gwendolyn Brooks," 21). As much as it surprises me, then, I turn to a politically self-conscious version of Cleanth Brooks's priority on poetic tension, as that tension hints at the social implications of poetic structures that enhance the implications of poetic "content," an ideal of apolitical literary reading that nicely, if paradoxically, corresponds well with attention to cultural mutation and the tensions between cultural traditions that inform such cultural practices. In other words, one of the ways scholars can and should enact Gilroy's mandate to theorize cultural mutation in African American poetry is to attend to how formalist poetic tensions mutate in the context of racial ideology to become simultaneously poetic achievement and protest, artistic genius and ethnic selfhood. I do not accept the conservative moral priorities of the original New Critics, but I follow the practices of reading that acknowledge that the literary text—no matter how traditional—is a hybrid cultural form constituted by aesthetic tensions that parallel and produce the cultural tensions that make African American cultural self-definition in traditional poetry a release from the fetters of which it is constituted.

In the rest of this book, I trace the emergence and enactment of this anti-epistemological agency of signification and cultural construction in the culture and cult of personality of five major figures and one movement. The result, I hope, is a vision of how traditional poetics presents a remarkable portrait of the entire interaction between poet and society as recorded in the mutually informing and simultaneous constructions of poetic genius and ethnic selfhood. In chapter 1, "'Bid the Gifted Negro Soar': The Origins of the African American Bardic Tradition," I define more fully what I call "bardic genius" by arguing that the antiracist practices and effects of the African American poetic tradition originate not in the abolitionist protest of nineteenth-century slave poet George Moses Horton, as some have argued, but with eighteenth-century slave poet Phillis Wheatley and her assimilation of the literary and religious culture of her time in ways that allowed her to participate in her society as a citizen by being accorded the status of genius. Not arguing for direct influence, I nonetheless also demonstrate that this model of assimilation is actually what made Horton's and Frances Ellen Watkins Harper's more explicit protest poetry effective and therefore a descendent, if you will, of Wheatley's work.

In chapter 2, "'Writ on Glory's Scroll': Paul Laurence Dunbar's Moral Heroism," I assert that Dunbar grudgingly initiated ethnic self-definition in African American poetry in his 1896 volume *Lyrics of Lowly Life,* in large part by opposing the moral heroism central to racial-uplift ideology to the failed parody of dialect poetry, constructing a bourgeois and ethnic form of British romantic genius. The concept of fettered genius helps us to see that, by predicating Dunbar's reputation almost exclusively on his dialect poetry, scholars have done a disservice to the full range of Dunbar's ethnic affirmation in his verse. In chapter 3, "'To Make the Poet Black': Constructing an Ethnic Poetics in Harlem Renaissance Poetry," I demonstrate how the Harlem Renaissance represents a coming-of-age of African American poetry, because the poets of the movement, though divided into genteel traditionalists and radical vernacular poets, were unified in making poetic genius "black" by fulfilling the promise of ethnic self-definition implied in *Lyrics of Lowly Life*. The construction of a New Negro in poetry was substantive, even if was historically dubious, because it constituted the impetus to define poetic genius as a self-assertive, culturally self-aware New Negro identity that was paradoxically that black person's claim to belonging in the nation.

In chapter 4, "'Weaponed Woman': The Modernist Heroism of Gwendolyn Brooks's Early Verse," I argue that, by paralleling her revision of traditional poetics to her characters' processes of self-definition, Gwendolyn Brooks defines the "feminine" heroism of existential cultural self-definition that makes African American identity what it is and that renders Brooks herself as a people's poet even in her early formalist verse. Recovering Brooks's early poetry as part of her commitment to community, I argue that her work complicates the defiant individual self of the Harlem Renaissance by locating its complexity, and the value of its representation, in the contingent value of the simultaneously folk and formal imaginative terms used to express it. I also suggest that this existentialism provides a central alternative in the bardic tradition to the masculinist terms of direct opposition by which Brooks's formalism has usually been found politically wanting. In chapter 5, "'Our Souls' Strict Meaning': Robert Hayden's Spiritual History," I demonstrate that Hayden was right to interpret his career as the ever-growing symbolic perception of the principles of his Baha'i faith, and that this practice constitutes a remarkable affirmation of ethnic difference as the ultimate symbol of humane values and spiritual meaning in history. Like Brooks, Hayden used the lived experience of African Americans, including prominent historical figures, in their pursuit of affirming identity, including his own, as the ultimate symbol of his spiritual ideals. By constructing individual spiritual transformation as metaphor for and motivating factor in the course of history, Hayden's verse articulates a politics of transcendence that suggests that the fetters of genius—historical fact for Hayden—were necessary for the poet to connect to the transcendent ideals that were supposed to make historical fact irrelevant.

Finally, in chapter 6, "A Port Worth the Cruise: Melvin B. Tolson's Epic Imagination," I argue that Melvin Tolson used high modernist allusiveness to write African and African American culture into the center of Western history ultimately through a representation of his own consciousness. Through the mind of his Curator in his most important poem, *Harlem Gallery* (1965), Tolson represents an African American dialectical imagination rooted in the cultural traditions of the African diaspora as the foundational ideal of the West. That "diasporic self," as I call it, synthesizes within itself the values necessary for the socially just vision of history with which Tolson concluded his career and with which the African American formalist poetic tradition fulfilled itself in the Civil Rights Movement. The port was indeed worth the cruise.

So this book is not a defense of cultural assimilation, nor is it a claim that all African American culture needs to be read in terms of its relationship to mainstream culture. Though I may be accused of validating a dangerous and ultimately self-defeating practice of cultural assimilation, then, the truth is that I am clarifying how that practice, as manifest in the formalist poetics of conservative African American poets, has never been entirely self-defeating and has in fact been at times a use of limited cultural resources for the ongoing process of African American ethnic self-definition in resistance to cultural hegemony. African American formalist poets are by no means offering radical challenges to their culture, but even in their conservatism, their work functions as a challenge to certain terms of racist exclusion. Though their art was circumscribed by their formal choices, then, their agency was facilitated by those same choices, a contradiction at the heart of their verse that dialectically resolved the perceived contradiction between race and art. Thus, the lesson of the bardic tradition is that culture is dynamic, that social change comes in part from changes in social and cultural meaning, and that all aspects of African American cultural production, including conservative to moderate ones like African American formalist poetic practices, have the potential to challenge inequitable terms of racial ideology. As a result, we cannot get so caught up in defining African American identity against "white" culture that we treat that cultural self as entirely static and primarily defensive, only a response to oppression. Such a definition reduces black people to victims and undermines some of the subtly transforming dynamics of our culture. But we can only see these dynamics of meaning if we turn to the poetry itself for the terms it implies. As Joseph Boone asserts, "To free ourselves from the often invisible grip of power or ideology, we need first to see—which is to say *read*, and read closely and well—the discursive strategies that imprison us with their prescribed meanings" (24). We can never escape ideology entirely, but perhaps we can, as Hall implies, participate more thoughtfully in its construction. And one way to do so is to recognize the agency of the African American bardic poet.

1 "Bid the Gifted Negro Soar"
The Origins of the African American Bardic Tradition

Listen all who never felt
    For fettered genius heretofore—
Let hearts of petrifaction melt
    And bid the gifted Negro soar.

—George Moses Horton, "A Poet's Feeble Petition"

In "A Poet's Feeble Petition," a poem he sent to the abolitionist Horace Greeley in a letter dated September 11, 1852, nineteenth-century slave poet George Moses Horton exemplifies in one quatrain the central claim to imaginative genius through poetic mastery and the accompanying claim to sympathy by which slave poets such as himself and African American abolitionist poets in general appealed to their white readers for an end to slavery. As such, the poem anticipates the way in which African American poets well into the twentieth century would construct poetic genius as the substance of an affirming racial self. It also provides the most persuasive terms for understanding eighteenth-century poet and slave Phillis Wheatley as the original African American poetic bard through her aesthetic, not just through her historical primacy. In the poem, Horton asks Greeley to recognize the slave poet's genius as an exemplar of Greeley's own imagination, an identification that would ideally melt Greeley's heart and motivate Greeley to bid Horton "soar" out of the fetters of slavery. And yet Horton's claim to be a "gifted Negro" implies that he has already transcended those fetters through the capacity to imagine that the poem exemplifies.[1] This capacity distinguishes Horton from other slaves, frees Horton's mind, and thus should justify the freedom of his body, if not the destruction of the entire system of slavery. This self-contradictory idea—that his imaginative freedom is in jeopardy from the slavery that it has already transcended—enacts a paradox in order to illuminate the fatal flaw of the ideology of absolute difference by which slavery operates. The poem implies that this fundamental and shared human capacity, even in Horton's generous portion of it, can be destroyed by lack of recognition or sympathy, even though Horton has cultivated that genius without recognition. Also, Horton's distinction from his fellow slaves paradoxically makes him representative of that community in the fundamental humanity they share with Greeley, since the implication is that if one African has imagination, all Africans might. Individuality and imagination defined personal value, racial difference, and human community. And as the poetic encapsulation of all three, genius became the chief political implication of Horton's art.

Thus, what matters about Horton's claim to genius is not exclusively the very conventional appeal it makes to sentiment or sympathy or its relationship to the explicit protest Horton offers in other poems; rather, what matters is the fact that such a claim implicitly depends upon the poem's construction of the poetic self as an ideal racial self. The significance of Horton's claim— characteristic of most abolitionist poetry and central to Wheatley's defining example—thus depends upon the fact that it constitutes a version of what Stephen Greenblatt called *self-fashioning*: "Self-fashioning is in effect the Renaissance version of . . . the cultural systems of meanings that creates specific individuals by governing the passage from abstract potential to concrete historical embodiment. Literature functions within this system in three interlocking ways: as a manifestation of the concrete behavior of its particular author, as itself the expression of the codes by which behavior is shaped, and as a reflection upon those codes" (4). A concrete historical embodiment of the slave's denied abstract status as person, Horton's concrete act of imagination initiates a reflection on the codes of behavior that render Africans into slaves and that should motivate Greeley's rejection of those codes based upon other, related codes in the same social system. Horton has an agency here, in other words, no matter the material effect of the poem, a capacity to participate somewhat in the construction of his identity in his culture. All African American abolitionist poets used a version of this early-modern construction of the individual to make claims upon society through their mastery of its social codes of imaginative and moral personhood, claims enhanced even as they were challenged by the poet's enslaved black body. For Wheatley, Horton, and Frances Ellen Watkins Harper, recognized poetic achievement was social participation, linking the abstract ideals of personhood and citizenship to the historically excluded black body, initiating through such conventionality the rewriting of conventional ideals of race, person, and nation. Scholars such as Henry Louis Gates have noted this association before but have not explored fully enough the aesthetic principles of the self-fashioning by which this association operates. Thus, the cultural agency of this mastery has been underestimated, since it has been linked primarily with literacy and self-defeating assimilation. By adapting ideals of sympathy and genius to their enslaved person, then, these poets made the poetic self a node of contention in the meaning of race, identity, and even nation. And Wheatley exemplifies this self-fashioning of genius, because the more fully these poets embraced communally shared literary standards of their time, the more fully their conventional poetics constructed an African self that was a convincing refutation of the ideologies of slavery.

In essence, I am suggesting that, paradoxically enough, the cultural assimilation of poetic mastery was the abolitionist poet's greatest act of resistance, an act exemplified by his or her self-constitution as genius as that self-concept was validated by the slaveholding and abolitionist reading public. Wheatley therefore became the originator of the central poetic practice of the African American formalist tradition because her work most fully engaged in the complicated antiracist meaning of literary genius. Unlike Horton's, Wheatley's claim to genius most fully associated her achievement with the cultural capacities of the entire race. By Wheatley's time, the term *genius* had come to mean a "personal quality . . . which was assumed to reside in the blood," a conception that incorporated an aristocratic notion of race as inherited gentility into an ideal of individual talent (Hannaford 188). At the same time, the meaning of "race" had also shifted from the idea of a pre-Enlightenment aristocratic hierarchy to Montesquieu's related but broader idea of race as species of humanity, so that elitist hierarchy and shared biology overlapped in notions of racial identity and literary genius. As a result, formalist poetics allowed African American poetic "geniuses" to enact the idea that, as Arthur Schopenhauer put it, genius is both "energy, creativity, originality, inspiration and the capacity to bring meaning to matter" for the individual artist and a common imaginative capacity that "must exist in all men in smaller and different degree; for if not, they would be just as incapable of enjoying works of art as of producing them" (3). And as Barbara Will asserted in her discussion of Gertrude Stein's genius, attributing genius to a marginalized person, whether avant garde white woman or slave, challenges the notion that the marginalized are absolutely different and inferior (8).

By simultaneously exemplifying both individuality and community, distinction and commonality, these poets could place African imaginative selfhood at the center of a culture that had rendered it an absence, illuminating the cultural conjunction between notions of shared natural rights and artistic achievement that made the imagination the chief challenge to racism. It also meant that these poets garnered the public voice that refuted the "social death" characteristic of all of the practices of slavery in the world. Reading this verse as an ongoing practice of self-fashioning, then, I can suggest ways in which the intersection of discourses in the construction of that self by poet and audience constituted a construction of shared national ideals that included the poet in literary culture and, given the centrality of that culture to certain notions of nation, that thereby included them in a model of social and cultural citizenship. And that antiracist participation depended not upon protest but upon recognized talent, which in turn depended upon assimilating social and cultural discourses associated with that mastery. Though perhaps in some ways a less persuasive notion today, a "gifted Negro" in the time of slavery was more politically provocative than an angry slave would have been.

This bardic genius—as I will call it—transformed poetic achievement into a racial voice of freedom through poetic conventionality, an ideal that made social inclusion a genuine possibility and a genuine antiracist act. Thus, this conception of Wheatley as the originator of a model of imaginative genius that was the basis of social liberty and democratic citizenship provides an alternative to the tendency in the study of African American literary culture to treat literary conventionality, ideals of social integration, and practices of cultural assimilation as only capitulations to superior cultural power, as if some original, authentic, and essential black self were always already limited by the ideology of slavery, even in slaves who knew no other culture. Only in the broadest terms is this true. But when scholars attempt to assign that fixed black self to individuals or to lament its absence, they tend to come to dubious conclusions. For example, such simple oppositions of race politics led M. A. Richmond to assert that Wheatley's poetic mastery was evidence of her personal and political "lobotomy," the erasure of her personality and self-awareness by oppression (81). Using the same binary logic, Terence Collins concluded that her poetry was an exemplary "gauge of the depths to which . . . self-hate by blacks [was] based on interjection of the dominant culture's estimate of . . . worth" (147). To suggest that Wheatley's self was lobotomized is to make the false biological argument explicit. Not only does such essentialism reduce the complexity of African identity, it also leads such scholars to neglect that fact that, as Greenblatt suggests, any reading of the intersection of individual and cultural selfhood in literary self-fashioning "must address itself . . . to the interpretive constructions the members of the society apply to their experiences" (4–5). In other words, in embracing the culture of its time, African

American poetic formalism *interprets* it, making such work evidence of something more than a lobotomy. This implicit interpretation is also more substantive than the idea that American culture is always an oppressive mask, a point through which scholars such as Rafia Zafar seek to rescue conventional writers such as Wheatley. Worse, scholars such as Richmond conclude that in the closing lines to his poem "On Liberty and Slavery," Horton "first struck the chord that has ever since dominated Afro-American poetry," a practice that, according to Richmond, made Horton a "pioneer" in black protest and black pride (81).

Instead of wearing early American culture as a mask or having her selfhood forcefully excised from her mind by some oppressive surgery, Wheatley constructed that self by wearing that culture as an ambivalent but ultimately empowering aspect of an ideal racial self worthy of poetic mastery and social inclusion. Therefore, a more persuasive conception of these dynamics of self-fashioning in general, and of Wheatley's remarkably successful case in particular, emerges when considered in terms of what Paul Gilroy aptly called the politics of fulfillment, the marginalized person's ideal that "a future society will be able to realise the social and political promise that present society has left unaccomplished," and that accomplished art can envision and motivate such fulfillment (37). Acting on the ideal that "bourgeois civil society [will] live up to the promise of its own rhetoric," Wheatley, Horton, and Harper fulfilled mainstream social codes in ways that provided an alternative—however miniscule—to the practice of those codes. After all, to be frank, the democratic ideals of the United States are well worth fulfilling, no matter how much racist social practices compromise those ideals, and that is exactly what these poets aspired to do by transforming poetic achievement into social participation. Certainly, it is more affirming to imagine that African American poets who were slaves would have created an ethnic tradition based on African culture, left to their own devices, but they were not left alone. To criticize them for not building an ethnic poetic culture seems to me to be worth doing only as a step toward understanding what they *did* build. Their politics of fulfillment was more self-assertion than abdication, a point conceivable only with a historically more persuasive attention to the meaning of poetic formalism in its time rather than in our own. It made good sense that slaves would want the nation to live up to its principles, and the African American poetic tradition is founded in this slightly self-deprecating but meaningfully self-assertive attempt to do just that. This pursuit is clearly a measure as much of their fettered situation as of their imaginative liberation.

I take the title of this chapter from Horton's poem, then, because, following the logic of Gilroy's assertion, the cultural assimilation that was a necessary precondition for inclusion into the imagined and historical body politic provided a rigid Eurocentric framework for African American identity and only the narrowest of spaces within which an affirming sense of self could be communally fashioned. But that space was broad enough to allow the "gifted Negro" to "soar" into public discourse through a mode of social participation derived from poetic self-fashioning and analogous to citizenship. It is the nature of this soaring that both unites and distinguishes these three poets as the progenitors of the African American formalist poetic tradition. In her 1773 volume *Poems on Various Subjects, Religious and Moral*, the first collection of poetry by a person of African descent published in the United States, Wheatley exemplified this soaring in her mastery of neoclassical poetics, Puritan religiosity, and discourses of natural rights. Her practice transformed the definition of African identity into the abstracted selfhood at the heart of what Andrew Burstein persuasively called "sentimental democracy"—"the connectedness of these people, their shared loyalty to national principles and the persistence of a common cultural idiom" as "zealous expressions of sympathy and affectionate ties joined with clear assertions of the reasoning intellect to promote national union" (xvii). For Horton, this self-fashioning was actually compromised by his claim to be an entirely distinctive poetic genius, a sense of individuality that resisted rather than confirmed this sentimental democracy and therefore compromised the politics of fulfillment. And Harper's advocacy for freedom through traditional moral integrity and explicit protest locates this sentimental democracy in the claim to conventional notions of womanhood. This self-fashioning of poetic genius was the central artistic and political achievement of these poets, and it is exemplified not by the more explicitly political Horton and Harper but by the still much-maligned Wheatley.

Thus I seek to reclaim Wheatley as an artist rather than an artifact by understanding more fully how her black body and slave status informed readings of her conventional artistic achievement as an expression of racial selfhood, allowing her claim to poetic gifts to function as the genius of citizenship. In these terms, the origin of the African American formalist poetic tradition starts with Wheatley's very existence. Brought to Boston from West Africa, a seven-year-old Phillis was bought by John and Susanna Wheatley in 1761 and soon proved herself to have intellectual gifts that refuted presumptions that Africans were incapable of higher thought, a contradiction to the racism of her society enhanced by her capacity to write poetry. The challenge was such that, as is quite well known by now, Wheatley had to prove to a panel of eighteen influential figures of the Massachusetts Colony that she was knowledgeable enough to have written her verse in order to get her volume published. As those worthies put it,

> We whose names are under-written, do assure the World, that the POEMS specified in the following Page, were (as we verily believe) written by Phillis, a young Negro Girl, who was but a few Years since, brought an uncultivated Barbarian from *Africa*, and has ever since been, and now is, under the Disadvantage of serving as a Slave in this Town. She has been examined by some of the best judges, and is thought qualified to write them.[2]

This oral exam, as Henry Louis Gates called it, was the beginning of her self-fashioning. Though the volume would not have been published without it, this authorization would not have mattered without Wheatley's mastered artistry and her personal capacity to justify it with her knowledge. As one nineteenth-century reviewer put it, "The classical allusions [in Wheatley's verse] are numerous, and imply a wide compass of reading, a correct judgment, good taste, and a tenacious memory" such that Wheatley's volume was "perhaps the most favorable evidence on record, of the capacity of the African for intellect." Wheatley becomes, in this construction of her identity, the "unassisted Genius" that her publisher Archibald Bell described her to be (Robinson 16). And Wheatley's self is constructed here as a passage from "barbarian" to slave to qualified poet, even genius, a progression that she accepts and manipulates to her advantage. Not only does this racist narrative of evolution make her "soaring" possible, it also creates a notion of her genius that makes that racist narrative the paradoxical basis for her claims to citizenship.

More than even Gates has recognized, then, Wheatley participated in this racist public fashioning of her genius not as much through Africanist wordplay as through identifying and defining as a component of her African heritage the imaginative gift that authorized her poetry and that was central to national unity. In her oft-anthologized poem "To the University of Cambridge, in New-England," for example, Wheatley revises the standard racist justification of slavery as the cultivation of barbarians by claiming that her imaginative life began before she was "cultivated."

> While an intrinsic ardor prompts to write,
> The muses promise to assist my pen;

'Twas not long since I left my native shore
The land of errors, and *Egyptian* gloom:
Father of mercy, 'twas thy gracious hand
Brought me in safety from those dark abodes.

(lines 1–6)

In addition to calling quite conventionally to the muses to motivate and authorize her artistry and requesting similar sanction from the Puritan God,
proving her "wide compass of reading," Wheatley declares that she can write
because she has an innate capacity that was ordained both by the muses and
by the Christian God and that arose from her African self. Moreover, as in the
spirituals in which slaves claimed biblical sanction for both spiritual and literal freedom by identifying with the Israelites and biblical Ethiopians, Wheatley's description of Africa as "Egyptian" and herself as an "Ethiop" later in the
poem root her poetic authority in biblical prophecy, as in Psalm 68:31, which
asserts, "Princes shall come out of Egypt; Ethiopia shall soon stretch forth her
hands unto God." Just as her African identity preceded her conversion, then,
and just as biblical ideals and prophecy preceded her enslavement, Wheatley's
imaginative "ardor" for writing preceded her acculturation. Her desire to
write—her imagination—is "intrinsic" to her personality and is thus a more
fundamental authority for her verse than is her more readily apparent mastery of the classical allusions and heroic couplets of poetic neoclassicism. No
matter its "errors" and "gloom," then; her "Egyptian" past was still the source
of her ardor. This intrinsic ardor actually functions, in ways that Wheatley
probably did not know entirely, as the substance of her claim to citizenship.

This claim to "intrinsic ardor" is one of Wheatley's most important antiracist gestures, because it ties her imaginative gifts to ideals of personhood
central to the terms of her reception and fundamental to the definitions of citizenship emerging in colonial America. In her 1774 letter to Samson Occum,
for example, Wheatley suggested as much. She declared herself to be "greatly
satisfied with [Occum's] Reasons respecting the Negroes, and think highly
reasonable what you offer in Vindication of their natural Rights." She goes on
to explain that the work of missionaries in Africa

reveals more and more clearly, the glorious Dispensation of civil and religious Liberty, which are so inseparably united, that there is little or no enjoyment of one without the other: Otherwise, perhaps the Israelites had
been less solicitous for their Freedom from Egyptian slavery; I do not say

they would have been contented without it, by no means, for in every human Breast, God has implanted a Principle, which we call Love of Freedom; it is impatient of Oppression, and pants for Deliverance; and by the Leave of our modern Egyptians I will assert, that the same Principle lives in us. (*Poems* 203)

Whether or not we here can equate sin directly with slavery, as Katherine Clay Bassard suggests, Wheatley clearly declares that the love of freedom, like her imaginative "ardor," is "intrinsic" to human personality, as it is "implanted" by God in "every human Breast" (42–44, 48). And Wheatley's conclusion to the letter emphasizes the relationship between her individual mind and these larger principles of human personality: "How well the Cry for Liberty, and the reverse Disposition for the exercise of oppressive power over others agree,— I humbly think it does not require the Penetration of a Philosopher to determine." Her ironic tone grants Wheatley the "Penetration" that she implies some of her alleged "superiors" lack, tying her intrinsic imaginative ardor to philosophical "penetration" and to a divine principle of freedom.

Likewise, seeing these antiracist effects of her assimilation of her culture, Betsy Erkilla and Houston Baker have discussed Wheatley's place in the rhetoric of the emerging democracy, but neither deals well enough with Wheatley as a poetic artist who used imagination and not the rhetoric of democracy as her ultimate authority. Erkilla has shown how Wheatley's poetry is invested in the rhetoric of democracy, offering admirable insights into the discursive context of Wheatley's art without examining aesthetic very fully. Baker, too, considers discursive effects, as in his persuasive reading of the frontispiece to Wheatley's volume, but has little to say about the poetry itself. In the context of her being an "Ethiop," Wheatley's capacity to speak becomes an assertion of individual personhood and of an intrinsic emotional capacity linked to the ideals of natural rights, two associations that render historically concrete in a slave's black body the abstract components of personhood that were denied her by her culture. And these terms of selfhood were so conventional that, in performing them, Wheatley makes the African self recognizable as a "human" self.

Even her otherwise conventional and apolitical verse participates in this self-fashioning as citizen, then, since this association between intrinsic imagination and the abstract personhood of sentimental democracy mirrored the transformation of social abstraction into social reality in Renaissance self-fashioning. In "On Imagination," for example, Wheatley might simply be read as defining the faculty of the imagination in the most boring of conventional gestures. But in the context of these ideological clashes created by her associations of African identity with universal human selfhood, her definition functions as a slave's link to her fellow Americans irrespective of race, class, or caste. So even though "*Winter* frowns to *Fancy's* raptur'd eyes / The fields may flourish and gay scenes arise":

> Such is thy pow'r, nor are thine orders vain,
> O thou leader of the mental train:
> In full perfection all thy works are wrought,
> And thine the scepter o'er the realms of thought.
> Before thy throne the subject passions bow,
> Of subject-passions sov'reign ruler Thou,
> At thy command joy rushes on the heart,
> And through the glowing veins the spirits dart.
> (lines 23–24, 33–40)

These lines declare the sovereignty of the imagination over "subject passions" in order to imply its central role in the creation of human identity and connection, upon which Wheatley depends to authorize her public address in "To the University of Cambridge, in New-England." As Horton suggests in "A Poet's Feeble Petition," the imagination can defy material conditions—including slavery—to transport the poet into the realm of the ideal and her poetry into the minds and hearts of her readers. This ideal itself could be called genius since, in ways she could not have known, her verse enacted the notion of artistic genius that Schopenhauer would articulate forty years later on another continent. It is both a distinctive creativity and a common human capacity. More important, this definition of the imagination transforms the neoclassical ideals of sentiment into ideals of democratic human connection best exemplified, as Ralph Waldo Emerson and Walt Whitman would later so famously attest, by the poet herself.

In other words, her poem effectively characterizes the sentimentalist's faith in what Bruce Burgett called "a universal and pre-political point of affective identification for individuals otherwise divided through the imposition of an ideological 'code'" (23). If, as Burgett argues, social codes and hierarchical socially constructed identities separate one person from another and potentially prevent the fulfillment of the abstract ideals of individual value and communal connection necessary for democracy, then what unifies people, especially in democratic ideals of citizenship based on natural rights and sentiment, is this "affective identification" (see Morris). Wheatley's conventional definition of the imagination may have come across as analogous to this compassionate, human spirit, this "pre-political point" of identification, a component of democratic self-fashioning easily overlooked because it was not likely a conscious political commentary.

> We on thy pinions can surpass the wind,
> And leave the rolling universe behind:
> From star to star the mental optics rove,
> Measure the skies, and range the realms above.
> There in one view we grasp the mighty whole,
> Or with new worlds amaze th'unbounded soul.
> ("On Imagination," lines 17–22)

This rhetorical "we," when warped and broadened by the lens of racial ideology and the conventions of sensibility, comes to include all poets and all people who share a common sympathetic reaction to common ideals of a sublime imagination, the capacity to "grasp the mighty whole." The poem is thus about a community held together by its members' equal access to the capacities of the imagination, a point that was the foundation of the poetic ideals of later republican thinkers like Percy Shelley, Emerson, and Whitman. Imagining new worlds in this context really means creating literary vision. But the experience of these literary creations can genuinely unite people, liberating them from the ideological codes that determine social identities. Perhaps a genuinely new world is therefore possible. Perceiving such sentiment in the *slave's* "unbounded soul" defied thinkers such as Kant, who claimed that "fundamental is the difference between [the black and the white] races of man, and it appears to be as great in regard to mental capacities as in color," or Hegel, who, when confronted with Africans, gave up on the universality of human experience and capacity so crucial to Enlightenment thinking. In other words, to paraphrase Greenblatt, Wheatley's literary self-fashioning revealed the construction of her social self as an extension of her "intrinsic ardor," which became embodied historically in her racialized and enslaved body. Its role as the source of community made this racialized ardor "democratic."

In these terms, Wheatley's very public cultivation of that ardor garners the force of subversive self-assertion because it constructs her poetic genius as a locus of cultural conflict and connection that both fettered and liberated her imagination. For example, "To Maecenas," the first poem in Wheatley's volume, transforms a conventional dedication to a patron into a construction of a sense of belonging based upon the "pre-political" identification that formed the foundation of literary expression as social participation and the cultural crossover that made that identification possible in art.

> Maecenas, you, beneath the myrtle shade,
> Read o'er what poets sung, and shepherds play'd.
> What felt those poets but you feel the same?
> Does not your soul possess the sacred flame?
> Their noble strains your equal genius shares
> In softer language and diviner airs.
>
>   While *Homer* paints lo! circumfus'd in air,
> Celestial Gods in mortal forms appear;
> Swift as they move, hear each recess rebound,
> Heav'n quakes, earth trembles, and the shores resound.
> Great Sire of verse, before my mortal eyes,
> The lightnings blaze across the vaulted skies,
> And, as the thunder shakes the heav'nly plains,
> A deep-felt horror thrills through all my veins.
> When gentler strains demand thy grateful song
> The length'ning line moves languishing along.
> When great *Patroclus* courts *Achilles'* aid,
> The grateful tribute of my tears is paid;
> Prone on the shore he feels the pangs of love,
> And stern *Pelides* tend'rest passions move.
>
>   (lines 1–20)

Cynthia Smith rightly asserts that in these two opening stanzas of the poem, Wheatley makes the patron Maecenas into a writer ("What felt those poets but you feel the same?") in order to affirm the nature of his sympathy for other writers. But even more important, this gesture reveals Wheatley's enactment of the literary-critical principles of sensibility and the sublime, which I am suggesting are central to a definition of citizenship implicit in her work. Her practice first implies that both she and Maecenas are great readers. Wheatley identifies appropriately what makes Homer great for a certain portion of neoclassical taste, gives credit to Maecenas for being able to discern this quality also, and, crucially, affirms her own authority as critic, since she too experiences the appropriate awe from the sublimity of Homer's poetry. When she actually sees Homer's portraits as if they objectively existed, she is "thrilled" as she should be, and the "grateful tribute" of her tears is "paid" where aesthetically and morally appropriate. Not only a celebration of her actual patron—whether her owner or the Countess of Huntingdon, who helped get the volume published—nor just a celebration of Maecenas's generosity and of Homer's poetry, this poem is also a celebration of Wheatley's own sensibility. It is one of her most explicit claims to the role of public leadership through poetic mastery, which I am calling "bardic genius," and it is also her clearest representation of the liminal space of cultural mutation that refutes the racial absolutism by which white Americans excluded her from the body politic.

In one of the many paradoxes of Wheatley's public self-fashioning, then, her evocation of this abstracted sense of commonality became the substance of her affirmation of her African identity, an affirmation that makes her version of poetic genius simultaneously conventional poetic mastery and unconventional ethnic self-definition. Even when she quite conventionally declares in deference to Virgil, "But here I sit, and mourn a groveling mind, / That fain would mount, and ride upon the wind" (lines 29–30), her poem belies that self-doubt with the affirmation of an African poetic tradition as a version of the national community she would like to join. She expresses her envy of

The happier *Terence*, all the choir inspir'd,
His soul replenish'd, and his bosom fir'd;
But say ye *Muses*, why this partial grace,
To one alone of *Afric's* sable race.

(lines 37–40)

Smith suggests that the Roman poet Terence, who was of African descent, is happier than Wheatley because, to Wheatley's eyes, he had a more appreciative audience, and this is certainly part of her point. But, more important, Wheatley is complaining directly to the muses that she has not been granted Africa's fair share of imagination and attention, effectively accusing her audience (as muses) of racism in their partiality. Without good reason, they fail to give Wheatley full credit. In this way, Wheatley implies a tradition of slave or African neoclassical artistry based in religious faith and the sublime, starting with Terence and including Scipio Moorhead, who was "Negro servant to the

Revd Mr. Moorhead of Boston, whose genius inclined him that way." In "To S. M. a Young African Painter, on Seeing His Works," Wheatley implores the African painter

> On deathless glories fix thine ardent view:
> Still may the painter's and poet's fire
> To aid thy pencil, and thy verse conspire!
> And may the charms of each seraphic theme
> Conduct thy footsteps to immortal fame!
> . . . .
> But when the shades of time are chas'd away,
> And darkness ends in everlasting day,
> On what seraphic pinions shall we move,
> And view the landscapes in the realms above?
> There shall thy tongue in heav'nly murmurs flow
> And there my muse with heavenly transport glow.
>   (lines 8–12, 23–28)

The function of such praise is to align Wheatley's own religious accomplishment with what she sees in Moorhead's work. First, she validates the ideal that his religious vision of "deathless glories" will aid the artist's "fire," making their shared religion and, potentially, their shared race the sources of their "immortal fame." But, second, she recognizes that this "fame" may genuinely be immortal, because it may not be fully acknowledged (due to racism) until they both are dead and are offered the greater recognition of heaven. Wheatley is waiting for the day when heaven will remove her physical and poetic shackles and grant her and Moorhead the voices and recognition they deserve. The criticism is clear: race and slavery prevent the African poet from being recognized despite faith, talent, and tradition. Wheatley's conventionality functions as a celebration of her Africanness and a scolding for those of partial grace who grant attention to only one of "Afric's sable race" at a time. Her American genius is once again shown to be African in its intrinsic ardor *and* in its cultural cultivation.

Nonetheless, the most important implication of this paradoxical claim of an African tradition, like all of Wheatley's references to being African, is that it constructs out of this subtle emphasis on cultural difference the "prepolitical" national self based upon inclusive social participation. And it does so in part and always by evoking the racist narrative of the cultivation of the barbarian. But since the barbarian's cultivation enhances an intrinsic ardor that also has a narrative of African cultivation, it enhances the politics of ful-fillment more fully than it embraces the racist narrative. Instead of losing her-self to cultural lobotomy, in other words, Wheatley was participating in what Phillip Richards describes as Wheatley's "gestures of self-deprecation," which were not just an African poet bowing to a superior white authority, though it was partly that. These gestures "were the rhetorical stock-in-trade of provin-cial American artists seeking to present themselves in [the] cosmopolitan tra-dition of English art" (170). Not only did such writers seek to bow down to that cosmopolitan tradition, as Richards emphasizes, they also implied their worthiness to join it. Wheatley's self-deprecation had a similar function, en-hanced by its challenge to the logic of race politics: "While blooming wreaths around thy temples spread, / I'll snatch a laurel from thine honour'd head, / While you indulgent smile upon the deed" ("To Maecenas," lines 45–47). In these lines, Wheatley is actively snatching a laurel from what is by now clearly a figurative Maecenas who embodies Horace's actual classical patron, an ideal reader, and the halls of poetic fame in one figure. Instead of emphasizing the patron's "indulgence," as too many scholars do, I am emphasizing the act of "snatching" the laurel, which implies that Wheatley deserves the laurel. As a young writer and a slave, Wheatley was probably genuinely unsure of herself, but the two poetic conventions she had mastered—self-deprecation before a patron and celebration of the poet's gifts to justify the patron's attention—come into conflict to reveal a subtle and self-contradictory affirmation of the African poet's gifts and her "pre-political" identity. Like the authorizing note from the dignitaries of Boston, this patron's approval depends upon the in-evitable recognition of Wheatley's verse that the poem implies. Not protest, this claim to fame still functions as a claim that she deserves social inclusion.

In effect, Wheatley's verse has constructed a hybrid African self that unites Homeric epic with an Ethiop's philosophical penetration, and the British tra-dition with an African poetic tradition, to suggest a "racial" self that is the sub-stance of her claim to literary merit, cultural memory, and the social inclusion that both imply. Wheatley's elegies—her most numerous and most explicitly public poems—offer the most explicit and consistent definition of this ideal of social participation and abstract selfhood through literary merit that made Wheatley, in her verse, a citizen. In poems requested by whites or dedicated to them of her own accord, Wheatley offered doctrinal consolation for the deaths of loved ones. She almost always begins such poems with some invocation either to the "heav'nly muse" or to the classical ones and parallels those invo-

cations to several implicit invocations to herself as African in order to authorize her most direct participation in public discourse. Moreover, Wheatley
adopts the conventions of the elegy to her own imagination: "The choice of
emphasis—celestial over terrestrial life, the Corporal Works of Mercy, the
ancestral-like abode that Heaven is, and the conception of happiness in terms
of the sense of sound over the sense of sight (Beatific Vision) as is traditionally
the case—helps to give Miss Wheatley's elegies a stamp all her own" (Rigsby
252). For example, in the poem to a dead evangelist, "On the Death of the Rev.
Mr. George Whitefield, 1770"—the poem that initiated her fame—Wheatley
exhorts her reader to "Behold the prophet in his tow'ring flight! / He leaves the
earth for heav'n's unmeasured height, / And worlds unknown receive him from
our sight" (lines 11–13). Also, Wheatley adopts the voice and character of
Whitefield in order to proclaim the joys of heaven and assert the exhortation to
peace and faith to the grieving. Wheatley even vocalizes the adored Whitefield's
heavenly advice to include Africans in the ancestral Christian community:

"Take him [Christ], ye wretched, for your only good,
Take him ye starving sinners, for your food:
. . . .
Take him, ye *Africans*, he longs for you,
Impartial Savior is his title due:
Wash'd in the fountain of redeeming blood,
You shall be sons, and kings, and priests to God."
(lines 28–38)

The poem posits Wheatley as a bard not just for Africans who were slaves; she
could also speak to and for whites and for God. In addition to associating her
imagination with the democratic spirit and her accomplishment with social
inclusion, in other words, Wheatley quite literally joins a mourning community as an equal or even as an advisor, as she had also done in speaking to the
graduating students at Cambridge. God will make Africans equals; and, by
speaking from the grave, Whitefield is implicitly attributing spiritual equality
to Africans in his godlike way. This is not militant resistance by any stretch of
the imagination, but it is a literal rewriting of a white divine's advice. The
shared religious vision to which Wheatley claims to have greater access than
her readers becomes the validation both of shared social ideals and values and
of the African poet's unique perspective on those shared values.

Thus, in the few explicit protests or references to freedom in Wheatley's verse, the main mode of self-fashioning is through this pre-political identity of sentimental democracy whose validity was enhanced by the poet's experience of oppression or exclusion. The poem "To the Right Honourable William, Earl of Dartmouth, His Majesty's Principle Secretary of State for North-America, &c." is the best example of Wheatley's soft but serious version of political protest. The poem opens with Wheatley declaring that the ascendancy of Dartmouth as governor promises that "in thine hand with pleasure we behold / The silken reins, and *Freedom's* charms unfold" while "hated *faction* dies" (lines 7–8, 10). Wheatley then implies that such liberty as "silken reins" is a contradiction analogous to her own situation:

> Should you, my lord, while you peruse my song,
> Wonder from whence my love of *Freedom* sprung,
> Whence flow these wishes for the common good,
> By feeling hearts alone best understood,
> I, young in life, by seeming cruel fate
> Was snatch'd from *Afric's* fancied happy seat:
> What pangs excruciating must molest,
> What sorrows labour in my parent's breast?
> Steel'd was that soul and by misery mov'd
> That from a father seiz'd his babe belov'd:
> Such, such my case. And can I then but pray
> Others may never feel tyrannic sway?
>
> (lines 20–31)

Torn between loyalty to pagan Africa and to liberty-loving America, her own intrinsic love of freedom allows her "to suggest that the British values at work in the Revolutionary crisis have a wider applicability than the reader thought," especially since that love of freedom even here is tied implicitly to her status as "saved" and to her capacity for the sensibility necessary to imagine her parents' pain (Richards 185). Her sense of common good that justified "dissolving the Political Bands which have connected them with another" had less to do with direct protests of slavery and more to do with the appeal to "feeling hearts" for her bereft parents, an appeal that is potentially more effective than an appeal for sympathy for herself. Resistance both to slavery and to an unjust parent were metaphors that dominated the public justifications of the incipient revolution. Such gestures effectively participated in the "democratic" functioning of literary sentiment, allowing Wheatley to join the "empty space" of republican citizenship despite her enslaved body. Her poetry thus enacts Burstein's "sentimental democracy."

So while Wheatley was clearly no radical, her verse still offers a sophisticated poetic genius as the foundation of an African self that was in turn the foundation of a claim to be a member of the nation. Wheatley's acts of assimilation were her most substantive acts of self-definition and protest, then, and granted to her mastery of traditional poetics an extra register of meaning as a component of a racial self that the verse constructed in conjunction with its readers. This self-fashioning also made her verse more fully capable of changing her material circumstances. It is rarely worth measuring such material effects of poetry, but in Wheatley's case her material circumstances prove the efficacy of her assimilation. Wheatley's travels to Britain after the publication of her volume confirm how it managed to transform her from slave to citizen, even while she was still in bondage. Wheatley garnered audience with dignitaries in England while also receiving a letter of thanks from George Washington and his apologies for the lateness of his reply. She also got to meet him, though no record exists of what happened at the meeting. There are obvious flaws in such politics of fulfillment, namely an acceptance that the principles of the status quo are good in themselves and that the fulfillment of those principles is possible. But in the specific democratic principles that Wheatley's art implicitly evokes, this acceptance is not entirely problematic. What would be wrong with a slave claiming an inherent intellectual capacity that transcends social roles and categories? This approach obviates the need of present-day scholars to make dubious claims about anagrams that might link Wheatley to an African past or that might portray her as a trickster. If "loyalty to national principles" is at the heart of "sentimental democracy," then her emphasis on her relationship to those ideals constitutes a rhetorically legitimate construction of her resistance to "tyrannic sway." And, of course, she was manumitted, becoming a citizen indeed.

This conception of "bardic genius" as a pre-political abstraction not only illuminates the means by which Wheatley successfully claims citizenship, it also clarifies how Horton's sense of romantic genius was not as full a protest of the fetters of slavery as was Wheatley's neoclassicism. Horton was an even more fettered genius than Wheatley, in part because his assimilation of mainstream culture was not as entire nor was his engagement in it keyed enough to its emphasis on the communal to refute fully the racist cultural constructions in which he was bound. So while it is easy to see that his poetry is "better" than Wheatley's, in that it conforms more fully to contemporary tastes shaped more by British and American romanticism than by neoclassicism, readers must not allow that closeness to contemporary taste and the easily recognizable protest to obscure the nature of Horton's most important aesthetic achievement and political claim and the limited social implications of that claim. "A Poet's Feeble Petition," his most persuasive poem in these self-fashioning terms, reveals how Horton's claim to individual genius paradoxically undermined his claim to belonging in the national community.

> Bewailing mid the ruthless wave,
>   I lift my feeble hand to thee.
> Let me no longer live a slave
>   But drop these fetters and be free.
>
> Why will regardless fortune sleep
>   Deaf to my penitential prayer,
> Or leave the struggling Bard to weep,
>   Alas, and languish in despair?
>
> He is an eagle void of wings
>   Aspiring to the mountain's height;
> Yet in the vale aloud he sings
>   For Pity's aid to give him flight.
>
> Then listen all who never felt
>   For fettered genius heretofore—
> Let hearts of petrifaction melt
>   And bid the gifted Negro soar.
>   (lines 1–16)

Claiming to be a "Bard," Horton begins his plea to Greeley—and to anyone who will listen—with the assertion that despair is the lot not primarily of the slave burdened by endless toil but of the *gifted* slave tied down by both physical and intellectual fetters. Unlike the transcendence of Wheatley's neoclassical genius and religious sublime, which links the gifted individual mind to an abstracted point of identification necessary for communal natural rights, Horton's images of thwarted transcendence are tied to the individual imagination alone. In this case, the "mountain's height" is an emblem of both artistic vision and physical freedom for the individual poet. The vale is therefore the poet's present condition as a slave, meaning that his characterization of limitation was less a matter of contradictions between social ideals and social practice than it was a matter of contradictions between the poet's individual ideal state and his reality. Horton is not engaged in pointing out a broad cultural hypocrisy through his social participation, in other words, and while Wheatley was not always aiming to do so either, her verse almost always did so because of the nature of her mastery. Horton's does not. In fact, he even calls on "Pity" to give him wings, as if the racist society could grant him poetic gifts as well as freedom.

In other words, the very effects of individual genius and self-assertive protest that make Horton's poetry "better" than Wheatley's essentially fetter its direct protest. As such, the images of flight and soaring, which John L. Cobbs rightly defines as the centerpiece of Horton's aesthetic, have their most significant appearances in his poems about poetry and the imagination, not in poems about freedom from slavery (446). Thus, Cobbs overstates their role in his direct protest. For example, Horton's poem "On the Poetic Muse," originally published in *Freedom's Journal* in the hopes of gaining subscribers before appearing in his volume *Hope of Liberty,* opens with what might be called this slave's "egotistical sublime":

> Far, far above this world I soar,
> And almost nature lose,
> Aerial regions to explore,
> With this ambitious Muse.
>
> My towering thoughts with pinions rise,
> Upon the gales of song,
> Which waft me through the mental skies,
> With music on my tongue.
>
> (lines 1–8)

The next three stanzas blend metaphors of fire, visual prospects of "wonders to survey," and the almost clichéd "quiet bliss of the soul / when in some calm retreat, / where pensive thoughts like streamlets roll" (lines 16, 17–19) to characterize the effects of imagination on mind, body, and soul. As such, Horton invests himself with the ideals of contemplation from which slaves would have been excluded. *His* ambitious muse provides music for *his* tongue as his wings gather the "gales" of that music in his individual "mental skies." Horton took his cue implicitly from the ideal that, as David Perkins put it, the romantic poem "ultimately . . . mirrors the struggle of genius against all limitation, and it leads to a glorification of yearning, striving, and becoming and of the personality of the artist" (8). What matters is the struggle of his genius against limitation, an ideal that other romantic poets successfully linked to democratic principles but that Horton does not, in part because of the nature of his conception and in part because of the ways in which he was constructed in the racial ideology of his time.

In fact, his conception of the pursuit of individual distinction even subtly compromises his explicit poetic protest. "On Liberty and Slavery" is not the communal voice Richmond and Collins make it out to be but is rather an assertion of individuality as a model for racial identity and political resistance. Any communal voice emerges as a secondary but compelling implication of the poet's individual and representative yearning:

Alas! and am I born for this,
    To wear this slavish chain?
Deprived of all created bliss,
    Through hardship, toil and pain!

How long have I in bondage lain,
    And languished to be free!
Alas! and must I still complain—
    Deprived of liberty.

Oh, Heaven! And is there not relief
    This side the silent grave—
To soothe the pain—to quell the grief
    And anguish of a slave?

Come Liberty, thou cheerful sound,
    Roll through my ravished ears!
Come, let my brief in joys be drowned,
    And drive away my fears.

Say unto foul oppression, Cease:
    Ye tyrants rage no more,
And let the joyful trump of peace,
    Now bid the vassal soar.
               (lines 1–20)

Clearly this protest is more likely to be stirring to the contemporary reader in its directness of resistance and the implications of pride in the poetic voice than Wheatley's more measured and even wimpish complaints. Moreover, given the insights Gates and others have offered about the inevitably public role of even the most private African American poetry, Horton's "I" here can easily be understood as a representative one rather than a personal one, and I suspect Richmond would concur with this reading (*Figures in Black* 4). After all, this poem clearly means to be representative as much as personal, claiming as Wheatley does that the individual genius of the slave poet is but a species of racial genius. The claim to genius justifies the "soaring" of the representative vassal in order to claim that soaring for the entire race. Nonetheless, there is a tension in this poem between that individual freedom and the eradication of slavery altogether, a tension that characterizes the space of discursive conflict into which Horton's poems enter. The speaker asks "Liberty" to drive away *my* fears," personalizing the otherwise generalized vassal being bid to soar, with the relief being only for the grief of "*a* slave" and not "*the* slave." Horton's outrage is more effective when coupled with the admiration we are expected to have for the imaginative poet. In these terms, Horton's pleas both appealed to and resisted the "pre-political" point of affective identification that would make it both an ethnic and a human self and that would write it fully into the principles of democracy.

In other words, Horton's verse actually conforms to the usually misguided critique of romanticism as entirely individualistic, undermining in part Horton's ability to push the nation to live up to its promise through his claim to genius. The individualism of his self-fashioning reinforced rather than challenged the construction of race in Horton's time. Rather than being seen as proof of African capacities against racist expectations of its absence, and rather than being offered as a genius the reader can assume along with the poet, as Whitman proposed, Horton's individualist "genius" sometimes rendered him as something of a comic novelty or buffoon, an exception whose perceived pomposity proved the rule that Africans were a pale imitation of white Americans. As Joan Sherman explains, partly in Horton's own words:

> Chapel Hill students, the sons of wealthy planters, seemed more interested in sports, gambling, and pleasures of the table than in their studies. . . . The collegians, Horton wrote, "for their diversion were fond of pranking with the country servants," and they "pranked" with him by insisting that he "spout"; they made him "stand forth and address" the collegians extemporaneously, "as an orator of inspired promptitude." . . . Since "oration was the highest type of literary effort developed in the ante-bellum South," it

was fitting that the students transformed Horton into an orator. At first, the slave felt proud of his performance, he wrote, "but soon I found it an object of aversion, and considered myself nothing but a public ignoramus." Consequently, Horton abandoned these "foolish harangues and began to speak of poetry." On one or two known later occasions, however, he again "spouted" to order for the collegians, and in his "Address" he called himself "your sable orator" and "your poor orator." (6–7)

This problem leads critics to take Horton lightly, and even some of Horton's white contemporaries believed that his "hope of liberty" was a matter of minstrel performance (Cobbs 443–44). But the problem with Horton's approach was less in his political consciousness, which J. Saunders Redding too simply characterizes as being that of a lackey for white pleasure, than in the difficulty he had challenging the roles into which he was placed by slavery and by the precursors to blackface minstrelsy, a role oddly reinforced by claims of individual rather than racial genius (17). If his individual capacity for expression sometimes distinguished him from the race, it did so by serving the sense among many slaveholders that talented slaves provided a mode of entertainment in their amusing and presumably inadequate imitation of white oratory or poetics. And because he was in the midst not of liberal-minded intellectuals, as Wheatley was, but of "pranking" college students, Horton's fame did not have the same broad cultural significance. These forces undermined the antiracist effects of Horton's self-fashioning as genius.

Horton did not strike the originating chord of the African American poetic tradition, then, because he did not fully engage in the construction of poetic genius invested in the mainstream culture of the time. By so successfully fulfilling the ideals of romantic genius, Horton did not embrace fully the range of social and cultural ideals available to link literary culture to the nation's political life. Horton's construction of bardic genius was thus an elaboration upon the artistic freedom of the individual genius without a thoroughgoing examination of the connections between that freedom and the racial discourses of the society. His protest, while stirring, was too narrow, as were his uses of formal innovation and individual distinction.

Frances Ellen Watkins Harper likewise did not originate the tradition. In fact, her artistry was fully a descendant of Wheatley's in terms of how its political effects—even its protests—depended upon its conventionality. Despite all apparent indications to the contrary, Harper's verse becomes perhaps the strongest proof of the primacy of Wheatley's model of poetic meaning as the origin of the aesthetic practice and political meaning of the African American formalist poetic tradition. On one hand, since she was freeborn and an abolitionist activist and lecturer; since she read her poetry as part of her lectures; since she was one of the most popular poets of the day; since she used proceeds from the sales of her books and her lecturing engagements to contribute to the Underground Railroad; and since she self-consciously devised her poetry explicitly for this purpose, her approach to poetry and politics comes closest to the twentieth- and twenty-first-century ideal implied by Richmond. In these terms, Patricia Liggins Hill is right: like 1960s poetic radicals Amiri Baraka, Haki Madhubuti, Nikki Giovanni, and Sonia Sanchez, who "base their oral protest poetry primarily on direct imagery, simple diction and the rhythmic language of the street to reach the masses of black people, Harper relies on vivid, striking imagery, simplistic language, and the musical quality and form of the ballad to appeal to large masses of people, black and white, for her social protest."

For Hill, this choice represents "an 'art for people's sake' aesthetic, rather than a Western Caucasian aesthetic assumption, 'an art for art's sake' principle." Melba Joyce Boyd concurs, declaring that Harper's consistent use of the ballad was central to her political purposes. The ballad, says Boyd, coincides with nineteenth-century mass culture and Harper's elocutionary format (67). Hill concludes that, even given her concern with all humanity—as in her temperance poems, for example—Harper "is primarily concerned with uplifting the masses of black people" (160).

Thus, her much-anthologized poem "Bury Me in a Free Land" bases its call to action on a claim to popular sentiments. It ends,

I ask no monument, proud and high,
To arrest the gaze of the passers by;
"All that my yearning spirit craves
Is—*bury me not in a land of slaves!*"[3]

Clearly this poem presumes an audience of like-minded people and suggests that, unlike Wheatley and Horton, the poet identifies more with the slaves than with the slaveholders. This poem also asserts a principle of direct resistance to the entire institution, not just to the individual condition of the slave. Such a stanza suggests a meaningful difference between the Harper's poetry and that of Wheatley and Horton.

But on the other hand, Harper's self-fashioning was based upon more than her claim of community with slaves. It was in fact a paradoxically radical pursuit of the politics of fulfillment, a self-fashioning predicated on being accepted in the mainstream as an embodiment of its moral and cultural principles pertaining to gender identity. Her poetry had its greatest effects, in other words, by articulating how the political principles and cultural mores of the nation should be transformed subtly in order to apply to slaves, especially slave women, creating community between Africans and white abolitionists through the contradictions in the morality that justified aspects of slavery. As such, the "genius" of the poet was as much her conventional moral sensibility as it was her political outrage, her formal mastery as much as her political protest. And these components of her poetic self came to be inextricable in the authorization of that self enacted by both the poet and the reading community. For example, the third stanza of "Bury Me in a Free Land" contains Harper's most characteristic gesture of protest:

I could not sleep, if I heard the tread
Of a coffle-gang to the shambles led,
And the mother's shriek of wild despair
Rise, like a curse, on the trembling air.
(lines 13–16)

Though the individual genius is foregrounded as it is in Wheatley's and Horton's verse, the authority of that genius depends upon slavery's effects on mothers, an appeal that participates very deeply in nineteenth-century conceptions of feminine sensibility. The greatest sin of slavery that a female abolitionist could identify is the way it deprived mothers of their capacity to act as mothers. And the most powerful expression of outrage was to provoke the reader to an awareness of his or her moral investment in the condition of slave mothers. Rather than simply detailing the wrongs of slavery, then, the poem challenges the reader to understand his or her own moral compromises. In effect, Harper's claims upon the social community of white women destabilizes the very terms of its claim to unity, using that destabilized notion of "woman" to rewrite the "feminine" morality into a feminist racial community.

As with Wheatley's claim to ideals of liberty, Harper's destabilization of the category of "woman" derived from her almost complete fulfillment of its conventional, even conservative, premises. As Hazel Carby points out, Harper revised the nineteenth-century discourses of true womanhood and its four cardinal virtues (piety, purity, submissiveness, and domesticity) for her own political purposes. These principles included a delicacy of constitution and modesty readable in the size and color of the female body, the manipulation of charm—titillating sexuality—rather than overt sexuality, the pursuit of wifehood and motherhood, and the dominion over private life. Black women—especially those who were slaves—were excluded from these categories, serving as the physical and moral antithesis against which true womanhood was defined, since black female sexuality was linked to capital accumulation and illicit sexual behavior rather than heirs, and since the work black women did meant that their less-than-delicate bodies did not bear the conventional marks of virtue. By making slave women into "women," Harper's poetry simultaneously undermines the terms of exclusion of the feminine and fulfills the claims of unity upon which her poetry is based. As Carby points out, "Women [such as Harper] who spoke in public to mixed audiences [in the nineteenth century] were considered by most people to lack good sense and high moral character"; and since political life had an investment in morality, most spokeswomen had to define their public advocacy as God's work with a high moral purpose and display knowledge of the Bible to do so (Foster 11). Hence Harper's numerous temperance poems and the following assertion in the lecture "Woman's Political Future," given at the World's Congress of Representative Women at the 1893 World's Fair: "If the fifteenth century discovered America to the Old World, the nineteenth is discovering woman to herself" (Foster 436). This newly self-aware woman now anticipates the coming of political power, says Harper, and with that power comes great responsibility, "for power without righteousness is one of the most dangerous forces in the world." While her habit of exercising moral authority in the domestic sphere does not guarantee moral political leadership, the nineteenth-century woman should prepare herself to maintain that moral authority in the public sphere. In these terms, Harper used conventions of womanhood to do what women were not supposed to do—speak in public—and to associate those same conventions with black women, who had been excluded from them. Her poetic genius thus genders genius, making the mastery of womanhood and poetic conventions associated with it—like sentimentality—a means by which she could revise racist and sexist exclusion.

The effect of this revision is a complex, hybrid notion of a "feminine" abolitionist community as the foundation of a just national community. Harper's practice also enacts a model of political poetic meaning through poetic conventionality that reiterates Wheatley's bardic genius. "The Slave Mother," one of Harper's most-anthologized poems, exemplifies Harper's broadening of conventional femininity to create this "national" community. The poem opens with a direct address to the reader that, formally, is perfectly appropriate to the kind of appeal Harper makes:

Heard you that shriek? It rose
   So wildly on the air,
It seemed as if a burden'd heart
   Was breaking in despair.

Saw you those hands so sadly clasped—
   The bowed and feeble head—
The shuddering of that fragile form—
   That look of grief and dread?

               (lines 1–8)

In keeping with the sentimental appeal associated with the literature of sensibility and with the fact that Harper probably read this poem at abolitionist meetings, the poem's opening question brings the reader directly into the anguish of the victim whose cry rose "so wildly on the air." It is also a way to place a woman's public address in a "proper" moral context. Posed as a series of questions, the poem's first three stanzas challenge the reader's ability to identify with this pain. If the implied reader does not hear the shrieks, the poem implies, the coldness of that reader's heart—its "petrifaction," if you will—will be revealed. In addition to this appeal, the poem asserts three times that the child whom the mother seeks to protect "is not hers," despite "the mother's pains"—presumably of labor—and despite the fact that "her blood / Is coursing through his veins!" (lines 19–20). Even among slaves, the poem argues, the bonds of family are real, the sympathy of mother and child is real, and the slave mother is a true woman, even if the society's laws and social practices do not recognize it. And the fact that the female speaker of the poem— Harper herself, of course—knows this moral truth authorizes the poem as much as its masterful ballad stanzas and crisp imagery do. This poem thus resembles Wheatley's poem to the Earl of Dartmouth, in which she refers to the suffering of her parents.

Community in this context is predicated on unifying sensibilities that are posited as universal, but instead of linking them directly to national community or to literary readership as Wheatley does, Harper associates those sensibilities with family. For example, the speaker points out that the defining horror of slavery derives from the fact that, in sending family members away from the mother, "cruel hands" have the capacity to "tear apart" the "wreath of household love / That binds her breaking heart" (lines 21–24). The poem concludes by associating the wreath with the natural beauty of sentimental human communion that becomes aligned in the poems with national belonging.

> His lightest word has been a tone
>   Of music round her heart,
> Their lives a streamlet blent in one—
>   Oh, Father! must they part?
>
> They tear him from her circling arms,
>   Her last and fond embrace.
> Oh! never more may her sad eyes
>   Gaze on his mournful face.
>
> No marvel, then, these bitter shrieks
>   Disturb the listening air:
> She is a mother, and her heart
>   Is breaking in despair.
>   (lines 29–40)

Slave women bear children and feel the emotional connections of motherhood, but they are not defined as such due to their race. But the speaker of the poem and the freeborn Harper are tied by bonds of race to these women, a contradiction that is revealed as one of the most fundamental horrors of slavery. Slave mothers *are* mothers, and once this fact is clear, the reader must acknowledge the astounding travesty that the family is destroyed by this peculiar institution. The great tragedy, then, is that the family "circle," hinted at in circle imagery throughout this passage, is torn asunder, meaning that the familial foundation of moral sensibility and national union is torn asunder. Most of Harper's poetic speakers, presumably Harper herself, thus occupy a space of "righteous" quasi-feminist moral self-assertion mirrored by Harper's conventional artistry and validated by this paradoxical appropriation of traditional domesticity for public unity. J. Saunders Redding is partly right when he notes that, though she was "immensely popular as a reader ('elocutionist'), the demands of [Harper's] audience for the sentimental treatment of old subjects sometimes overwhelmed her" (40). But he misses the fact that this sentimentality was a trenchant political use of poetic achievement. Sentimentality was for Harper the substance of the moral heroism of black female selfhood, of the moral character women were bringing to the public sphere and national life, and thus the terms by which abolitionists should move to end slavery and all people should embrace female sensibility as the foundation of nation.

In these terms, the individualism central to national identity became the foundation of a mode of "feminine" heroism in which Harper yokes "true womanhood" to masculine heroic ideals of adventure and self-assertion to validate this simultaneously conventional and alternative model of womanhood. For example, in "Eliza Harris," Harper transforms the sentimental moral martyrdom that is the substance of the meaning of "The Slave Mother" into a brave and active heroism that otherwise would be considered masculine. As Eliza escapes from slavery by crossing the Ohio River with her child, Harper writes:

> She was nearing the river—in reaching the brink,
> She heeded no danger, she paused not to think!
> For she is a mother—her child is a slave—
> And she'll give him his freedom, or find him a grave!
>
> ("Eliza Harris," lines 5–8)

It is telling that the only reason Harper gives for Eliza's motivation is simply that she is a mother. In the similarly titled "The Slave Mother (A Tale of Ohio)," Harper elaborates upon the apparently "heroic" story of a different slave mother—a historical one rather than one from *Uncle Tom's Cabin*—who did in fact find her children a grave, an act depicted as heroism twisted by the horror of slavery, but heroism nonetheless. In these passages, Harper has articulated the moral source of heroic action in the implications of "true womanhood" for a slave woman presumed to be capable neither of morality nor of heroism. No longer damsels in distress awaiting knights, these mothers act, and they do so in the best interests of their children within the circumscribed circumstances in which they find themselves. And in finding themselves, these characters become like the poet in their capacity to destabilize the boundaries and conventions of womanhood by daring to serve as a public example of the moral principles—"the zealous expression of sentiment" and the "reasoning intellect"—necessary for national union.

What mattered for Harper's use of poetry to protest slavery, then, was not primarily outrage but mastery. She assimilated conventions of womanhood in order to define a black female consciousness exemplified by the poet that asserted the slave's individuality and collective human commonality in the terms of rationality and sensibility, imagination and genius, that were current at the time. As with Wheatley's sublime, Harper's moral outrage, channeled through bardic mastery, presupposes and pursues the "pre-political" point of identification on which to build the political ideal of citizenship for the slave. So when Maryemma Graham pointed to Harper's use of the vernacular in her Aunt Chloe series, she was partly right to emphasize the heroism of folk wisdom in Harper's verse. But since this emphasis on folk culture functions as an ethnic authenticity that excludes a consideration of femininity, it does not tell the whole story. Also, since Graham implies that Aunt Chloe's wisdom is alternative simply because it is asserted in an early version of vernacular speech, her claim underestimates how fully conventional Aunt Chloe's wisdom was and how fully that wisdom was a component of the alternative "true womanhood" that Harper offered as a Reconstruction extension of her abolitionism. All of these elements of her verse are predicated in some substantial part on the "bardic genius"—the antiracist implications of the "gifted Negro"—that is the centerpiece of African American abolitionist verse.

In essence, for the African American abolitionist poet, especially the poet who was a slave, artistic self-assertion became an effectual challenge to the racist exclusion of the poet from ideals of national belonging, including the notions of absolute difference that allegedly justified slavery. Where Wheatley constructed citizenship from religiously authorized poetic genius, and where Horton constructed an artistic subjectivity that almost entirely authorizes itself (and almost fails) in its resistance to limitation, Harper authorized her protest through her role as a conventional woman. These three poets together exemplify the broad continuum of antiracist meaning available to the African American formalist poet from the public self-fashioning enacted through his or her mastery of traditional poetics. This range of "protest" is best illuminated by the terms of the literary conventions these poets mastered as those terms related to the racial ideology current at the time. Given this continuum, it becomes clear that, whatever we think of the actual quality of Wheatley's verse or of her conservative politics, her verse and public role exemplify the potentially subversive character of formalist poetic mastery and its associated cultural assimilation, anticipating the central forms and function of African American formalist poetics well into the twentieth century. In this verse, cultural assimilation is the locus of conflicting ideas about race, culture, and cultural achievement that transforms the self-assertion of artistic creation into the agency of racial protest. This practice also transforms the mainstream culture, becoming instrumental in the freedom of the slaves. This complex relationship between formal poetic structure and political effect is the defining antiracist effect of the African American poetic tradition. And it is built upon Wheatley's construction of herself as bardic genius.

2 "Writ on Glory's Scroll"

Paul Laurence Dunbar's Moral Heroism

But ah, the world, it turned to praise
A jingle in a broken tongue.

—Paul Laurence Dunbar, "The Poet"

In chapter 1, I argued that the originating antiracist aesthetic practice of the African American formalist poetic tradition was eighteenth-century poet and slave Phillis Wheatley's self-fashioning as a bardic genius. I suggested that her mastery of traditional poetics and her public status as poetic genius transformed her assimilation of mainstream religious and political beliefs—even the ones that justified her enslavement—into a claim to social inclusion as a citizen. In his most important volume of poetry, the 1896 *Lyrics of Lowly Life,* nineteenth-century poet, novelist, and journalist Paul Laurence Dunbar garnered his fame by broadening the effects of Wheatley's model of political poetics to include a fairly explicit ethnic self-definition, enacted as much through his neglected Standard English verse as through his more well-known dialect poetry. In its arrangement of Dunbar's two modes of verse, that volume created a paradoxical public perception of Dunbar as a romantic, bourgeois poet connected to the oft-disparaged folk, an image that was a more fully empowering African American ethnic identity than the ambivalent folk cultural self articulated in his dialect poetry alone. Many critics have noted that Dunbar's use of dialect was compromised due to his partial acceptance of the parody of African Americans that was central to the plantation tradition, which was the source of the conventions he used. But none have recognized that Dunbar's ideal of an empowering bourgeois ethnic self was a justifiable alternative that articulated the moral values through which an African American bourgeois self heroically transcended the stereotypes associated with dialect poetry and black folk culture to fulfill national ideals. As with Wheatley, then, Dunbar's representation of an ideal poetic self

as an ideal racial self effectively challenged ideologies of absolute racial difference and inferiority, in Dunbar's case transforming poetic mastery from the
fulfillment of conventional ideas of citizenship into the practice of ethnic self-
definition based paradoxically on national ideals. And, like Wheatley, Dunbar
did so using a vision of cultural evolution, in his case from folk to bourgeois
culture. Equally as important as Dunbar's innovative use of black language, in
other words, his poetry's construction of this paradoxically bourgeois ethnic
self is his greatest legacy.

In these terms, Dunbar initiated self-conscious ethnic self-definition in
African American poetry not primarily through his dialect poetry, as most
scholars claim, but through the relationship between his two modes of verse
in the 1896 volume, as they ultimately validated Dunbar's ethnic bourgeois
self. These modes effectively if provisionally resolved the newly emerging fis-
sure between folk and bourgeois culture in the African American cultural self-
concept, a resolution available only if Dunbar's dialect is read in the context of
the romantic idealism and bourgeois identity defined in his heroic odes in
Standard English. Dunbar's ideal ethnic self is located not in black language
but in his commitment to racial uplift ideology, the dominant black political
principles of the time predicated on ideals of economic self-assertion and
moral rectitude. Thus, I read Dunbar not primarily as a folk cultural poet but
as a poet who elaborated upon a mode of heroism in the ideology's "emphasis on self-help, racial solidarity, temperance, thrift, chastity, social purity,
patriarchal authority and the accumulation of wealth," which he construed as
"black" versions of the national ideals of individualism and social mobility
parallel to the individualism of the poet. His adaptation declared with some
justification that the cultural and aesthetic value of African American folk culture was as a precursor to the fulfillment of these ideals, the beginning of the
"uplift" to bourgeois achievement (Gaines 2, 5). This ideology therefore transformed poetic self-assertion into a theory and enactment of a unifying moral-
istic ethos for African American people that motivated the pursuit of higher
class status that, in Dunbar's aesthetic practice, reconciled folk to formal culture. As a vision of political engagement, Dunbar's poetics of racial uplift is
not to my mind entirely persuasive and has therefore rightly been criticized.
But these critiques have underestimated its admirable function as an aesthetic
self-definition that refuted the caricatures associated with the racist dialect
poetry of the plantation tradition and that redefined national values as racial
ones through a complex artistic redefinition of traditional heroic forms.
These complex artistic practices rescue Dunbar from his political ambiva-

lence and even hypocrisy. As a result, Dunbar's validation of racial uplift in *Lyrics of the Lowly* effectively expressed the spirit of an ethnic place, primarily the African American communal cultural self, making his ambivalent poetic and ethnic self genuinely empowering.

Two components of Dunbar's aesthetic are clarified in light of his conservative moralism. First, Dunbar's primary mode in dialect was parody rather than affirmation, and his primary mode in Standard English was the heroic ode. Second, this construction of romantic poetic genius as an alternative to folk cultural identity produced substantive antiracist effects. In the simplest terms, Dunbar's poetic self-fashioning enacts the process of ethnic self-definition that African American sociologist and cultural critic W. E. B. Du Bois suggested would resolve the problem of "double consciousness," the potentially debilitating psychological dynamic created when disempowered African Americans evaluate themselves in terms of the oppressive white society (Story 34). Just as Wheatley's status as poetic genius brought the ideology of racial inferiority in conflict with her achievement, Dunbar's poetic self in *Lyrics of Lowly Life* brought bourgeois ideals and folk cultural practices and values into conflict with one another by seeking to assert the cultural values that united African Americans simultaneously to each other and to the nation. By simultaneously engaging in and reflecting this problem, poems in both modes of verse enacted what Stuart Hall would describe as the spaces of "ideological struggle" in the dynamic, ever-changing ideological structure of society, spaces that "rearticulate" existing cultural discourses—in this case of folk cultural identity and bourgeois cultural norms—into alternatives that emerge from the dialectical synthesis of those discourses. In the case of *Lyrics of Lowly Life,* this space of psychological double consciousness and cultural transformation emerges from the fact that Dunbar's oft-neglected Standard English became the ideal fulfillment of the set of shared values that unified African American "lowly life" and that were asserted by implication in Dunbar's parody and more directly in his odes. Thus, as in Wheatley's construction of her genius, Dunbar's poetic self "rearticulated" racial difference by adapting a quasi-racist narrative of cultural evolution to the antiracist purposes of the ideal bourgeois, ethnic genius. The commitment to simple pleasures and moral self-cultivation in his dialect poetry became the themes of heroic self-assertion in his odes in Standard English. While revealing Dunbar's subtle disparagement of the folk, this representation of cultural evolution substantively redefined black identity in poetry as an ambivalently self-conscious process of ethnic self-definition.

I offer this ideal of moral heroism and this attention to Dunbar's dynamic rearticulation of race through class hierarchy in order to posit Dunbar's claim to and actual achievement of poetic glory as an alternative to the idea in most Dunbar criticism that his bourgeois elitism compromised the potential authenticity of his dialect poetry. These approaches to Dunbar tend to treat African American ethnic identity as fixed, purely vernacular, and inherently opposed to both bourgeois culture and formalist poetics, suggesting that the traditional poetic glory Dunbar pursued was opposed to African American ethnicity. While it is true, for example, that more of African American culture is folk than formal, the two are in no way simply opposed, meaning that Dunbar is in no real way a sellout or entirely divided against himself. Neither simply the self-hating poet capitulating to the dictates of a racist poetic tradition that such scholars as Jean Wagner and Emeka Okeze-Ekigbo make him out to be nor the poet of vernacular authenticity that Marcellus Blount suggests he was or that Henry Louis Gates suggested he could have been but failed to be, Dunbar was actually a slightly self-hating poet who resisted the dictates of not one but two racist poetic traditions by mastering both of those traditions. What the concept of bardic genius reveals, in short, is that Dunbar's achievement enacts the contradictory cultural mutation that, as Paul Gilroy, Werner Sollors, and others have acknowledged, is the defining component of what Sollors called the "process" of ethnicity. If ethnic identity is not actually fixed, then we can read Dunbar's verse as a construction rather than a reflection of an ethnic self and see in that construction and its dynamic contradictions the dynamic workings of ideology and power, within and against which Dunbar asserted his ambivalent but empowering self. This idea therefore reveals how socially disempowered Dunbar was and how fully he made the most of the genuinely narrow space of cultural navigation made available to him. Thus, I shift the blame for Dunbar's compromises more to society's misreading of his identity and his achievement then and now than too simply to Dunbar's alleged lack of nerve or political savvy. Though certainly conservative, Dunbar was no fool. Rather than reflecting poorly on an authentic self, Dunbar's work ambivalently revealed how poetry in general, and romantic poetics in particular, could participate in constructing that ethnic self, within and against vigorously oppressive terms in formal literary culture. This revelation challenged even as it accepted the notion that African American folk culture was absolutely other and lesser.

What is needed for a fuller appreciation of Dunbar's verse, then, is a new set of terms for Dunbar's ambivalent engagement in African American double consciousness that acknowledge how his representation of this divided self also implicitly and provisionally resolved it. The idea of bardic genius reclaims traditional artistry as self-assertion rather than sellout and evokes what Gilroy called the politics of fulfillment rather than the self-defeating politics of assimilation. In this real distinction, the artist did not seek to join a corrupt mainstream, as assimilation implies. Rather, the artist acts as a Jeremiah, a prophetic spokesperson who identified where society was not living up to its ideals and ideally helped motivate it to pursue those ideals anew. And in Dunbar's case, this jeremiad also implied that black people were already living up to those ideals, despite racism and poverty. As a former elevator operator, Dunbar knew firsthand this ideal position of transformation. Thus, on this point Darwin T. Turner was partly right: "Dunbar's noble sentiments and protagonists [in his short stories, through whom Dunbar 'repeatedly emphasized the ability and willingness of Negroes to forgive white Americans for previous injustice'] reveal not only a naïve political philosophy but also a romantic and idealized concept of society. He believed in right rule by an aristocracy based on blood and birth which assured culture, good breeding and all of the virtues appropriate to a gentleman" (3). Though Dunbar was not as naïve nor as interested in inherited or biological aristocracy as Turner suggests, he was indeed interested in "good breeding," the cultivation of allegedly universal moral values that would ideally justify social inclusion, which he portrayed as being central to the heroic process of cultural unity and self-definition that African Americans were enacting in Dunbar's time. If, as Du Bois put it, "the history of the Negro is the history of this strife" between two opposed cultural traditions in one ethnic mind, then Dunbar construes this historical strife to be resolved by the artistry of the bourgeois poet as an extension of the moral ideals of the folk. Thus, in *Lyrics of Lowly Life*, Dunbar can indeed intersperse poems of both sorts on equal footing. Racial uplift was not just the economic self-sufficiency and acceptance of social segregation that Booker T. Washington made it out to be. It was cultural self-sufficiency as well, a self-sufficiency best exemplified by poetic romanticism, not by the parodies of dialect.

In other words, cultural cultivation was moral cultivation for Dunbar, and both were components of the heroic self-assertion of racial uplift and therefore of heroic self-definition. And the two together also validated the artist's gifts and achievements, which in turn validated the race's capacity for uplift, a point Dunbar averred in "The Negro as Individual." As such, Dunbar believed, as Du Bois put it, that being a "co-worker in the kingdom of culture" was an answer to the divided African American self. In his essay "Representative American Negroes," Dunbar makes this role of culture quite clear: "In the Luxembourg gallery hangs [African American painter Henry O. Tanner's] picture, 'The Raising of Lazarus.' At the Academy of Fine Arts, Philadelphia, I saw his 'Annunciation,' both a long way from his 'Banjo Lesson,' and thinking of him I began to wonder whether, in spite of all the industrial tumult, it were not in the field of art, music and literature that the Negro was to make his highest contribution to American civilization" (*Dunbar Reader* 59). For Dunbar, Booker T. Washington's philosophy of accommodation through industrial training, social segregation, and economic self-assertion was inadequate because it did not deal with the full complexity and highest faculties of the African American self. Thus, the corresponding representation of the race in Tanner's "Banjo Lesson," where an elderly black man teaches his son or grandson how to play the banjo, was inadequate as well. Ultimately, African Americans must acknowledge that folk culture and manipulate that accommodation to move a "long way" beyond the pursuit of wealth and from an old-fashioned culture of the folk to the individual and communal validation available in representation in the Academy of Fine Arts and the portrait of grand biblical themes of Lazarus in African American life. Traditional artistic achievement mattered because the social values necessary for full racial harmony were best articulated and most fully enacted in art. And Dunbar suggested that African American cultural identity was defined centrally by the moral character that made ethnic self-definition into national self-definition.

While Dunbar can be read ideologically as having his subjectivity entirely determined by racist ideological forces, I prefer to see the complex ways in which this vision of "cultivation" reveals the flexible and complex nature of racial selfhood, a set of ideas always already invested in mainstream culture and constantly in self-contradictory flux even as they oppress. This idea is particularly important for recognizing how formalist poetics constitutes as much a foundation for ethnic selfhood in Dunbar's verse as dialect. And that empowerment emerges from Dunbar's cultivation of assimilation. Even an elevator operator can embody the nobility of national ideals that would lead to social inclusion.

Readings of Dunbar must take this ideal of moral heroism more fully into account in order to understand the true, parodic function of Dunbar's dialect and its backhanded affirmation of the moral values that constitute the substance of his more directly affirming heroic portraits in his Standard English odes. Even though his dialect poetry arguably owes at least as much to the realism of the Hoosier dialect of James Whitcomb Riley that Dunbar idolized as to the racist plantation tradition, it ultimately owes more to Dunbar's personal economic necessity (he could not get published without them and he wanted to live as a man of letters) and the conventions of parody than to authenticity or realism. As Wagner points out, "In the revival of the plantation tradition a scant ten years after the Civil War had ended[,] . . . there came the new southern resentment of the Negro, who was regarded as primarily responsible for four years of bloodletting," so that "the writers of the New South place[d] the Negro in the foreground" (50–51). As many scholars have noted, the images of this plantation tradition were originally based on misreading of black language and on the myth of the "happy darky," the stereotype of the slave who was happy in slavery or of the sharecropper who yearned for the genteel relations of that slave past (Revell 32–33). Both the misreading of the language and the "happy darky" stereotypes were read as realistic conceptions of black people. As a result, as J. Saunders Redding observes, "By a sort of natural development the 'darky' sketches, now so intimately a part of American minstrelsy, hardened into the recognized speech of the Negro" and "set up the limits to the Negro's media of expression . . . as a slapstick and a pathetic buffoon" (50–51). These conventions included comparisons between the wealth of whites and the poor imitations blacks offered, as in the slave's banjo versus the white's piano. And these comparisons became the basis for celebrating and even prescribing the loyalty of the happy darky to the plantation system, since that system included an alleged aristocratic love from white owners that was better than capitalist indifference (Revell 32–33). Finally, the poetic conventions of this tradition involved a portrait of the race's need for moral guidance, for the paternal leadership that the Old South patriarch gave to slaves he knew by name in order to guide them in life, more generously and helpfully than the absentee capitalist could. And, according to these conventions, black people knew it.

It is remarkable that scholars such as Wagner, Okeze-Izigbo, and Gates know of these compromised conventions of dialect but have not fully and properly assessed how this odd combination of realism and parody made the representation of any "authentic" identity impossible and undermined the moral idealism that both modes of verse tried to celebrate. A closer attention to how these ideas functioned in Dunbar's time is needed. For example, the publishers of African American dialect poet Daniel Webster Davis used an image called "The Negro as He Is" to introduce his 1895 pamphlet *Idle Moments*, taking the caption from the title of one of Davis's poems. In the image, this allegedly representative black man, sitting on a small satchel in rustic garb in front of his rustic cabin, puzzles out the words on his two placards, "the ballot" and "education." He seems to prefer the ballot to education, since he holds that placard in his hand while the one for education is at his feet. A press clipping from the *Richmond Times* claims that "'Idle Moments' depict[s] the Negro in his transition stage from slavery to his present station" (*Idle Moments* v). The implication is either that the thinker is headed in the right direction, toward enfranchisement, or that he is moving too fast, skipping a step in his evolution. Similarly, in the preface to Campbell's 1895 *Echoes from the Cabin*, northern journalist Richard Linthicum claims that "the evolution of the Negro is fast destroying the unique types of the race" and that "the author of this volume has caught the true spirit of the antebellum Negro, and in characteristic verse has portrayed the simplicity, the philosophy and the humor of the race" (9). William Dean Howells, who wrote the introduction to Dunbar's 1896 volume, located Dunbar's value in Dunbar's "ironical perception of the negro's limitations" (xviii). Thus, in the racist nostalgia of the progressive, dialect preserves the differences of African Americans which were dying out in their admirable assimilation. In the racist nostalgia of the apologist, the image represented a better past condition for blacks. For both, folk cultural difference meant comic inferiority, and neither saw African American culture as heroic. Any representation of the folk was subject to this compromise, clarifying how the dynamics of cultural imperialism make the recovery of an authentic folk self for the marginalized minority a dubious pursuit, as Homi Bhabba has suggested. Though not a sophisticated cultural theorist, Dunbar clearly recognized the limitations these discursive conditions entailed.

Given their commitment to racial uplift, which exacerbates these stereotypes, African American dialect poets like Dunbar and Davis were not as interested as they could have been in asserting some heroism in folk culture itself. But they were interested in the moral heroism of uplift and did use it awkwardly to reclaim some small dignity from portraits such as the one described above, positing morality as an alternative to the false and disparaged "authenticity" of the folk. For example, Davis offered his poem "The Negro as He Is" as an assertion of the terms of moral heroism by which bourgeois black people such as Davis himself superseded the genuinely uncultivated folk, though the folk revealed some of those same values in their disparaged culture. Davis's poem proposes in its epigraph to reveal "our true condition and the remedy apply" and contains such lines as "We boast of education but the masses still plod on / In grossest superstition, and for bread prefer stone," lines which articulate the ambivalence black elites such as Davis felt in their conflicted space between bourgeois assimilation and racial unity (Gaines 8). As Joan Sherman points out, "Davis . . . follows [Booker T.] Washington's practice of criticizing his own race, pointing out that its faults and foibles, [which were] the legacy of slavery, cause much of the discrimination and prejudice they suffer." Davis also thought that the race was ultimately judged by its lower class, whom "he described as . . . shiftless, extravagant and showy, untidy, dishonest, untruthful, unreliable, imitative, suspicious, superstitious, and immoral," people who "must be regenerated by their teachers and ministers," of whom Davis was one (459, 471).

In effect, the conventions of dialect poetry did indeed seem as though they were a fixed game, as Ralph Story suggested, and, in the hands of dialect poets less talented and of less subtle aesthetic minds than Dunbar, were in fact just that. When Davis's dialect poems attribute the same bourgeois moral values to the masses as he claims for himself, he does so through the parodic figures of dialect stereotypes in ways that do little to undermine the authority of the stereotype. For example, the last stanza of Davis's poem "The Biggis Piece ub Pie" reads as follows:

> Fur when tiz mine to go alone
>   To de happy hom' ub love,
> I kin not take de smallis' piece
>   To dat bright lan' above;
> An' when I reach de gol'en gate,
>   In glory lan' on high,
> I'll not be axed how much I had,
>   But how I used my pie.[1]

This portrait of the modest ambition of a comical minstrel figure, a thrifty and chaste happy darky, moves from selfishness to generosity in order to reveal not only how this stock figure is placated in his deprived "present station" with pursuits of animal satisfaction but also how this moment of self-satisfaction reinforces the bourgeois principles that make this figure comical. According to the poem, what matters is not accumulation but use, with the proper use of material goods ("how I used my pie") being construed as admirable moral action.

The entire race would be worthy of both the Christian heaven and the heaven of the American cultural mainstream if it would follow this moral plan of "economic" self-sufficiency, which is also validated in "Stickin to de Hoe":

I 'spose dat I'm ol'fashun',
   But God made man to plow,
An' git his libbin by de sweat
   Dat trickles down his brow.
While larnin' an' all dem things
   Am mighty good fur sho',
De bes' way we kin make our pints
   Is—stickin' to de hoe.
             (lines 49–56)

Here is virtuous self-help as opposed to unnecessary "book-larnin'," a version of the alleged anticapitalist moral authority of the Old South. These portraits affirm the principles of racial uplift by attributing them to these comic figures, both asserting and undermining the idea that these characters are acting properly out of that ideology or that they could serve as the ultimate affirmation of the race. The race may be judged by its lower classes, but Davis hopes to change that by associating the race with the upper class, by reinforcing the parody of dialect. Davis's verse did not fully enact the cultural contradictions and synthesis that constitute what I have called bardic genius and thus is less successful than Dunbar's as a practice of affirming ethnic self-definition.

But Davis's case illuminates how narrow was the discursive space these black dialect poets navigated and how we should be particularly sympathetic to Dunbar, who offered the fullest affirmation of African American identity that was possible in this parodic form. Though subject to some of the same flaws as Davis's work, Dunbar's dialect poetry does manipulate opposing cultural discourses by manipulating opposing cultural practices and aesthetic conventions within the dialect tradition. Dunbar's parody in dialect functions similarly to Davis's, then, with the exception that Dunbar validates this moral heroism more complexly by subtly undermining the parodic conventions he uses, a practice that, while innovative, could of necessity have only limited success. In other words, Dunbar transforms the minstrel "sounds" of dialect, to paraphrase Houston Baker in *Modernism and the Harlem Renaissance,* into the voice of a tragic-comic moral heroism in which the poet's virtuosity allows for fuller validation of African American folk culture in its own right than the characters in the poems could realize (15–16). Unlike Davis's or Campbell's, then, Dunbar's dialect participates more fully in what Eric J. Sundquist rightly identified as a "tradition of performative subversion of white authority that reached back into slave culture" (8). It is what Gates famously defined as "signifying": "If blacks were the subject of this sort of racist Signifyin(g) parody [of nineteenth-century white society's use of dialect] they were also quite capable of establishing the necessary distance between themselves and their condition to Signify upon white racism through parody" (*Signifying Monkey* 94). Just as African Americans Bert Williams and Herbert Walker donned blackface and parodied the practice by calling themselves "Two Real Coons," Dunbar offers a parody of a parody either by exaggerating the stereotypes to the point of incredulity or by using a mode of realism to excavate from beneath the comic stereotypes the moral ideals that inhere in the folk culture being simultaneously represented and parodied. Not only is his art more fully a refutation of stereotypes without a primary recourse to authenticity, it is also more fully an affirmation of the moral codes of the nation by which, for Dunbar, the African American bourgeois self is constituted in the process of ethnic culture being enacted in Dunbar's turn-of-the-century society.

Instead of implicitly comparing Dunbar's dialect to that of such later, more assertive, and prideful dialect poets as Langston Hughes, as is too often done, I am suggesting that the flaw in his art was also its greatest strength: its manipulation of the limited, self-defeating power of parody to validate the moral heroism of the romantic bourgeois poet that is his ultimate ideal. In "The Party," for example, Dunbar fully embraces the stereotype of the happy darky for sheer enjoyment of it, while humanizing it to some extent by elevating animal satisfaction to the level of a morally admirable commitment to the joy of living in the face of implicit oppressive circumstances. The poet, through his speaker, occupies the duality of being one of the parodied and one doing the parodying, an observer appreciating the culture and a participant, something Davis never does. With less of a condescending edge than Davis presents, Dunbar's poem recounts a celebration that the addressed "you" of the poem missed, cataloging the stereotypical behavior and pleasures of the stereotypical black people who donned fine clothes and put on airs for comic enjoyment. Parody is relevant here because the party itself is thus based in part upon the cakewalk, an African American folk practice in which African Americans, especially slaves, imitated the pretensions of their white owners for comic effect. That ritual competition, in which the best imitators were awarded with the cake, also functioned to elevate the antics of the African parodist into its own kind of pretension. Thus, it is a version of the signifying performative subversion Gates and Sundquist discuss in which the pretensions of whites are both fulfilled and undermined in the same gesture. While such practices as these were prime evidence for the slavery apologists that Africans had been

happy as slaves, they were more accurately evidence of the self-awareness of
and playful satire enacted by those blacks. By portraying such figures enjoying their food and their false pretensions, the plantation-tradition poet could
poke fun at the African's allegedly failed imitation of white culture while celebrating the former happier state. Like the preacher spouting malapropisms or
the "cullud Gentlman" or other such stereotypes, the happy darky of the cakewalk was a parody of black claims to inclusion. But Dunbar's use partially
affirms and enacts the capacity of African Americans to manipulate stereotypes for comic and pecuniary purposes.

These cross-purposes simultaneously enliven and compromise the poem.
The nine-page poem addresses "you" in the poem as both another "darky"
who missed the party and the more genteel, presumably white, reader who
was even less likely to be in attendance. As such, Dunbar's parody addresses its
dual audience explicitly.

> Ain't seen no sich fancy dressin' sence las quah'tly meetin' day
> Gals all dressed in silks an' satins, not a wrinkle ner a crease,
> Eyes a-battin', teeth a-shinin', haih breshed back ez slick ez grease;
> Sku'ts all tucked an' puffed an' ruffled, evah blessed seam an' stitch;
> Ef you'd seen em' wif deir mistus, couldn't swahed to which was which.[2]

On one hand, both blacks and whites share the desire for aristocratic hierarchy, for sartorial finery, and for pomp and circumstance. Both blacks and
whites enjoy the comedy evoked when black people imitate pretentious
whites. This commonality of vanity and pretension also places Dunbar as poet
in a position to exaggerate the conventions of the stereotypes to such an
extent—with the eyes and teeth in stereotypic poses—that it would ideally
undermine it. But the poem's extreme versions of this stereotype function like
Chinese boxes, producing regressions of meaning that ultimately trap the parody in its own terms. The implication of commonality across the boundaries
of race and class is a challenge to racist social exclusion, but the comic associations of the misspelling of dialect itself, along with the stereotypical pleasures
of the flesh that follow, emphasize the quaint ways in which the lack of certain
resources renders the black version of this pretentious culture a lesser imitation. And even as Dunbar hits the deeper note of the joy of living, "The Party"
ends in separation: "Y'ought to been dah, fu' I tell you evahthing was rich an'
prime, / An' dey ain't no use in talkin', we jes had one scrumptious time!"
(lines 97–98). Many of Dunbar's poems operate in this fashion; with poems

such as these, Dunbar confirms for the other part of his audience their comic preconceptions. While other scholars lionize Dunbar's capacity to speak to two audiences, I agree with Dunbar that this forked tongue divides the poetic self falsely and undermines more substantive ideals of poetic achievement that would offer more substantive resistance to racism.

In fact, even Dunbar's dialect poetry is most effective when it combats this inherent parody with an assertion of the moral principles of self-definition associated with racial uplift as exemplified by artist figures. This affirmation of morality created the spaces of cultural conflict through which Dunbar's verse at its best substantively "rearticulates" the meaning of these stereotypes. Such poems also point toward the fuller achievement of these ambivalent ideals in Dunbar's Standard English verse. A good example is "When Malindy Sings," in which Dunbar takes on the stereotype of natural musical gifts and offers a persuasive celebration of a vernacular cultural tradition in which joy of living becomes artistic self-definition. Instead of looking for laughs, this poem affirms the greater power of the natural musical talents of Malindy over the schooling and precision of Miss Lucy, who could be read either as an educated black person or as a white mistress. The poem therefore celebrates the capacity to express oneself as the most valuable means by which to make oneself, to validate communal mores, and to heighten communal morale.

> Who dat says dat humble praises
>   Wif de Master nevah counts?
> Heish yo' mouf, I hyeah dat music,
>   Ez hit rises up an' mounts—
> Floatin' by de hills an' valleys,
>   Way above dis buryin' sod
> Ez hit makes its way in glory
>   To de very gates of God
>
> Oh, hit's sweetah dan de music
>   Of an edicated band;
> An' hit's dearah dan de battle's
>   Song o' triumph in de lan'.
> It seems holier dan evenin'
>   When de solemn chu'ch bell rings,
> Ez I sit an' ca'mly listen
>   While Malindy sings.
>   (lines 41–56)

The praise for Malindy here and as it is repeated throughout the poem is Dunbar's subtle attempt to work through the minstrel affirmation of the comic naturalness and unlearned talents of blacks into an affirmation of a vernacular cultural practice. Malindy's gift is a native and untutored appreciation of the divine that redeems the divine itself. After all, the voice is holier than religious rituals ("chu[r]rch bells"), elevating these "humble praises" to an ideal mode of worship. And this portrait of voice is much more directly an affirmative alternative to the stereotypes than reckless eyeballing because it locates that value as much in the possibility of an actually affirming black folk culture as in the conventions of dialect. In other words, this is one of the few dialect poems where Dunbar's sense of folk culture is substantially different from the stereotypes of the plantation tradition. Not only is the affirmation genuine, it also could be claiming that natural genius as a version of Dunbar's own.

In these terms, "When Malindy Sings" offers an empowering racial identity not through the address of opposed audiences or even through the persuasive and pervasive analogy of cultural masking but through the best fidelity to the vernacular culture available in dialect poetry. The poem creates a space in which the folk cultural protagonist can be constructed as a version of the poet himself and can bring the assumptions of dialect in conflict with one another to suggest that even bourgeois African Americans have a greater source of voice and values from folk culture than is sometimes acknowledged. This space of conflict has to do with artistic self-definition, creating what John Keeling called "a space in addition to the discourses of the Plantation Tradition . . . and of the blues protestor [who challenges racism more directly and didactically] . . . where an author such as Dunbar can wear a mask that 'grins and lies' in order to expose [the] blues realities." "Blues realities" for Keeling are the implications of social limitation that a dialect poem suggests through what it does not say. For Keeling, that space is the artistry itself, since Dunbar's adaptation of the conventions of dialect allows him to posit the limits of those conventions. But Keeling argues that this excess of meaning depends upon the idea that Malindy does not exist, since she makes no literal appearance in the poem, so that "a much bleaker vision rupture[es] the surface" (28). That bleaker vision is an implication that there is a lack of genuine culture because of the implied oppressive social conditions that produce that lack. In this way, the poem becomes a kind of mask analogous to the parody of "The Party."

The problem with this reading is that it assumes a specific black reality that the poem disguises and assumes that reality to be entirely a lack, offering one of the most unfortunate consequences of the priority on authenticity in the study of African American literature: authenticity as victimhood. Keeling assumes or implies that slave or folk culture is a lack for Dunbar, entirely debilitated by racism. I reject this implication altogether. It seems to me that, though the blues realities implicit in the poem are associated with social deprivation, the real "blues" meaning of the poem—if the association with the blues is even appropriate—is in the function of the speaker. Like a blues singer, Malindy can sing the community's pain, bringing it the heaven of emotional solace with her voice. Poems such as "Banjo Song" and "When the Cone Pone's Hot" imply a tradition of modest solace to the horrors of oppression available through the artist figure. Thus, in "An Ante-bellum Sermon," Dunbar asserts that the artist figure speaks for the race in a masking subtlety that is more than adequate to the task. It is almost not masking at all, but rather the claiming of moral authority that, if expressed too directly, could lead to physical violence. In the poem a minister preaches to a largely black audience, with his gestures of careful wording suggesting that white listeners are around. Keeling's "blues realities" are more relevant to this poem than to "When Malindy Sings," since what is absent is a sense of security and an inviolate communal space. Blackness is always infiltrated, and submission to that infiltration can only be a viable response for a time. This assertion of a need for evolution and even revolution is most evident in the preacher's comparison of the slave's situation to that of the Israelites, while insisting that he is only talking in metaphors.

> So you see de Lawd's intention,
>   Eva sence de worl' began
> Was dat His almighty freedom
>   Should belong to evah man,
> But I think it would be bettah,
>   Ef I'd pause agin to say
> Dat I'm talking' bout ouah freedom
>   In a Bibleistic way.
>   (lines 57–64)

Such disclaimers as the one that concludes this stanza are frequent in the poem and only serve to emphasize the implication that the preacher is talking about material freedom. It also serves to enhance the poem's sense of the censorship of white power that undermines the truthfulness of the happy darky. Of course the slave would express content in the presence of whites! But given other references to biblical prophecy in Dunbar's work, this preacher is meant to be suggesting genuine freedom soon to be ordained by God. Its being "Bibleistic" does not make the pursuit of freedom any less real. In fact, Dunbar clearly implied that he prefers shedding the mask, that manipulations of the cakewalk, while enjoyable, are limiting, and certainly writing dialect poems about them is even more limited.

Thus, Dunbar's self-awareness as a poet and his construction of a poetic persona both of and separate from the folk is more politically savvy than is sometimes suggested in political studies of him, especially those which pay little or no attention to the foil of the Standard English verse. For example, Baker vilifies Dunbar for failing to "adopt masking as self-conscious gamesmanship in opposition to the game white America has run on him," arguing,

> Someone as proximate to the abhorrences of slavery as Dunbar—whose father was a fugitive and whose mother recounted stories of slavery to her young son—should know [as did Booker T. Washington, that masking is subversive performance]. Anyone with Dunbar's background who did not realize the guile and game of minstrelsy for what they were, who could in fact whine that the most powerful literary critic of his era had done him "harm" by praising and ensuring the publication and sale of his dialect poetry—any black writer of this stamp had to be naïve, politically innocent or simply "spoiled." (*Modernism and the Harlem Renaissance* 46)

In essence, Dunbar had the wrong intentions in wanting to be a romantic poet, according to Baker, because that pursuit undermined the capacity of his poetry to "signify" on white racism through performative subversion. But what Dunbar knew, perhaps in a naïve way, was that his romantic ambitions were more substantively antiracist than his dialect poetry, especially given the terms by which Howells praised his dialect. Dunbar knew that the parodic subversion of masking that Baker valorizes was inherently caught in the tension in what Linda Hutcheon called the paradox of parody:

> This paradox of legalized though unofficial subversion is characteristic of all parodic discourse insofar as parody posits, as a prerequisite to its very existence, a certain institutionalization which entails the acknowledgement of recognizable, stable forms and conventions. These function as norms or as rules which can—and therefore, of course, shall—be broken. The parodic text is granted a special licence to transgress the limits of convention,

but, as in the carnival, it can do so only temporarily and only within the controlled confines authorized by the text parodied—that is, quite simply, within the confined dictated by "recognizability." (74–75)

In these terms, Dunbar's dialect had to be recognizable as the representation of the limitations of black people and therefore was inherently circumscribed by the preexisting dialect conventions. Moreover, since parody shifts the reader's attention from the world to the literary text, as Hutcheon also points out, an appeal to authenticity will not obviate these limiting effects of parody. First of all, Dunbar would be read for whether or not he mastered the existing conventions before his parody could work, not whether the conventions were true to black people. Worse, the parodic effects already built into dialect actually were already read as "authentic" to African American culture. These effects were self-canceling.

As a result, Dunbar offers his most substantial affirmation of African American ethnic identity not in his dialect poems—not even in "When Malindy Sings" or "An Ante-bellum Sermon"—but in the Standard English odes in which the joy of living and the hints of moral heroism in African American folk culture reach their fullest fruition in the valiant figures Dunbar explicitly lionizes without the paradox of parody. Moreover, those odes also clarify in their construction of the poet why the bardic genius of the romantic poet was potentially more substantively antiracist than was African American folk culture. As often anthologized as his dialect poems, Dunbar's "Ode to Ethiopia" is perhaps the best example of this fuller affirmation. The poem opens by declaring that the race is the poet's muse:

O Mother Race! to thee I bring
This pledge of faith unwavering,
    This tribute to thy glory.
I know the pangs which thou didst feel,
When Slavery crushed thee with its heel,
    With thy dear blood all gory.
                    (lines 1–6)

The poet pledges faith to the race and pledges that he will sing its glory, transforming praises normally reserved for God in the Christian tradition or the muses and gods in the classical tradition into an aspect of this epic invocation of a historical ethnic identity. Also, by referring to the biblical prophecy of

Ethiopia stretching forth her hands to God (Psalm 68:32), Dunbar places newly freed blacks in a glorious biblical history that substantiates the race's and the poet's place in the mainstream traditions of heroic poetry. Here the speaker is talking freedom both in a material and in a "Bibleistic" way. Moreover, as in the heroic tradition of the West, in which individual heroes almost literally embody their community's values, Dunbar attributes to every individual of the race, including the poet himself, the heroic endurance, the long-suffering pursuit of justice, and the prophecy of future liberation asserted here in collective terms. After all, the poet gets to claim a voice central to that Ethiopian community's values. Crucially, this heroic ancestry is of both the Christian tradition of the West and a distinctive African prophetic faith. The cultural assimilation of traditional poetic mastery and Christian religious faith coexists well with the affirmation of ethnic difference in this ideal Ethiopian self.

And those new Ethiopians are the African American masses who distinguish themselves from racist stereotypes of dialect poetry and from white Americans by embodying the ideal values by which they will heroically uplift themselves simultaneously into Ethiopia's glory and into American national belonging. What makes them heirs to the legacy and prophecy of biblical Ethiopians, in other words, is their slow but discernible fulfillment of Booker T. Washington's version of racial uplift, the black versions of national ideals of individual effort and economic and social self-sufficiency:

No other race, or white or black,
When bound as thou wert, to the rack,
    So seldom stooped to grieving;
No other race, when free again,
Forgot the past and proved them men
    So noble in forgiving.
                                (lines 37–42)

As biographer Peter Revell put it, Dunbar is "establishing in the mind of the reader, black or white, the belief that the black citizen has a deserved and meritorious place in the life of the nation" (66). Rather than being predicated on the humor of dialect or the revelation of a truer folk culture sometimes enacted through the parody of parody, that meritorious place depends here upon how, given this resistance to bitterness, "Proud Ethiope's swarthy children stand" and "stir in honest labor" as "They tread the fields where honor calls" and as "Their voices sound through senate halls / In majesty and power" (lines 14, 18, 19, 20–21). While the poet joins the heroic tradition of the West through his formal mastery, the race distinguishes itself as heroic and divine through the manual toil of farming. As awkward as this "nobility" sounds to post–Civil Rights ears, it is a substantive antiracist stance. Bitterness against oppression is no more inherently a proper response to racism than this noble suffering and self-sufficiency. And even if we grant the fact that such bitterness usually emerges from a greater sense of urgency, such bitterness is not necessarily poetically or politically better than the validation of achievement.

Oddly enough, then, Dunbar derives a heroic vision out of the portrait of the race implied by the image of "The Negro as He Is" and in Davis's poem of that name, tying it to a more directly self-assertive version of that vision and to the heroic achievement of the poet himself. Without the comic frame of dialect, that bourgeois selfhood was more substantively heroic, even if it is still a partial submission to the superior power of white society. The suffering of oppression, like the suffering of honest labor, is ennobling in part, obviously, because it is not a direct challenge to white power, truly a limited and limiting mode of affirmation. But this accommodationist vision validates the reality of the masses of African Americans by tying such patience to the prophetic faith with which the poem opens:

Though hast the right to noble pride,
Whose spotless robes were purified
 By blood's severe baptism.
Upon thy brow the cross was laid,
And labour's painful sweat-beads made
 A consecrating chrism.
     (lines 31–36)

Social inferiority and segregation are part of a divine plan in which the principles of self-help will produce substantive resistance to social oppression. That faith is heroic, as are the acts pursued in its name. Those acts may include more direct opposition, though that opposition is not stated here. But the "consecrating chrism" of the "severe baptism" testifies to the social and spiritual "holiness" of this biblical race ordained for its freedom, a race that started with "spotless robes" and was purified even more by its moral heroism. As politics, this vision is accommodationist. As poetry, it is quite beautiful, broadening the accommodation into self-assertion and validating a set of values that motivate Dunbar's genuine if ambivalent version of cultural self-determination. The poem therefore articulates what was called in antiquity the "heroic ethos" of a "heroic society," declared and enacted by the poet, an ethos tied both to the passive moral heroism of uplift and the potentially more active biblical prophecy (Bowra 15).

In addition to being more direct, then, liberated from the fetters of stereotypes and parody, the affirmation of this preordained heroic vision through poetic genius also more fully claims a very public place for this celebration by evoking the conventions of the ode. Dunbar is still potentially addressing two audiences here, one with the "content" and one with the "form," but both are getting the same message: the heroic history of the race is being recorded in the very instance of the poem as well as in the world around the poem.

> Be proud, my Race, in mind and soul;
> Thy name is writ on Glory's scroll
>   In characters of fire.
> High 'mid the clouds of Fame's bright sky
> Thy banner's blazoned folds now fly,
>   And truth shall lift them higher.
>   (lines 25–30)

Even though the choice of form and language implies an implicit attention to a white audience, the traditional formalism functions to enhance the themes surrounding the idea that the race has been given divine place on the "scroll" on which the last judgments are recorded. Divine "Glory" and secular "Fame" become aspects of one another, two sides of the coin of historical memory, because the poet is doing as much to write the race's name on the scroll as is the historical and religious prophecy. By being directed to an audience on a presumably more august occasion than in any of the dialect poems, "Ode to Ethiopia" has the effect of identifying, calling into existence, and spreading to the world the "truth" of the race's banner and the poet's fame, both of which are currently obscured by the clouds of racism. Moreover, as Revell observes, the poem is written in *rime couee*, a characteristic stanza of the eighteenth-century ode: "It is not just the formal language that dignifies the subject. The mere choice of form asserts a claim that the race and its sufferings and achievements merits the language usually accorded to heroic events in the nation's history, and makes that suffering a religious dedication to endure and to prevail" (65). While this notion of elevating the race to the level of the nation accepts the racial hierarchy of white supremacy, it also suggests that African Americans are their own measure of this heroism, enacting black versions of national ideals that shall be remembered for how much more fully they embodied national possibility in society and, of course, in art.

> Go on and up! Our souls and eyes
> Shall follow thy continuous rise;
>   Our ears shall list the story
> From bards who from thy root shall spring
> And proudly tune their lyres to sing
>   Of Ethiopia's glory.
>
> (lines 43–48)

The race should rest assured in its heroism and in the fact that a host of bards of this racial and historical tradition will sing Ethiopia's glory, including this poet himself. Crucially, it will take a black bard to sing this heroism and the poem makes Dunbar one of the first in that line. The declaration of an ethnic tradition of poetic bards—a bardic tradition not unlike the one I am describing in this book—these assertions are more than accommodation alone. Given its investment in an ethnic vision of biblical prophecy and its claim to an ethnic tradition, this vision of accommodation is also ethnic affirmation and clarifies how William Dean Howells did indeed do Dunbar wrong to suggest that his Standard English verse could have been written by a white man. The cultural perspective and the conception of the poetic self here make it quite clear that, though rooted in principles of social integration, accommodation, and assimilation, this poem is about a distinctive ethnic culture worthy of a race's pride and central to inclusion in the nation.

In essence, "Ode to Ethiopia" exemplifies how these Standard English odes create a vision of poetic meaning and poetic selfhood that unifies Dunbar's two opposing audiences and his two visions of moral heroism into the ambivalently empowering cultural self resolute in its ethnic community. On one hand, the poem verifies Dunbar's assertion that it was through the arts, not "industrial tumult," that African Americans would make their greatest contributions to society. On the other, the greatest contribution his people are currently making is their labor and patience, their forgiving adherence to the ideals of economic uplift through individual effort. The bourgeois elitism of uplift need not be that of the intellectuals alone, in other words, nor do the intellectuals need to be entirely alienated from the masses for them to attribute to those masses the affirmation accorded to the virtue of the intellectuals. Both elites and masses share common ideals of valor and achievement and they share a common heroic destiny. Representing this pursuit of assimilation as heroic functions is a poetically effective way of linking the poetic self to the racial self and the national self in common ideals without any hints of parody or compromise. It is ultimately more effective than offering versions of these same ideals through the comic parody of dialect. Neither would qualify entirely as heroic from the perspectives of the Black Nationalism from which so much African American literary and cultural thought emerges, but this vision of poetic artistry as an extension of racial heroism is, in its very ambivalence, a rejection of stereotypes and, more important, an empowering fulfillment of the possibilities of bardic genius initiated by Phillis Wheatley.

This ambivalent reconciliation of bourgeois elitism to the uplift of the masses and the assimilation of national values to the validation of a distinctive ethnic culture in the figure of the ethnic bard enlivens his otherwise very conventional poetics and complicates his accommodationism by transforming it somewhat into aesthetic self-definition. In "The Colored Soldiers," for example, which is a direct address to an explicitly white audience ("In the early days [of the Civil War] you scorned [the colored soldiers]" [line 9]), the speaker clarifies how heroic African American soldiers were in the war, paralleling that heroism with the moral heroism of uplift in ways that use accommodationism to resist accommodation (lines 9–16). The poem is a textbook case of the politics of fulfillment. The speaker declares his pride that the soldiers "fought for Uncle Sam" (line 78) and ties that pride to the obvious valor of the war itself:

> And where'er the fight was hottest,
>   Where the bullets fastest fell,
> There they pressed unblanched and fearless
>   At the very mouth of hell.
>   (lines 29–32)

In effect, the soldiers are braver than the "you" who ignored them and were therefore not white at all ("unblanched") in their culture or in their bravery, their skin color being a positive and indelible sign of their ethnic distinctiveness and their distinctive embrace of the cause and the fighting of the war.

Tellingly and, to my mind, admirably, the race's distinctive expression of traditional heroism during the war is an extension of the moral heroism that is the foundation of Dunbar's poetics of uplift and his bardic genius.

> Then distress fell on the nation,
>   And the flag was drooping low;
> Should the dust pollute your banner?
>   No! the nation shouted, No!
> So when War, in savage triumph,
>   Spread abroad his funeral pall—
> Then you called the colored soldiers,
>   And they answered your call.
>   (lines 17–24)

One central irony of the poem is that the people for whom the war was being fought and who turned out to be the saving participants of the war were originally excluded from fighting by the racism the war was meant to defeat. But because those soldiers believed in "your banner"—the ideals of the nation—more than the whites did, they were loath to have it dusty, even though the dust was caused by their exclusion from the war in the first place. They were willing to offer the noble sacrifices of a disparaged race. Fulfilling the nation's cry to clean the banner of compromised national belief, the "colored soldiers" arrived right on time. Moreover, like the long-suffering people of "Ode to Ethiopia," the "colored soldiers" eschewed bitterness in favor of higher ideals of liberty that would make national unity possible:

> They were citizens and soldiers,
>   When rebellion raised its head;
> And the traits that made them worthy,—
>   Ah! those virtues are not dead.
>   (lines 61–64)

In fact, their acceptance of the call constituted the act that made those values of unity manifest. The moral heroism of the soldiers precedes the traditional heroism of fighting in the war and makes the latter heroism possible. This moral heroism thus constitutes the fulfillment of the ideals for which the war was being fought and clearly justified the inclusion of African Americans in their society.

By fulfilling these national ideals, both the soldiers' heroism and Dunbar's poem broaden the implications of accommodation from an entire self-sacrifice into a call for the society to make its social practices conform more to their articulated principles. In this way, the unfortunate self-deprecation of the poem coexists with the genuine self-assertion of the poet's jeremiad. And it also broadens accommodation to the politics of fulfillment wherein, instead of giving in entirely to the status quo, this accommodation was a call to live up to ideals, something well worth doing as an aesthetic practice in poetry, and certainly one mode of expression and social practice of the romantic poet. Also, the poem contains another instance of Dunbar's implicitly ethnic bard—again Dunbar himself—identifying and recording the race's fame, thereby calling it into being. The bard in the poem provides the memorial for which he calls:

> And their deed shall find a record
>   In the registry of Fame;
> For their blood has cleansed completely
>   Every blot of slavery's shame.
>   (lines 71–74)

The ambivalence here is that, as Wagner put it, "all the soldiers in these poems are American heroes, not racial heroes—even if the black fighters in the Civil War happened to battle to free the slaves" (99–100). But that ambivalence is exactly Dunbar's point and his ideal. These soldiers *should* be American heroes because they did honor to the nation, leaving behind that shame of slavery that Dunbar, unfortunately, attaches to blacks rather than to whites. That sense of shame aside for the moment, if the ideals of freedom and equality for which the Civil War was allegedly fought are only "white" values and not black "racial" values, as Wagner suggests, then what alternative should Dunbar have asserted? If Wagner is arguing, as so many other critics imply, that Dunbar should have addressed a different audience, then he is right. But if he is talking about the values Dunbar is affirming, then why are those values "white"? Such an idea reinforces white supremacy—democracy belongs only to the descendants of Europe.

This is exactly why "politics of fulfillment," which still acknowledges accommodation to aspects of the status quo, is a better term than "assimilation" for what Dunbar is up to. Rather than calling on whites to accept blacks as white people with white values, Dunbar's poem asks the following questions:

How can the values of the nation be "white" values if it is the black soldier who embodies those values most fully? How can they be white when it is the former slave who stands to benefit the most, both in terms of physical freedom and in terms of the all-important affirming sense of self? The implicit hope of the poem is that the recognition of this heroism will change the meaning of heroism from being exclusively white, like the rest of white society, and broaden the meaning of nation, which, as Gilroy has persuasively suggested, has long been too closely associated with the ethnic culture of the dominant people to be genuinely inclusive (7–15). So even though Dunbar does compromise his message somewhat by locating the moral responsibility of racism primarily on African Americans and by accepting the notion that slavery was a shame for black people rather than for white, he does manage to suggest ways of "rearticulating" the national values, as Hall would put it, as characteristics of a distinctive and distinctively heroic racial self (Hall 112).

To be clear: My claim that Dunbar is effectively characterizing a heroic ethnic self through moral heroism is not primarily an endorsement of Dunbar's politics. It is rather a validation of the artistry through which he conveyed those politics, an artistry whose complexity mirrors the complexity of Dunbar's politics. That artistry participated in the collective societal construction of an affirming ethnic identity that largely considered these uplift principles to be genuinely heroic. Moreover, I am suggesting that this complex interaction between antiracist if conservative politics and traditional artistry is crucial for understanding the African American bardic tradition, especially since it is in the construction of the poetic self that his verse's challenge to aspects of the ideology he accepts to write it is most clear. As with "Ode to Ethiopia" and Dunbar's other odes, and unlike most of Dunbar's Standard English poems, the poet in "The Colored Soldiers" is clearly identified as black, since he affiliates himself with the soldiers.

> If the muse were mine to tempt it
>   And my feeble voice were strong,
> If my tongue were trained to measures,
>   I would sing a stirring song.
> I would sing a song heroic
>   Of those noble sons of Ham,
> Of the gallant colored soldiers
>   Who fought for Uncle Sam!
>   (lines 1–8)

This conventional gesture of poetic self-deprecation, too easily misread as a simple capitulation to an audience the speaker considers to be superior, actually has three affirming functions. First, it ironically tempers the poet's hubris, since, while Dunbar is not justifying the ways of God to man or anything like that, he is claiming a mode of epic nobility for a disparaged race and for a humble poet in the public forum implied by the conventions of the ode. Second, then, such apologies also function to call attention to the poet's remarkable craft, since the ensuing nine stanzas of accomplished verse (eight-line stanzas composed of two quatrains rhyming *abcb* with an intricate, largely anapestic and trochaic rhythm with subtle variations adapted from Greek and Latin tragedy) belie that self-deprecation, as does the heroism of the represented characters.[3] Clearly his tongue is trained to "measures," since the unrhymed lines in the poem are all of eight syllables of more consistent anapestic meter while the rhymed ones are of either six or seven syllables, with trochaic and iambic irregularities preventing the potential singsong or monotonous effects of short trochaic lines in English.

In other words, Dunbar knows his poetics. Like the songs that epic poems once were in their original oral forms, this poem attempts to capture a literal song of these soldiers without undermining the heroism, adapting a meter that was used for tragedy to the weighty subject of validating an excluded people. Third and finally, the poem uses this invocation to revise traditional proslavery Christian imagery with the reference to the "sons of Ham," using the literary, as Milton did, to humanize Christian doctrine. In this case, the soldiers' valor and the poet's gifts contradict Noah's curse on the sons of Ham to be slaves. It picks up on the holiness of suffering and transforms it into a defiance of a part of Christianity used to justify racism. Moreover, the poet's artistry would recuperate it all. In effect, the contrast between the humility of the invocation and the virtuosity of the poem simultaneously writes the poet and his people into the highest ideals of the "rearticulated" nation. And the bard's song is an example of this vision and a memorial to the ways in which the soldiers enacted it.

Such simultaneous and virtuoso validation of the moral heroism and poetic achievement of the formalist poet and his African people can be read as effectively tempering even Dunbar's most ambivalent odes, usually referring to the actual African American masses rather than to ideal abstractions or literally heroic people. In "Not They Who Soar," Dunbar uses these conventions to suggest that such public honor, while necessary and affirming for the masses, is not to be privileged entirely over their private suffering: "Not they who soar but they who plod / Their rugged way, unhelped, to God / Are heroes" (lines 1–3). The masses, in their oppression, are nobler:

'Tis they whose backs have felt the rod,
Whose feet have pressed the path unshod,
May smile upon defeated care,
    Not they who soar.
                    (lines 6–9)

Tying this striving to the ideal of Christian suffering embodied by Christ bearing his own cross, Dunbar's speaker suggests that these meek and humble people are the chosen of God who shall inherit the earth by dint of suffering toil. Even in losing, they smile; even with beaten backs and unshod feet, they continue on. The "they" who are privileged do not know this honor.

Of course, there is a problem with this idea that *being* lowly is heroic, a problem that Dunbar tries to address:

High up there are no thorns to prod,
Nor boulders lurking 'neath the clod
To turn the keenness of the share,
For flight is ever free and rare;
But heroes they the soil who've trod,
    Not they who soar!
                 (lines 10–15)

Part of the problem with this vision of heroism is that it is unclear whether or not flight is an ideal, an alternative. On one hand, flight seems like the easy, privileged life for which "they" strive, in which case this poem is justifying the pursuit of something that the dishonored privileged have without appreciating. Flight is what those who are unshod desire and will appreciate, something they can achieve, as the poet has already, to an extent. On the other hand, though, the poem implies that such "flight is ever free and rare," not really existing except through oppression. In these terms, flight requires someone's labor and is inherently the consequence of oppression. Heroism is accepting the grounded life we must all live, but especially those who do not soar, also in this case including the poet. This ambivalence reveals contradictions in the ideology of uplift and, by extension, the racial ideology of segregation, because it suggests that time itself will end the oppression that makes people noble in enduring even as it suggests that such oppression is inevitable. Either way, the poet's fate is tied to that of the masses; and either way, both are rescued by their enduring heroism.

At its best, then, this association of moral heroism, poetic heroism, the conventions of the ode, and the idealism of the poet suggests that the difference between the poor who must be uplifted and those that uplift them is only in the degree of heroism. They do not differ in kind. Thus, in his odes to Frederick Douglass, of whom Dunbar wrote three times—one instance of which is in *Lyrics of Lowly Life*—the moral unity of the race belies the class hierarchy that Dunbar validates, allowing him to imply through such heroes as Douglass that the entire race, from folk to bourgeois, will come to embody national ideals and values. In "Frederick Douglass," Dunbar writes,

> A spirit brave has passed beyond the mists
>   And vapors that obscure the sun of life.
> And Ethiopia, with bosom torn,
> Laments the passing of her noblest born.
>   (lines 3–6)

The speaker laments the loss of a leader who could literally lift the race up: "When Bondage held her [Ethiopia] bleeding in the dust, / He raised her up and whispered, 'Hope and Trust,'" and since "he was no soft-tongued apologist; / He spoke straightforward, fearlessly uncowed" (lines 11–12, 19–20). He lifted the race both by addressing its own nobility and by defending its interests through direct address to the oppressors. Douglass is the "noblest born" of this religiously noble Ethiopia because he used his oratory as a mode of direct resistance. Unlike the masses of "Ethiopia" who plod, Douglass lifted the race with his words, something the poet also claims to do in this and other odes. More important than Douglass's physical escape from slavery, then, was his voice. Though there are real contradictions between the uplift heroism Dunbar asserts elsewhere and the more traditional heroism here, the poem presents them as equivalents or at least as being of a piece. The implication is that everyone in the race is capable of this heroic stance and everyone should use the lamenting and memorializing of Douglass's passing to motivate them to pursue that ideal.

In fact, it is this gesture that justifies calling this poem an ode instead of an elegy. In the next-to-last stanza in the poem, the speaker turns from his chronicling of Douglass's representative heroism—his place in the pantheon of

Western greats—to a first-person plural explanation of what that example means, creating the link between the hero and the people that allows them, and the poet, to become part of one another. It also reiterates the public occasion associated with the ode that is not always associated with elegy.

> We weep for him, but we have touched his hand,
> And felt the magic of his presence nigh,
>   The current that he sent throughout the land,
> The kindling spirit of his battle-cry.
> O'er all that holds us we shall triumph yet,
> And place our banner where his hopes were set!
>
> (lines 49–54)

In this stanza, the reaching for God is closer to fruition than it was in "Ode to Ethiopia." Having metaphorically touched the hand of Frederick Douglass, the people have garnered a moiety of his spirit, a portion of heroism that will be "kindled" into the fire by which "we" will triumph. I cannot help but think of the Sistine Chapel painting of God reaching his finger down to Adam, something Dunbar seems to have had in mind.

Moreover, given Dunbar's romantic inclinations, it is tempting to read Douglass's "hand" as his writing. Douglass thus functions as an artistic figure in this poem, a more traditional bard than Dunbar, who nonetheless rides along the liminal spaces between black and white cultures. Like Douglass and his godlike hand, then, the poet is a kind of translator or mediator, even medium, identifying specifically what legacy "we" have gained from Douglass and actually transferring it to the people, calling into existence both in the poem and, ideally, in the audience this revolutionary spirit. The poet is a kind of lightning rod or electrical conduit, both declaring the existence of the current between Douglass and the people and serving as the conductor of that current, again writing into existence an aspect of ethnic culture and heroic ideals alleged to be preexisting. In this way, again following the example of Douglass, Dunbar's speaker hopes to motivate his people to live the ideals for which Douglass died, declaring, "She [Ethiopia] will not fail, she heeds thy stirring cry, / She knows thy guardian spirit will be nigh" (lines 59–60). Like Douglass, the poet has a voice that could speak for all and a power to identify the root source of oppression and to articulate the possibility of the heroism in response.

Thus, it is not appropriate to consider Dunbar simply a bourgeois sellout, nor does the logic of political opposition that characterizes masking suit the construction of ethnic identity through traditional poetic mastery that Dunbar enacts most prominently in his Standard English odes. In fact, Dunbar's self-constitution enacted a substantial antiracist agency implicit in the public response to him. First of all, Dunbar was wildly popular and was able to make a living. Second, even after suggesting that Dunbar's claim to fame is his capacity to capture the "negro's limitations," Howells claims that "I accepted [Dunbar's verse] as an evidence of the essential unity of the human race, which does not think or feel black in one and white in another, but humanly in all" (xvii). Dunbar aspires to just this ideal, and though the vision of commonality is too often associated with a white bourgeois cultural norm, Dunbar's version of it recasts this ideal somewhat to be associated with a more inclusive norm. At the same time, Dunbar's continued popularity among black people and, most important, among black poets, suggests that, though his poetry may not have motivated the social activism the poet claims in "Frederick Douglass," it did create a unifying sense of heroic cultural self-definition as one mode of social inclusion. For Dunbar and much of his audience, such conventional notions of achievement, cultural assimilation, and common values transformed the stereotypes of "The Negro as He Is" into the basis for what thinkers of the time saw to be empowering terms of African American self-definition. While that portrait was ambivalent, invested in a class hierarchy that was an extension of the hierarchy of white supremacy, it was also a self-assertive attempt to rewrite that hierarchy. Given the complexities of the failure of parody and the powerful public role of the ode, Dunbar's artistry was more than conventional mastery—it was a complex and contradictory conception of poetic genius as racial genius that made ethnic self-definition in formalist poetry possible.

For Dunbar and his contemporaries, and for every poet since, the emergence of an artistic representation of a distinctive black culture and of a local-color realist literary tradition led to a crucial question: What role should that emerging culture play in art, and how should art accommodate that difference? While Dunbar's answer was incomplete, it did suggest fruitful ways in which formalist artistry and traditional poetic achievement—even romantic genius—could be informed by the distinctive experiences and modes of expression of African American people. And that construction of genius was by far more effective in the Standard English verse than in the dialect poetry. In

3 "To Make a Poet Black"
Constructing an Ethnic Poetics in Harlem Renaissance Poetry

Yet do I marvel at this curious thing:
To make a poet black, and bid him sing!

—Countee Cullen, "Yet Do I Marvel"

In his 1925 poem "Yet Do I Marvel," Harlem Renaissance poet Countee Cullen did more than identify the African American poet's characteristic need to resolve the tension between a potentially liberating ethnic culture and the potentially strangulating conventions of the Anglo-American poetic tradition, as I suggested in the introduction to this book. His poem also characterizes the defiant romantic imagination by which poets of the Harlem Renaissance—that remarkable flowering of African American literary culture in and around Harlem in the 1920s—constructed the conception of poetic genius commensurate with the "New Negro" cultural identity that they rightly claimed had provisionally resolved the aesthetics and the politics of this problem. Like the heroic odes of nineteenth-century dialect poet Paul Laurence Dunbar that I discussed in the last chapter—conventional poems that celebrated a heroic ethnic communal version of national cultural ideals exemplified by the moral heroism and aesthetic persona of the poetic bard—the verse of the Harlem Renaissance predicated its celebration of African American identity upon the poet's capacity to elevate African American folk culture into the pantheon of traditional literary fame through a combination of traditional and vernacular poetic techniques. But unlike in Dunbar's verse, in Harlem Renaissance poetry this provisional unity of folk and formal more fully articulated a distinctive and hybrid ethnic cultural self that also more fully transformed as it embraced the mainstream social and cultural values of which it was partly constituted. In other words, instead of being the heroic culmination of communal racial uplift, moral heroism, and national becoming, as they were for Dunbar, poetic genius and ethnic selfhood in most Harlem Renaissance poetry were the culmination of a marvelous construction of an empowering *individual* ethnic self whose distinctive cultural heritage became the necessary foundation for its claim to fulfilling national ideals. Enacting the paradox that individuality created community, the marvel of Harlem Renaissance poetry was that this pursuit of individual distinction did indeed make poetic genius black.

In other words, the bourgeois cultural model and romantic poetic ideals of Countee Cullen more accurately illuminate the construction of ethnic selfhood in Harlem Renaissance poetry and, by extension, in the study of African American poetry than do the models of vernacular self-definition or political activism that dominate the studies of this movement. Instead of seeking to find in the Harlem Renaissance a commitment to the vernacular entirely analogous to that found in contemporary literary and cultural thinking, I am suggesting we view the complex negotiation of individuality and poetic achievement as the means to construct a communal cultural identity, as exemplified by Cullen. While Harlem writers defined cultural identity as a cultural intersubjectivity, a shared communal mind-set, their artistry constructed that intersubjectivity through the pursuit of individuality and through traditional poetic glory. In "Yet Do I Marvel" Cullen posits his own imaginative questioning as an answer to the injustice of God of which the poem speaks. The speaker questions God by wondering why

> The little buried mole continues blind,
> Why flesh that mirrors Him must someday die,
> Make plain the reason tortured Tantalus
> Is baited by the fickle fruit, declare
> If merely brute caprice dooms Sisyphus
> To struggle up the never-ending stair.[1]

But the closing couplet quoted above posits this perfectly achieved Shakespearean sonnet as the answer to this injustice. It suggests that the very unjust burden that threatens to silence him as it blinded the mole or punished the Greek figures is also the most productive inspiration for his empowering ethnic voice. Even without claiming an ethnic tradition, then, Cullen's poem enters a claim by suggesting how the genius of the African American poet, exemplified by the production and perfection of this poem, is constituted in substantive part by the distinctive version of traditional poetics by which Cullen's speaker wishes away the burden. As James Weldon Johnson asserts,

"It is because Cullen revolts against these 'racial' limitations—technical and spiritual—that the best of his poetry is motivated by race" (220). By rejecting the imposition of a shared political voice for black poets, Cullen identifies the shared aesthetic and cultural issues by which an ethnic poetics was implicitly constructed. Cullen's speaker was really marveling at himself, in other words, and this individual self-affirmation is the signal gesture of the ethnic poetics of the Harlem Renaissance.

For the Harlem Renaissance poet, then, this bardic self was the exemplar of the entire movement's New Negro ethnic self, its implicit or explicit fulfillment of Alain Locke's assertion in his defining 1925 essay "The New Negro" that African Americans were "shaking off the psychology of imitation and implied inferiority" in order to express themselves with "renewed self-respect and self-dependence" by defining communal unity not as a "common problem" of racial oppression but as a "common consciousness and a life in common" (25). The meaning of that common consciousness was up for complex debate in the movement, leading to a wide variety of literary practices dedicated to expressing it that were unified by their diversity. But one point remained consistent throughout: it was through the claiming of an individual voice, in part by claiming a shared problem *and* a shared culture, that these poets resisted the homogenizing function of stereotypes and the silence that comes with those stereotypes. Whether traditionalists such as Cullen or jazz and blues poets such as Langston Hughes and Sterling Brown, the major Harlem Renaissance poets transformed the "intimate self-revelation of the poet" that "mirror[ed] the struggle of genius against all limitation," and the romantic poet's "glorification of [the] yearning, striving, and becoming . . . of the artist" into a model of ethnic communal becoming (Perkins 8, 3, 4). This practice made Harlem Renaissance poetry a record of its own making through the construction of the individual poetic mind, fulfilling the pursuit of social inclusion that Locke described: "The Negro mind reaches out as yet to nothing but American wants, American ideas," a pursuit in which African Americans were "forced" to build their "Americanism on race values" (29–30). When read in its entirety, the range of Harlem Renaissance poetics reveals just how fully Harlem Renaissance poets did indeed base their Americanism on race values while validating that same Americanism as the ultimate affirmation of those race values. By adapting racial experience and African American vernacular culture into poetic form, these poets were defining a new way to become American. Individualism became a pursuit of both social mobility and ethnically specific personal distinction. Aesthetically and therefore politically speaking, the self was "new" because it enacted "new" versions of poetic formalism that, for the first time, made traditional poetics a defining component of an explicit and individualized ethnic self and made the ethnic self an entirely distinctive Americanism.

This conception of the "New Negro" bardic genius provides more persuasive terms for characterizing the poetry of this movement because it captures the full hybridity and existential self-definition of the African American self represented by each individual poet and by the movement as a whole. And it does so by becoming an implicit manifestation of the idea, expressed by scholars such as Werner Sollors and Paul Gilroy, that the difference between racial identity and ethnic identity is that ethnicity is a social process that produces codes for its own definition, a process that rejects the logic of biological and social fixity and static opposition that still almost inexplicably dominate discussions of African American cultural production. George Hutchinson summarizes these problematic assessments well:

> The interpretations [of the Harlem Renaissance] tend to divide up like this: If the renaissance failed (the most common view in the major scholarly studies), it did so because white influence steered it in the direction of the "primitive and exotic," and/or it was motivated by bourgeois assimilationist desires to minimize cultural differences between blacks and whites, to win acceptance according to white cultural norms. If it succeeded, it did so to the extent that it cannily took advantage of neurotic (and racist) white patrons and audiences to promote an independent cultural movement without their realizing how radical it was and/or it succeeded in overtly detaching black from American or Western literary tradition, anticipating later black nationalist and Afrocentric cultural movements. (16)

On one hand, such assessments include Richard Wright's characterization of Harlem Renaissance formalism as "the knee pants of servility" in his "Blueprint for Negro Writing" and Amiri Baraka's conclusion in his essay "The Myth of a Negro Literature" that there was no such thing as a distinctive or valid African American literary tradition. On the other hand, the defense of the Harlem Renaissance is typified by Houston Baker's claim that the movement was an alternative modernism predicated on self-conscious and strategic manipulation and rejection of mainstream cultural values and norms. Every Harlem Renaissance writer was an ethnic trickster rather than an ethnic myth. Either way, critics claim one political perspective for the entire movement and neglect both the numerous political ideals and numerous aesthetic approaches by which the New Negro self was constructed.

Instead of primarily taking sides in Harlem Renaissance debates about authenticity and political protest, then, as too many scholars do, I start by tracing the dialectical synthesis of the oppositions of vernacular and formal that is central to the process of African American ethnicity in general and therefore central to the ethnic self-making of Harlem Renaissance poetics in particular. Thus, I join scholars such as Sterling Brown among others in distinguishing the artistry of the movement from its primary locale, calling it a New Negro Renaissance, because the locale tends to suggest a greater homogeneity of literary practices than is accurate. Moreover, as J. Martin Favor has suggested, the claimed "newness" of the New Negro had at least as much to do with bourgeois culture as with folk culture, to which I add the idea that both traditional and vernacular formalisms—not just the bourgeois culture Favor emphasizes—incorporated components of an African American bourgeois self into the hybridity of the ethnicity that made its New Negro poetics possible. Finally, this construction of New Negro selfhood need not be verifiable by demographic statistics, nor does its politics need to be verified by material change, as David Levering Lewis asserts, since what matters is the fact that the genuine innovation of the artistry practiced much of what it preached, making the New Negro an artistic if not a social reality. Thus, instead of reflecting a preexisting New Negro, ethnic identity with varying degrees of accuracy, as some scholars suggest, or being exclusively a movement dedicated either to proving oneself worthy of assimilation or to affirming folk culture, the New Negro poetic self was actually all of these, a site of cultural crossover clarified by Homi K. Bhabba's observation that "[t]he social articulation of difference, from the minority perspective, is a complex, ongoing negotiation that seeks to authorize cultural hybridities that emerge in moments of historical transformation" (2). And the New Negro poetics fulfilled the process it claimed to represent, enacting a politics of individual self-definition rather than of material resistance as part of the historical transformation of the discourse of race in African American verse to the discourse of ethnicity, even if the term "race" was still used. This transformation through racialized Americanism was a subversion of the movement's own misguided claims about the political meaning of their art in order to become a subversion of racist and racialist notions of absolute difference that the very existence of an ethnic self refuted.

This hybrid vision of the intellectual process of individual poetic selfhood made ethnicity American because of the particular character of its individualism. That hybridity proposed that the practices, ideals, and issues of cultural difference substantively framed a universally shared human consciousness, redefining the ideal of the universal as something that may have "transcended" the false binary logic of race but that did so only by being deeply invested in and expressed by the practices and forms of ethnic cultural heritage. On one hand, the verse of genteel formalists such as Cullen, Georgia Douglas Johnson, and Claude McKay enacted this defiant construction of the individual imagination in ways that exceeded their various ideals of cultural assimilation and bourgeois individualism. Their choices suggested that the distinctive African American poetic romanticism characteristic of a black gentility reconciled that individualism with ethnic culture within the individual mind, effectively making internal hybridity a more persuasive foundation of cultural assimilation than the homogenizing self-erasure usually associated with the practice and, sometimes, with their poetics. On the other hand, folk cultural formalists Langston Hughes and Sterling Brown (and, to a lesser extent, Jean Toomer) did more than offer their admirable and influential definition of the poet's self as an extension of African American vernacular culture in ways that subordinated individual selfhood and individualism to a communal identity. Their artistry also asserted or implied that this otherwise subordinated individual imagination was the source of the forms of the cultural expression that unified communal cultural identity. Still seeking poetic distinction, in other words, Hughes and Brown celebrated themselves by celebrating their community, likewise establishing poetic distinction as the reconciliation of ethnic culture with the individual mind. This continuum makes this romantic and defiant New Negro self a manifestation of what Mark Sanders aptly called "Afro-modernism": the "claim of historicity, of change, development[,] . . . and finally both social and psychic complexity [as] the salient rejoinder to assertions of black absence, antithesis, stasis" (75). In effect, formalist ethnic self-definition rewrote inherited discourses of race by rewriting the "universal" human subject as a black ethnic self, becoming a kind of existentialism that predicated communal cultural identity on the internal processes of the individual mind. New Negro poetics therefore initiated a central strain of existentialism in African American poetics in which self-definition constituted a powerful validation of the most fundamental component of democracy, the individual imagination capable of assimilating and articulating a dual communal heritage.

The New Negro poetics of the Harlem Renaissance is therefore the construction of this self-contradictory individualism whose rootedness in social

exclusion and a distinctive cultural heritage led to the transcendence into social inclusion based upon the interaction of shared and distinctive values.
In poetry, this Americanism of race values was constituted by a dialectical
or synthetic construction that implicitly reconciled—or implied a unity between—opposed racial ideals and opposed arguments about the nature of the
relationship between race and culture *in the individual mind*. As such, all of
the poems fulfilled the mandate described by critic, poet, and statesman
James Weldon Johnson: "What the colored poet in the United States needs to
do is something like what Synge did for the Irish; he needs to find a form that
will express the racial spirit by symbols from within rather than by symbols
from without. . . . He needs a form that is larger and freer than dialect but
which will still hold the racial flavor" (41). Though Johnson uses the word
"racial" here, he is referring to what Sollors described as the "codes of social-
ization" by which the "process" of ethnicity both enacts and constitutes the
"common consciousness" of the movement. In other words, "racial flavor"
has to do with the simultaneous recognition, identification, and creation of
the codes by which ethnic identity is defined, allowing each Harlem Renaissance poet to become the bard that Johnson describes, even given the broad
range of strategies these poets used. All "New Negro poetics" developed "symbols"—common codes, images, language, and poetic form—from "within"
their own heritage to convey the "racial flavor" of individual African American experience, so that even when claiming to be the voice of the collective,
that collectivity found its voice usually in the validated individuality of the
poetic persona or the poetic character of a dramatic monologue. These are
multifaceted and dialectical rather than hierarchical, including components
of gender and sexuality that were seldom explicit in the movement's verse but
were nonetheless one of the means by which the hybrid New Negro self was
constructed. And this construction of the bardic self straddled two cultural
worlds in ways that made it a full and sufficient New Negro self.

I will make this case by suggesting the particular ideological context in
which the formalism of Harlem Renaissance poetics garnered its capacity to
construct Americanism through race values. The ethnic poetics of the New
Negro emerged as poets of the movement used their representation of individual self-definition as their primary means to negotiate the fluctuating and
self-contradictory conceptions of racial and cultural identity in the science
and popular culture of the twenties. Thus, on one hand, the assimilationist
ideals of the genteel formalists and their representations of a transcendent self
were valid responses to such observations as those offered by Brenda Moryck,

a white Harlem Renaissance supporter: "Without stressing the unpleasant and dismal element of race-prejudice and its cursed results, it would be impossible to construct a Negro theme as such, from the daily tragedies and joys and ordinary pursuits of colored people, except of those belonging to the untrained and inexperienced groups, who through continued lack of enlightenment and contact with refining influences have reverted to the African type, which I frankly admit is peculiarly different from all other race types" (248). For Moryck, as for many supportive whites of the time, African Americans were the same as whites only after being refined to transcend their primitive African heritage and race type, a racist notion of inherent difference that contradicted the claim that there were no differences between the races. This link between biology and culture had already begun to undermine to an extent the stranglehold that racial uplift ideology had on the African American political imagination, since that ideology was flawed by its similar acceptance of the premise that blacks needed to be refined. Nonetheless, African Americans of the movement made similarly contradictory assertions about how race type and primitivist essence were defining components of ethnic literary beauty. For example, while critic and fiction writer Jessie Fauset wrote novels about bourgeois African Americans in order to prove the falsity of absolute difference, she also claimed that African Americans have a distinctive "gift of laughter" that is "racial" in nature and that should contribute to powerful theater and thus to social inclusion ("Gift of Laughter" 162). While "racial" sometimes meant "cultural" in the lexicon of the movement, Fauset more likely had in mind inherent but positive difference. To assert a transcendent, bourgeois romantic poetic self, as the genteel formalists did, was to constitute a sound aesthetic that would resist and refute such notions of inherent difference. Individuality undermined racialism and therefore resisted racial hierarchy.

On the other hand, scholars and poets of the movement were mounting the opposite and equally persuasive argument that the individual self made its culture out of its distinctive past, an argument that validated the work of the vernacular formalists as a subversion of the same racialist argument. Thus, Locke felt compelled to declare in a lecture called "The Concept of Race as Applied to Social Culture" that the biology of race had no necessary connection to culture: "Far from being constants, these important aspects of human society are variables, and . . . though they have at all times significant and definite relationships, they nevertheless are in no determinate way organically or causally connected" (423). Similarly, Franz Boas was producing scholarship that debunked the notion that races evolve along the same path, with some being more advanced than others; instead, cultures developed their own internal logic for the needs of their people and could therefore develop on parallel tracks. Though Boas accepted some aspects of racial hierarchy, he ultimately argued for the idea that a culture's internal coherence was valid in itself and should not be measured by the terms of other cultures. Similarly, from W. E. B. Du Bois's combination of African American spirituals, European poetry, and opera in his famous 1903 explanation of black culture, *The Souls of Black Folk*, to Locke's numerous articles on African art to bibliophile Arthur Schomburg's collections, writers and intellectuals in this group saw themselves as identifying and participating in a coherent, historical culture that needed to be embraced and celebrated. Nonetheless, each would have agreed to some extent with Du Bois's assertion that such practices would fulfill "the ideal of human brotherhood, gained through the unifying ideal of *Race*" by "developing the *traits* and talents of the Negro not in opposition to . . . but rather in large conformity to the greater ideals of the American republic" so that "two world-races can give each to each those characteristics both so sadly lack [emphasis added]" (16). Even at its most reasonable commitment to ideals of social construction, then, the emerging cultural self-awareness of the New Negro was predicated on what Locke described as "the racialism of the Negro" which "is no limitation or reservation with respect to American life; it is only a constructive effort to build the obstructions in the stream of his progress into an efficient dam of social energy and power" (29–30). An authentic African American identity was predicated, paradoxically, on transforming African Americans' social exclusion into either absolute or almost absolute difference in order to join the cultural mainstream. And from these contradictions emerged the ideal, self-assertive hybrid individuality in Harlem Renaissance poetics that fulfilled all of these requirements.

With this framework in mind, I conceive of the affirming implications of Harlem Renaissance poetics as much through the visions of poets such as Cullen as through Hughes. Even the most romantic and bourgeois of Harlem Renaissance poets implicitly asserted an ethnic source to their attempt to transcend race into either an American or a universalist cultural mainstream, thereby implying the separation of race from culture that leads to the illumination of the true hybrid process of African American ethnic selfhood. This conception justifies our attention to poets who do not receive as much attention, even those whose work is considered to be of lesser quality than the major figures of the movement. For example, even though Georgia Douglas Johnson was very resistant to political obligation in poetry, her most important verse transformed her idealism into ethnic self-definition by complicating the link between race and culture with her conception of gender. That verse actually has a more central place in the movement than is recognized because of the very conventionality by which it is often excluded. On one hand, she declared her resistance in a 1941 letter to Arna Bontemps: "Whenever I can, I forget my special call to sorrow and live as happily as I may. Perhaps that is why I seldom elect to write racially. It seems to me an art to forget those things that make the heart heavy. If one can soar, he should soar, leaving his chains behind. But, lest we forget, we must now and then come down to earth, accept the yoke and help draw the load" (quoted in Hull 169). Like Dunbar, Johnson compares the poet's reluctant acceptance of this burden of being a racial spokesperson to the implied nobility of manual labor to which African Americans were consigned and by which they garnered the admiration of the nation necessary for citizenship in the logic of racial uplift. Her first volume, *The Heart of a Woman* (1918), was filled almost entirely with love lyrics that had little to do with race, and a number of readers, including Locke and Du Bois, were critical of her neglect of social problems and cultural heritage. Her love poems tended to be about the yearning for lost love, a yearning often associated with the imagination and almost always expressed in short lyric poems in couplets and quatrains. And when she took on the yoke of race in her next volume, *Bronze* (1922), the central focus remained on yearning and loss, to which she added a fuller elaboration on her version of the Americanism of racial uplift.

Even when turning outward to historical figures rather than inward to the internal life of the poet or the problems of women in love, Johnson still emphasizes the ultimately liberating relationship between this imagination and its claim to dignity on one hand and its circumscribing, oppressive world on the other. In "To Mary Church Terrell—Lecturer," one of her sonnet odes to African American heroes in the "Appreciations" section of *Bronze,* for example, Johnson claims a public voice of the ode analogous to Dunbar's. She declares that this African American educator and abolitionist exemplified how a romantic individualist could take on the yoke of race through a transcendent genius. This is the kind of poem that scholars of Harlem Renaissance poetry have often criticized. While its conventionality does compromise some of its effect, that conventionality is also its most important "innovation."

A pioneer, she blazed a trail of light
Through murky shadows, with a lithesome tread
Unto forums, where Hope's beams are shed:
Straight through the mighty cordon of the night,
Rapt with a vision, soul-born, clear and bright.

                              (lines 3–8)

Replete with Johnson's signature romantic clichés about the horrors of night, the possibilities of day, and the insights of light, this poem reveals a poet seeking to elevate the achievements of one hero and the possibilities of a people through the poetic sublime. Terrell's vision of freedom is "soul-born, clear and bright" and cuts "[s]traight through the mighty cordon of the night" in much the same way that the imagination of the romantic genius recorded the struggle of genius against limitation or the resistance of the poet to her "special call to sorrow."

Though Johnson sometimes substitutes convention for clarity in such poems, as in calling slavery and segregation in the South a "frigid wrong," the implication is that such conventionality is a manifestation of both poetic and political genius, the defiant and transcendent self. As such, the poem leads to "hope's liquid piping," a cliché of nature's music of possibility, of sexual freedom associated with Pan, of orphic song and of the bardic traveling poet, all of which suggest that the individual mind is a source of freedom for the black poet and the black woman leader. If one did not know who Mary Church Terrell was, then one would be hard-pressed to see this sense of individual selfhood as an ethnic self. But clearly this validation of a racial freedom fighter—like Cullen's anxieties about race—required the honored tradition of the sonnet. The sonnet—that icon of Western poetics—becomes a central pillar of African American antiracist poetic expression. While this ideal clearly suggests that Johnson has accepted the value of this "white" form, that acceptance nonetheless constituted a resistance to the racist implication, articulated so well by Baker, that the form itself inherently erased the black self in the name of a putative universal that was actually a white liberal humanism. Instead, the "universal" self is rooted uncomfortably but genuinely in the works and mind of a racial freedom fighter.

When read in light of the idea that the individual self was the defining component of the political mandate that motivated Terrell, then, such a poem does indeed conform in the broadest sense to the principles of the New Negro that were articulated by Locke and that are also principles of New Negro poetics. Even Johnson's most famous love poem, published before *Bronze,* was ultimately as much about this paradoxically transcendent ethnic female self of the poet as about lost love. In the title poem to that first volume, Johnson makes clear how an archetypal African American woman yearns to transcend conceptions of physical differences and the associated social hierarchy, not unlike Cullen's speaker in "Yet Do I Marvel." And, like that speaker, Johnson finds in the imagination the best means to do so and finds in the hated dilemma of social limitation an inspiration for powerful self-expression and self-definition.

> The heart of a woman goes forth with the dawn,
> As a lone bird, soft winging, so restlessly on,
> Afar o'er life's turrets and vales does it roam
> In the wake of those echoes the heart calls home.
>
> The heart of a woman falls back with the night,
> And enters some alien cage in its plight,
> And tries to forget it has dreamed of the stars,
> While it breaks, breaks, breaks on the sheltering bars.[2]

The loss in the poem is attributed to gender identity itself rather than to an inability to meet someone compatible, as would be typical of a love lyric. The use of "heart" instead of "mind" and the gendered implications of the dangers of night root this consideration of the romantic genius in stereotypes of love, intuition, and frailty that are the strangling expectations of modern domesticity. She evokes and resists the patriarchal conceptions of gender identity that privilege silenced women over articulate ones and that also, paradoxically, disparage private, "silent" expressions of love in poetry in favor of vocal poetic protest. Such are the fetters on the imaginative woman. In short, the social category of womanhood is what limits the heart of a woman, which makes self-expression a defining act of resistance. Not just about love, then, the poem is about the imagination as the defining aspect of the self, as it is circumscribed by race and gender.

Johnson validates this imagination through the anapestic meter of the poem. She borrows from the light or popular verse of the English tradition in order to claim her ability, like those poets, to translate this difficult meter from the Greek to the English language. With an occasional iambic foot in each line, Johnson resists what is often seen as the "jog-trot" rhythm of the anapestic meter, adapting its "song" to the lament of this lone and lonely woman.[3] The contemplative tone associated with iambic pentameter remains, but the implicit lightness of the poem's anapestic tetrameter could be meant to contrast with the seriousness of the woman's dilemma. If such practices are read only as "white" forms, as is often the case, then the representation of a woman's desire for imaginative freedom—and, by extension, freedom from encumbering gender roles—would not carry the analogy to racial justice. This is still a love poem, in other words, one that aligns love and poetry and that asserts that a woman's heart needs room to roam and does indeed roam, finding the ability to love in part in the ability to imagine. But rather than being opposed to racial protest, this association of love and imagination *is* the protest here, as this poem aligns the poet's imagination with that of Mary Church Terrell and others. Juxtaposed to the sublime of the freedom fighter's mind in the sonnet quoted above, "The Heart of a Woman" becomes a gendered version of the self-assertive New Negro and the fetters of convention that also potentially liberate.

To my mind, this negotiation of the possible connection between poetic imaginativeness and political and cultural self-definition rescues the sometimes frustrating commitment to proving bourgeois cultural worth that guided some of these poets. For example, when Cullen—often seen as a poster boy for the genteel Harlem Renaissance, given his Harvard education and award-winning poetry—declares that African American artists would be better off hiding the "racial idiosyncrasies" of folk culture to protect the image of the race, he was consciously sacrificing an aspect of the racial self for the sake of only the most modest political gain. And when Cullen declared in his preface to *Caroling Dusk,* his anthology of "poetry by Negroes," as he put it, that African American poets would owe more to the English and American traditions than to any African culture, he was only partly right. But such statements come from a poet falsely surer of himself in prose than in poetry, where he was much more inclined to suggest the complex difficulty of claiming the individual, nonracial identity he asserts so cavalierly in his prose.

Cullen's most important poem, therefore, is "Heritage," because it takes as its themes the pitfalls in Cullen's own philosophy and moves well beyond Johnson's conventionality and abstraction into an exemplary construction of the hybrid New Negro self and the bardic poetic persona that exemplifies it. In it, Cullen defines the marvel of the African American poet, his or her remarkable struggle to balance self and culture, racial heritage and bourgeois gentility, into a better and truer self. Evoking and perhaps even embracing the primitivism he denies himself in his preface, Cullen makes clear that those stereotypes have a real allure as explanations for the racially and sexually divided black self. The poem thereby enacts the heroic pursuit of individual dignity in an innovative version of conventional poetics that is, I am arguing, the founding gesture of New Negro poetics.

That this self-affirmation remains potential throughout the poem actually enhances rather than undermines its power, revealing how poetic virtuosity provides complications to bourgeois assimilationism that constitute the self-assertive and hybrid process of ethnicity that the poem's ambivalence enacts. It also shows that the agency of self-definition is not based upon a static affirmation of cultural authenticity but on the construction of that "authenticity" in a process that never closes itself off in any falsely authentic self. Not knowing the answer to the question of "What is Africa to me?" the speaker admits,

> So I lie, who find no peace
> Night or day, no slight release
> From the unremittant beat
> Made by cruel padded feet
> Walking through my body's street.
> (lines 64–68)

That internal beat urges the speaker to "'Strip! / Doff this new exuberance. / Come and dance the Lover's Dance!'" (lines 80–82). Divided between present and past, memory and action, restraint and release, decorum and passion, the speaker cannot complete the expected iambic tetrameter quite common in verse, nor can he fully comprehend his own heritage. Each of these seven-syllable lines is in trochaic catalectic tetrameter or evokes it, as Cullen adapts a classical mastered verse that sounds to my ear like a metrical version of the speaker's irresolution in the face of this question of Africa. After all, if that heritage includes passionate self-expression, it would potentially be an atavistic yearning for a primitive past that the speaker implicitly rejects as racist. But in rejecting that, not only does he potentially reject a part of himself but he also rejects an explanation for the repressed sexuality implied in the "unremittant beat" and the "Lover's Dance," an explanation that would help him release feelings he must now restrain. That release could be tantamount to the freedom of the heart of a woman, but fear keeps him behind the sheltering bars of decorum. So he "lies," writing poetry that is the alternative to expressing physically the passion that may be as much his African heritage as his skin color, as much his (homo)sexuality as his transcendent imagination.

Thus, this poem is simultaneously about writing poetry in the face of racial stereotypes and a racial past and about the construction of the African American ethnic self based on an ideally unifying individual imagination freed from stereotype and, perhaps, from the very past it would need to define itself. It therefore incorporates into its pursuit of a transcendent individuality the components of sexuality that complicate race but that are still too often ignored in studies of the Harlem Renaissance. And this hybrid affirmation is especially telling since, even though the speaker ultimately rejects his African heritage, he portrays it and its potentially liberating sexuality as the ultimate solution to his dilemma. Thus, after vacillating between Africa as passion and the West as civilized restraint, the poem concludes with an examination of religion as a mode of passionate self-expression analogous to a mode of ethnic self-definition the poet finds both tempting and dangerous.

> Quaint, outlandish heathen gods
> Black men fashion out of rods,
> Clay, and brittle bits of stone,
> In a likeness like their own,
> My conversion came high-priced;
> I belong to Jesus Christ,
> Preacher of humility
> Heathen gods are naught to me.
>   (lines 85–92)

For the first time in the poem, the speaker identifies with the Africans rather than distancing himself from them. Significantly, this identification is predicated on the fact that Africans are defining their own religion as opposed to accepting the Christianity by which the poet's Western bourgeois culture—a symptom of colonization, to be sure—restrains his passion. In other words, the source of the identification is not the religion itself or even some primitive passion by which Africa is oddly and awkwardly defined in the rest of the poem; rather it is the Africans' resistance to the imposition of a potentially false Christianity, their creation of culture in their own image, a practice characteristic of the self-defined New Negro.

Contrary to Brenda Moryck's assertion, then, the African cannot revert to

type in some unconscious way, nor is that type some uncomplicated or inferior essence. It is rather a practice of an antiracist, ethnically self-affirming
cultural self-definition that the poet would like to claim. Thus he must con-
fess in his "idle boast" that

> Lord, I fashion dark gods, too,
> Daring even to give You
> Dark despairing features.
> (lines 107–8)

The speaker imagines a dark-faced god in order to believe that "Surely then
this flesh would know / Yours had borne a kindred woe" (lines 105–6). Seeking forgiveness for his "human creed," the speaker hints at the biblical assertion of the weakness of the flesh, tying this desire for "dark gods" to the restrained sexual passion and the even more restrained ethnic self-affirmation.
The speaker cannot resolve the contrast between his "blasphemous" passion
for self-definition and the restraining force of his Christian training because
he cannot resolve the relationship of that passion to "the struggle of genius
against all limitation," including the opposed limitations of race and civilization. With this lack of resolution, the poem implies that the ideologies of the
racist society that Cullen is so frequently accused of accepting are the villains
here. The poem declares that the Western claims of superiority through civilized restraint—religious and sexual—are the central causes of the poet's ambivalence and pale in comparison to the rich self-assertion of the disparaged
Africans.

With the loss of heathen gods, then, the speaker lost an assertive sense of
self, a control over his own image in culture, perhaps even a fairer control over
his sexuality—a control the passionate heathens have. He also lost a means by
which he could resist the ideologies of white supremacy that are the origin of
this tension between past and present, passion and restraint. It is here that the
poem takes on the existential cast that signals the complication to the romanticism caused by the alienation of racism. This is Cullen's ethnic poetics. Thus,
at the end of the poem, the civilized restraint of the West is represented as inadequate, even as the poem itself belies its claim of inadequacy. As in "Yet Do
I Marvel" and in the later poems "The Shroud of Color" and "The Black
Christ," Cullen posits in "Heritage" the limitations of race as the primary evidence of the injustice or, worse, the nonexistence of God. Thus, the speaker
laments the fact that, if he had the passion and bravery of his African ances-

tors, he would rewrite it in an entirely new kind of poetry. This is not the kind of self-assertion prized in contemporary African American poetry or critical thought, but it is a stirring and honest rendering of the divisions of a bourgeois black person's soul. In short, one powerful version of the New Negro was Cullen's portrait of this self-conscious failure of nerve in which the poem's final declaration is purposefully an empty one:

> Not yet has my heart or head
> In the least way realized
> They and I are civilized.
>   (lines 126–28)

In this conclusion, the meaning of civilization is called into question, because if it cannot accept both pagan Africans and Christian African Americans, then which is to be preferred? And how can the poet admit both are civilized without therefore admitting his elitist investment in the West's idea of civilization? Rejecting both primitivism and, to an extent, his own bourgeois gentility, the poet maintains them as separate, implying the falsity of the "civilization" that separates them. And if neither is civilized or properly passionate, what is the poet to write? The effect of even this self-doubt is validation, since the poem does offer an artist figure who does in fact have control over his own image. By enacting this brilliant contradiction of New Negro selfhood, Cullen captures his complex heritage, as the poem promises, without resolving it too simply in a sense of self the poem admits it cannot deliver. It fails to reconcile its Americanism and its race values, a failure that is one defining internal component of African American ethnic selfhood. And since Cullen provides an innovative mastery of traditional poetics, his poem is an instance of New Negro ethnic poetics.

It is only if we read Cullen's speaker too simply as Cullen himself that we miss this affirmation of the culturally self-defining possibilities of traditional poetics and the ways in which Cullen's best poem shares this plea for cultural self-determination with the work of Claude McKay, the most politically militant Harlem Renaissance poet. Rejecting the ambivalence of Cullen's speakers, McKay effectively embraces the same practice of revealing the process of ethnicity rather than the stasis of racialism and primitivism in order to illuminate analogous concerns about passion and restraint. McKay takes the limitations of traditional formalism, Western culture, and the circumscribed New Negro self head-on by using the sonnet explicitly to make poetry in his own militant image of the dignified individual black self. For example, in his best-known poem, "If We Must Die," McKay manipulates the grand traditions and high poetic diction of the form to lend grandeur and dignity, and, concomitantly, a cultural authority, to his anger at racist violence. Not "literally baffled" by form, as Stephen Henderson put it (20), nor masked for subtle self-assertion, as Baker suggests (*Modernism and the Harlem Renaissance,* 85), McKay's militancy, like Cullen's gentility, is in fact *enhanced* by the way he balances passion and restraint in his manipulation of traditional artistry.

Instead of treating the form as "a forced adoption of the standard" (Baker 85), McKay treats it as an aspect of his resistance to violent oppression and he is right to do so:

> If we must die, let it not be like hogs
> Hunted and penned in an inglorious spot,
> While round us bark the mad and hungry dogs,
> Making their mock at our accursed lot.
> If we must die, O let us nobly die.[4]

With this honor, in poem and militancy, "even the monsters we defy / Shall be constrained to honor us though dead!" (lines 7–8). The classic honor attributed to the sonnet, alleged to be universal, is transferred to the honored resistance to racism, making the sonnet itself and the "universal" nature of such heroism part of that resistance. One need only point to Winston Churchill's use of the poem in a 1942 radio address to inspire his citizens to endure the German blitzkrieg, and to its presence in a cell of one of the prisoners who participated in the takeover of Attica, to recognize how powerfully the poem conveys its political import. While it is clear that revolutionary passion would have perhaps been honored more fully in a revised sonnet, the mastered sonnet does not entirely contradict the passion it conveys, especially since an aspect of that passion is a kind of noble restraint and focus of the anger. Here is a version of transcendent individualism analogous to Johnson's in "To Mary Church Terrell—Lecturer," a claim to militancy whose claim to ethnicity is expressed only in knowing the poet and the situation of the 1919 race riots that inspired the poem.

But, like Johnson, when McKay turns to explicit ethnic self-definition, not only does he write better poetry but he also frames that self-definition in analogous terms of honor and passion through what Jean Wagner called "self-mastery" (Wagner 163). Even more important than the sonnet's capacity to honor rather than compromise revolutionary passion, then, is its capacity to locate the roots of that revolutionary passion in the individual imagination, a capacity through which McKay defines individual ethnic selfhood as the most militantly revolutionary component of his militant art. Most of his sonnets, written in a very personal first person, align the individual, representative mind of the poetic speakers both with the honored community of the race and with McKay himself, celebrating, paradoxically, an honorable restraint as the individual's defining practice of McKay's revolutionary ideal. Jean Wagner argues persuasively that McKay's art is a response to hatred and its consequences for spirituality, a pursuit dependent upon a preexisting, if resisted, faith in God through "self-mastery" (163). The best example is "To The White Fiends," which, in its opening lines, reverses what Mark Sanders would have called the "tropic vocabulary" of the Western poetic tradition by turning whites into uncivilized fiends and savages and blacks into the civilized. Instead of being strangled by the tropes of color and race in the African American poetic tradition, McKay "rearticulates" them, as Stuart Hall put it in his definition of the agency inherent in the conflicts in the ideological structure of society. McKay turns the web of these associations upside down to cling to new meanings (112). For McKay in this poem, this rearticulation constitutes the individual self that is capable of such reversal. Clearly, McKay's poem does not revise these ideological terms in the society altogether, but they are transformed within the logic of the poem itself, an act at least as militant as the explicit protest by which McKay is usually understood.

In these terms, the New Negro selfhood that is McKay's ideal finds its greatest affirmation in a version of the moral heroism of racial uplift, uncompromised by class hierarchy, a version in which the revolutionary's forbearance from violence testifies to his superior moral inheritance from his African past. It is a paradox that has been masked by the emphasis in scholarship on McKay's militancy. This revision starts with the title and is amplified in the first quatrain:

Think you I am not a fiend and savage too?
Think you I could not arm me with a gun
And shoot down ten of you for every one
Of my black brothers murdered, burnt by you?

(lines 1–4)

The speaker adds, "Am I not Afric's son, / Black of that black land where black deeds are done?" (lines 6–7). Here, the victim declares his capacity for violence that can match that of the colonizing whites, especially since that violence is, in racist terms, associated with Africa and especially since that violence is a justified response to being killed while unarmed. The implication is that whites are truly "fiends" and "savages." And yet, in addition to being the justification for the speaker's incipient violence, Africa is also the basis for an honorable, even divine, restraint that keeps the "savage" passion at bay. His restraint is not the ambivalent limitation that Cullen's speaker experiences but a manifestation of the unity of his sense of self. It is a "self-mastery" that is ordained by God, since "the Almighty from the darkness drew / My soul and said: Even though shall be a light" (lines 9–10). Transforming revolutionary passion and Christian oppression into justification for stoic resilience graced by the Divine, the speaker will not become a fiend. In the words of God as expressed in the poem,

Thy dusky face I set among the white
For thee to prove thyself of higher worth
Before the world is swallowed up in night,
To show thy little lamp: go forth, go forth!
(lines 11–14)

The light of the poetic and ethnic self here is the strength of revolutionary passions and just restraint. McKay is not simply a revolutionary poet on an opposite pole from Cullen. "To The White Fiends" is McKay's version of "Heritage" in which the speaker claims the self-defining ability of Africans to resist the ideologies of race in Western society while using that African ability to embody more fully than the whites "their" values.

The central role of this complex individual imaginative self in McKay's militancy is quite remarkable, but even more remarkable is the fact that this imaginative self constitutes one of the defining ideals of the poets of the movement directly invested in African American vernacular cultural forms as models for poetic expression. While these poets clearly shift the emphasis of poetic expression from bourgeois individualism to communal affirmation and from traditional terms of literary achievement to innovative uses of ethnic cultural forms, their artistry still ends up framing an ideal of the individual poetic self that enhances the implications of their ethnic affirmation. Poets such as Jean Toomer, Langston Hughes, and Sterling Brown used the same contradictions and divisions of self as the traditionalists to construct their vision of an affirming African American self. Thus, Jean Toomer offered in *Cane* (1923) an ideal of African American cultural evolution toward individuality that, while rooted in vernacular culture, prizes cultural assimilation. The implication of his choices was that the "New Negro" was indeed evolving from an "Old Negro" of folk culture and stereotype, but the New Negro needed to remember the true folk culture as distinct from the stereotype.

Toomer's "Kabnis," as a figure for Toomer himself, arises from his remarkable journey through *Cane* as the ambivalent, mixed-race potential bard of a new racial community. Because *Cane* is such a hybrid text, with more prose than poetry, at least strictly conceived, it does not completely belong in this study. Nonetheless, Toomer's attempt to memorialize African American culture in verse, in part as a way of ushering in what for him was not just a New Negro but a new American, does suggest the transformation of the individual racial self into a national ideal. In Toomer's words, "A family of back-country Negroes had only recently moved into a shack not too far away. They sang. And this was the first time I'd ever heard the folk-songs and spirituals. . . . But I learned that the Negroes of the town objected to them. They called them 'shouting.' They had victrolas and player-pianos. So, I realized with deep regret, that the spirituals, meeting ridicule, would be certain to die out. . . . 'Cane' was a swan-song. It was the song of an end" (xxii). But that end becomes a beginning for Toomer in a hybrid new American race of which he claimed to be the first conscious member. If Kabnis's transformation at the end of *Cane* is genuine, then he would be the new bard. Like Toomer himself, Kabnis will have imbibed the dying black culture in order to articulate more fully the pride of his black ancestors as the basis of this new American self.

But the best proof of this individual New Negro imagination as the foundation of an ethnic poetics is the fact that, when Hughes and Brown sought to validate the folk culture in its own terms, they both did so in part by validating the quasi-modernist existential capacity of the individual imagination to make sense of its world in distinctive cultural forms. In his jazz and blues poetry, Hughes creates characters who are sometimes versions of the poet himself, characters whose self-expression in vernacular forms mirrors both the race's ethnic self-definition and the poet's distinction. Thus, for Hughes, the contradiction of the New Negro came to be the capacity of subsuming the individual into the collective in order for individual artistic figures to gather their validated voices from the community as Kabnis might. In these terms, "The Weary Blues," the title poem from Hughes's groundbreaking 1925 volume, is perhaps his greatest and most important poem. The volume as a whole was the first to use African American folk cultural forms as models for its entire representation of African American culture. As Locke suggested in his review of the volume, and as most scholarship emphasizes, this turn to folk culture, with a fuller and richer appreciation than the dialect of Dunbar expressed, is the source of a more direct affirmation of communal identity than the representative bourgeois romantic genius. Says Locke, "[I would not] style Langston Hughes a race poet merely because he writes in many instances of Negro life and consciously as a Negro; but because all his poetry seems to be saturated with the rhythms and moods of Negro folk life. A true 'people's poet,' he has their balladry in his veins; and to me many of these poems seem based on rhythms as seasoned as folk songs and on moods as deep-seated as folk ballads" (24). Not just "poetizing" the substance of racial experiences into the universally human moods of life, as Locke suggested of Cullen, Hughes comes to embody in form and in his person the beauty of the folk culture itself, out of which those universally human moods emerge. This mode of genius is less a matter of mastery and more a matter of capturing the spirit of a place, making that otherwise disparaged space the locus of the same shared ideals as bourgeois individualism.

In other words, by identifying what unifies African Americans in their own cultural terms, Hughes is able to identify what African Americans share with all humanity, building his Americanism on genuinely "racial" values. The second half of the poem reveals how Hughes takes the question of artistic motivation and possibility that Cullen roots in classical traditions and roots it in black vernacular culture, in a communal voice that becomes individualized. That individualization characterizes the function of art, a function analogous to the potential catharsis of Cullen's "Heritage" or Johnson's "The Heart of a Woman."

> With his ebony hands on each ivory key
> He made that poor piano moan with melody.
>   O Blues!
> Swaying to and fro on his rickety stool
> He played that sad raggy tune like a musical fool.
>   Sweet Blues!
> Coming from a black man's soul.
>   O Blues!
> In a deep song voice with a melancholy tone

I heard that Negro sing, that old piano moan—
  "Ain't got nobody in all this world,
  Ain't got nobody but ma self.
  I'se gwine to quit ma frownin'
  And put ma troubles on the shelf."
Thump, thump, thump, went his foot on the floor.
He played a few chords then he sang some more—
  "I got the Weary Blues
  And I can't be satisfied—
  I ain't happy no mo'
  And I wish that I had died."[5]

Here the blues are the "eternal tom-tom beating in the Negro soul," as Hughes described jazz in "The Negro Artist and the Racial Mountain," with actual blues lyrics expressing the individual soul both of the blues singer himself and of the poet-speaker who is the observer in the poem (58). Accepting to an extent the primitivism of the era, Hughes posits this mode of cultural expression as practically inherent.

Improvising on the two lines of repetition, the third line of closure, and the *aab* rhyme scheme characteristic of the standard twelve-bar blues stanza (including the one the piano man sings), the passage transforms the blues into a ballad of the oral and written traditions of Americans, African Americans, and the British. This formal overlap locates Hughes's speaker and his blues singer in several traditions at once, just as with Cullen's speaker in "Heritage." Moreover, as scholars such as Steven Tracy have pointed out, Hughes's transformation of the twelve-bar blues stanza into quatrains and sestets creates more numerous line breaks, which enhance the emotional power of the blues by muting the repetition and, according to Tracy, by replicating the pauses of the blues singer's performance (155). Tracy even declares that Hughes invites us as readers to "hear" a guitar or harmonica riff at certain line breaks or caesurae, a riff meant to encapsulate the painful pleasure that makes expression itself the central effect of blues artistry. Finally, by replicating the communal function of the ballad in his use of the traditional poetic quatrain, Hughes unites the vaunted communal function of the blues and the ballad to his own poem, implying that the blues singer, the traditional balladeer (both oral and written), and Hughes himself share a role of communal affirmation through their distinctive musical gifts.

In other words, the brilliance of Hughes's practice here is the overlap of different communities—the blues audience, the ballad audience, the poetic audience—and the overlap of artistic selves in ways that produce an affirming individual identity derived from the existential individualism of blues music itself. If the blues is, as Houston Baker suggests, an assertion of an affirming "intersubjectivity," then the creation of that communal mind-set is, as Hughes realized, dependent upon individual artistic distinction (*Blues, Ideology,* 7–9). The blues song enacts for the speaker and the poet the same cathartic effect, one described well by Ralph Ellison: "The blues is an impulse to keep the painful details and episodes of a brutal existence alive in one's aching consciousness, to finger its jagged grain, and to transcend it, not by the consolation of philosophy but by squeezing from it a near-tragic, near-comic lyricism" (78–79). In other words, as Ellison suggests, the blues singer's impetus is personal, not communal, though the singer and the audience know that some pain will be shared, as will be the consoling function of expression. Scholars of the blues have too often reduced the blues only to its communal function and therefore they have neglected the process of individual creation that poems such as Hughes's enact. And in the transformation of individual and communal in "The Weary Blues," the speaker of the poem gains the tough-mindedness of the blues singer. Sleeping "like a rock or a man that's dead," as the blues singer does at the end of "The Weary Blues," is not the transcendence through beauty or self-mastery that the genteel New Negro poets emphasize or that traditional romantics imagine. It is instead a mode of individual affirmation that secularizes the divine romantic imagination without losing all of the sanctity of that imagination. The speaker cannot transcend but he can endure and inspire, becoming a locus of what Baker calls "adequate cultural understanding," his or her mind a "matrix" that produces alternative cultural meanings. The blues song or poem substantiates the poet's gift and places that gift, and the mind that created it, into a tradition of artistic and cultural expression that is ethnic in nature. After all, both the poem itself and the song the bluesman sings are "The Weary Blues." Hughes does the same thing in "The Negro Speaks of Rivers," where an individual poetic speaker—"*The* Negro"—compares the race's soul to the world's longest and most historically significant rivers. Though a communal voice, the speaker of the poet is individualized for all of its readers.

While most directly affirming and more explicitly communal, these overlaps in Hughes's verse are analogous to the construction of poetic genius in Cullen's and Johnson's work, an analogy that illuminates Hughes's similar adaptation of traditional thematic poetic conventions of Western poetry to the blues' communally valid individual self. Rejecting the idea that blackness is the antithesis of civilization and the concomitant sense of the universality of whiteness, Hughes still recognizes how African American life contains and even transforms those so-called universals. And since Hughes has turned to the tradition of his people, he can adapt those traditional poetics without lamenting the limitations it puts on him or the alienation it creates. In "Song for a Banjo Dance," for example, Hughes rewrites carpe diem for the black urban folk by adapting the same stereotypes of the folk that trapped Paul Laurence Dunbar.

> Shake your brown feet, honey,
> Shake your brown feet, chile,
>
> Sun's going down this evening—
> Might never rise no mo'
> The sun's going down this very night—
> Might never rise no mo'
> So dance with the swift feet honey,
>   (The banjo's sobbing low)
> Dance wit swift feet honey
> Might never rise no mo.
>
>   (lines 10–19)

Like "The Weary Blues," this poem improvises upon the blues stanza by incorporating blues features in order to give the poem its organizing structure, where again the blues is both individual and collective. In this case, the poet becomes one with the people through the unidentified speaker who is potentially collective, as ballad speakers sometimes are, and through the direct address of the reader. Moreover, with an ethnically specific cultural referent such as the banjo, which was associated with both southern rural and northern urban African American culture, Hughes locates the poem's themes in an African American cultural context (D. Lewis 29–30, 206–8).

The poem moves beyond the association of the banjo with the lesser cultural capacities of the "happy darky" stereotype that Dunbar sought to parody by celebrating the banjo in its own terms rather than in implicit terms of what it should have been without oppression. Not just about the inevitability of death and the necessary pursuit of full lives, as other carpe diem poems are, these lines imply the stoic response to *ongoing* and *present* deprivations that constitutes the backdrop of many blues songs. The sobbing of the banjo, sometimes seen as a poorer alternative to "higher" instruments, implies a lack in terms of social and cultural resources, but not a lack of creativity or voice for these characters. In other words, carpe diem has elements of privilege, which, in this poem, includes the possible lust for pleasure and the capacity to forget their deprived circumstances. To put it still another way, however satisfying it may be to pursue coy mistresses with threats of death, as Andrew Marvell's speaker did, carpe diem is in fact a gesture of privilege dangerous to black folk and a luxury garnered by racism or other forms of social advantage for whites such as Marvell's speaker. For these presumably black speakers, the coming death is not as hypothetical or distant as Andrew Marvell's. It is immanent, expanding the theme of carpe diem into a critique of the racist social forces that necessitate this potentially self-destructive attitude.

The effect of this combination is to temper as it enhances the anticipated joy of a Herrick or a Marvell poem, since such joy for poor blacks seems always to be deferred. The option here is not a potentially fulfilling sexual relationship but cultural expression. Thus, carpe diem becomes a mode of the blues, the consoling fingering of the jagged edge of African American experience by which Ellison defined the blues. Hughes's contemporary Jessie Fauset appreciated the validation of cultural expression as full living in these terms: "Now this [poem] is very significant, combining as it does the doctrine of old Biblical exhortation, 'eat, drink, and be merry for tomorrow ye die,' . . . and Herrick's 'Gather ye rosebuds while ye may.' This is indeed a universal subject served Negro style and though I am no great lover of dialect I hope heartily that Mr. Hughes will give us many more such combinations" ("Our Book Shelf" 39). Meaning more than "style," Fauset implies, against her otherwise genteel taste, that Hughes has created an ethnically specific version or manifestation of a traditional poetic theme. In "Shakespeare in Harlem," for example, Hughes declares that bringing Shakespeare to Harlem would make "The Bard" into a bluesman. Here, eating, drinking, and being merry have particular manifestations in the black community that balance the universal mandate to live and the particular social circumstances that circumscribe that mandate.

Rather than being alienated from one another, the poet and the people are alienated from the social resources needed to give them greater self-fulfillment. Such thinking gives complex meaning to the ethnic poetics of poems such as "Epilogue" or "Theme for English B," since this ambivalent selfhood is more explicitly central to those poems. Hughes is at his best, then, when he resists the temptation to submerge the individual self entirely to the communal self. When he does so, he creates a powerful interaction between individual and community that validates the folk New Negro selfhood as an extension of the poetic persona of Hughes himself. It is a combination that becomes the foundation for the identification of commonality that makes social inclusion possible. In other words, Hughes's fame as a poet proves the blues possibilities of both individual voice and communal self-fulfillment defined in his best poems.

In these terms, Sterling Brown exemplifies "New Negro Aesthetics," because his volume *Southern Road* (1932) brings the logic of the defiant romantic imagination full circle by characterizing it as a blues existentialism that makes ethnicity readable through individual imaginative "transcendence," including that of the bourgeois poet. The volume also provides a unique tension between the folk modernism of Brown's blues poems and the sardonic bourgeois achievement of his traditional formalism at the end of the volume that reiterates beautifully how American identity is exemplified by African American ethnic self-fashioning. Part of Brown's distinctive achievement is that he creates more fully realized characters in his blues poetry than Hughes did. Brown's richer characterization enhances the means by which the blues affirms the individual imagination and by which Brown's poetry was read then and since as an ideal ethnic self verified by distinctive artistry. Wagner was correct that Brown "is not satisfied, as Hughes had been, to borrow only the forms of his verse from the storehouse of folk poetry. He imbues himself with its spirit, its practical philosophy, its humor, and its speech—which for him, have lost none of their validity, and have permitted him to handle the present-day themes with undeniable originality" (476). Like Hughes's characters, Brown's speakers can be read as an African American Everyman. In fact, given his research into folklore, Brown is often read as an ethnographer who writes poetry. But, unlike Hughes's speakers, Brown's have enough of a life of their own both to exist independently of the poet and of the community and to convey to the reader a sense of the poet's mastery as an extension of the interior life, cultural practices, and vision of life of his characters. Many of Brown's characters are artist figures who personally enact Brown's cultural practice. So even though Brown rightly separates himself from the bourgeois norms of the genteel Harlem Renaissance, providing probably the first substantive argument for the term "New Negro Renaissance," his poetic artistry shares with that movement the validation of the African American ethnic self through the contradictory individualism of the bardic imagination. Calling Brown an ethnographer does not actually do justice to his role as bard.

As much as *Southern Road* is about a communal history of the Great Migration that helped make the Harlem Renaissance possible, in other words, its central import is its representation of the journey of the individual consciousness as both parallel and integral to that historical communal journey. The journey of that consciousness is ultimately that of Brown himself, as he seeks to reconcile his own bourgeois upbringing and poetic aspirations to his appreciation of the folk. In the volume's title poem, for example, Brown does with the work song what Hughes does for the blues in "The Weary Blues," placing the song in the mouth of a single, distinctive, and yet representative character in order to validate how that personal story becomes archetypal. The poem tells of a representative individual singing an explicitly communal song (sung by slaves and prisoners to keep time with their work) about his reason for being on the chain gang. The alternation between individual and communal voice in the alternating lines enhances the possibility of individual expression motivating communal work.

Instead of (in addition to, actually) providing its traditional function as the soundtrack to the work on a chain gang or railroad, the song here becomes an opportunity for the song leader to receive the affirming response of sympathetic listeners to his life-sustaining call. Calling for patience in the first stanza ("Swing dat hammer—hunh— / Steady, bo'; / Ain't no rush, bebby, / Long ways to go" [lines 3–6]), the speaker goes on to explain how he shot someone, got a life sentence, and thereby left his daughter on the streets, perhaps as a prostitute. Moreover, his son "done gone," perhaps because his father cursed him, leaving the mother to suffer in anguish for her lost family.

Doubleshackled—hunh—
Guard behin';
Doubleshackled—hunh—
Guard behin';
Ball an' chain, bebby,
On my min'.

White man tells me—hunh—
Damn yo' soul;
White man tells me—hunh—
Damn yo' soul;
Got no need, bebby,
To be tole.[6]

The weight of racism is added to the weight of imprisonment, allowing this individual prisoner to link his individual woes to historical and institutional problems and practices of racism that probably contributed in some unspecified way to his act of violence. Here Brown thrusts a killer—one who may even be self-hating, accepting his "damnation"—into the face of the genteel Harlem Renaissance as a kind of hero, refuting the bourgeois logic of the romantic individualism of poets such as Cullen and McKay while going even further than Hughes in asserting a self-defining and valid cultural self in ordinary African American people. Like the bad man of the blues tradition, the speaker here accepts his badness and accepts oppression, using expression rather than a call to action for solace. Rather than ending racism through direct resistance or positive, genteel images, Brown's representation is meant to defy stereotypes of black criminality by rendering the full humanity of an actual criminal through his complex consciousness. The speaker's resistance to assimilation and to the social costs of the institutional exclusion makes his self-reflection a mode of integrity.

Not at all concerned with making good impressions, as he asserted in "Our Literary Audience," Brown uses such "Bad Men" to exemplify how traditional American aesthetic and cultural ideals must be substantively transformed to account for African American experience and to motivate truly just social inclusion, especially since folk culture is both a subversive act and evidence of deprivation. Sanders aptly argues, for example, that Brown's presiding image of the "southern road" in this poem and in the volume revises Whitman's "Song of the Open Road," offering a narrative of compromised possibility and contradictory transformation that complicates Whitman's almost naïve optimism: "Whitman's lack of self-consciousness, the unexamined racial privilege he exercises in order to conceive his road of perpetual promise, displays a racial myopia Brown cannot afford" and that he corrects (40). But Sanders wrongly concludes that, in the poem "Southern Road," early in the volume, and on the road, "the entire spirit of revolt is already snuffed out and transcended, since it is seen as useless, and there is a stoic acceptance of destiny" (41). Brown does indeed complicate the implications of an open road in American literature, especially since the title poem is about physical imprisonment. But his narrative is of an African American consciousness that allows for both stoicism and optimism since it is both victim and agent simultaneously.

Direct revolt may be impossible, but self-sustaining self-definition is quite possible and quite a valid response, even though that response hardly changes the conditions that necessitate it. The speaker lacks the privilege to "assume" as Whitman does. Nonetheless, the call-and-response characteristic of many African American folk cultural practices substitutes for that assumption and provides a more realistic, sustained, and sustainable interaction between self and community. For Brown, then, the "Southern Road" is about the road of the mind in conversation with a like-minded community that assumes nothing but rather builds its unity together, even though its unity is sometimes as much a problem as a possibility. True democratic interaction is found on the chain gang, not in parlors, and derived not from some divine spirit but from a shared experience of woe and a shared value in the catharsis of expression. In this way, Brown's speaker and strategy in "Southern Road" resembles McKay's in "To The White Fiends"—it is a reversal of literary and political expectations for the validation of the African American mind and, like that poem, ultimately posits individualistic self-mastery as the ultimate subversive act.

In the end, then, Brown may not be so different from Whitman after all. Thus, the African American artist figure is Brown's ultimate hero not because he or she mastered traditional poetics or accepts political mandates to represent the race positively. Rather, these figures are heroes because they sing their songs in the language appropriate to them, providing themselves solace and offering that same solace to the listeners, though that solace does not pretend to lead to social inclusion or transformation. Instead, those songs unite a democratic black community that can, if it will, accept all of its people into collective memory and collective self-definition. In the process, it provides a space to validate the individuality that is a necessary resistance to racism and a foundation for the cultural self-determination necessary for genuine inclusion into the national body politic.

This is part of the reason that the volume opens with "Odyssey of Big Boy," a poem that transforms a folk artist into an epic hero by combining blues, ballad, and epic conventions into one unique song form, announcing a new approach to black imagination. Big Boy wants to join African American legends:

An' all dat Big Boy axes
   When time comes fo' to go,
Lemme be wid John Henry, steel drivin' man,
    Lemme be wid old Jazzbo
      Lemme be wid ole Jazzbo.
                     (lines 61–65)

Transforming epic heroism from violent action and nation building to imaginative self-assertion and ethnic self-definition, the first-person narrative of "Odyssey of Big Boy" is not, as Sanders asserts, a collective voice, but an individual voice yearning to be included among collectively celebrated heroes. After all, what Big Boy celebrates about himself is the forced migration from job to job and place to place that was his limited version of the open road. Due to injury and demeaning labor, Big Boy *chooses* to travel, granting to his itinerant life both the epic quality of being driven by the gods and the claim of political agency associated with choice. Though his life would not have been admirable to Cullen and his ilk, the speaker of the poem claims the self-defining capacity for which the speakers of "Heritage" and "The Heart of a Woman" yearn. That agency may be through womanizing and he may idolize womanizers and clowns, but at least his self-image is his own. And the song that Big Boy sings of his life substantiates the agency of his life, even if that agency is but a retrospective creation of his song. As Sanders rightly observes, "'Odyssey of Big Boy' concerns itself with the present moment of vocalization with the ongoing dynamic of self-articulation and re-creation, and the ability of voice to project and reconstruct" (45). Nation building here is about the exploits of another bad man, this one an artist like Brown, who, also like Brown, hopes his song of his exploits will carry him to the heaven of cultural memory.

This capacity of the outcast individual to be accepted democratically into an outcast community constitutes the defining distinction of the blues people that Brown celebrates. These people are also central to his capacity to articulate a multifaceted cultural self that is his version of the New Negro. In this way, as in the poem "Ma Rainey," the artist figure is one of these democratically accepted outcasts.

> When Ma Rainey
> Comes to town,
> Folks from anyplace
> Miles aroun',
> . . . .
> Flocks in to hear
> Ma do her stuff.
> (lines 1–4, 7–8)

The Everyman speaker of the poem pleads, "O Ma Rainey, / Sing yo' song" and "Git way inside us / Keep us strong" (lines 27–28, 31–32). Her individual voice gets *inside* her hearers, articulating something in them, creating moments of collective identity through individual pain to keep them strong.

The communal role of this outcast and yet accepted artist is made absolutely clear at the end of the poem.

> An' den de folks, dey natchally bowed dey heads an' cried,
> Bowed dey heavy heads, shet dey moufs up tight an' cried,
> An' Ma lef' de stage, an' followed some de folks outside.
>
> Dere wasn't much more de fellow say:
> She jes' gits hold of us dataway.
>
> (lines 48–52)

Though exalted for her capacity to "git hold of us," she actually follows the community, meaning both that she is embraced and that her inspiration is the community. She follows their growth and their pain and sings it, getting hold of her community as they hold on to her. It is hard to imagine a more appropriate model for Brown's own ideal. In fact, by the end of the poem, the speaker of the poem has shifted from an objective third party into the poet himself so that, by the concluding two lines, the "us" undoubtedly includes the poet. Each validates the other and each is affirmed in individual distinction. Perhaps there actually is an open road of the mind, a point that is the most substantial conclusion to the logic of New Negro poetics. And these poems reveal most fully how New Negro poetics subverts the racialism both of white outsiders and black insiders by emphasizing this simultaneously individual and communal process of self-constitution. The communal self that Ma Rainey sings is not a finished authentic self but a complex emotional life that evolves and changes with the immediacy of the Mississippi flood of which Ma Rainey sings in "Backwater Blues."

This validation of the folk artist's role in the community creates a possibility that the bourgeois self can be redeemed in its similar construction in ethnic poetics, allowing someone such as Brown himself, whose background is closer to Cullen's than to that of the real Big Boy Davis, to fit into this ideal ethnic community. In "Vestiges," the concluding section of Standard English sonnets and traditional formalism, Brown recognizes the alienation of the bourgeois blues poet from his own craft, as well as potentially from his own people, the representation of which at the end of *Southern Road* brilliantly complicates the trajectory of Brown's own argument about cultural progression in ways intentional and unwitting. The strength of the section is Brown's awareness of his problem in writing himself into that community, his acceptance both of his alienation from those people and his refusal simply to be strangled by the bourgeois culture of his birth and that was supposed to be of his aspiration.

For example, Brown's sonnet "Challenge" adapts the Shakespearean tradition of immortalizing love in poetry to the blues condition of blues people.

> I said, in drunken pride of youth and you,
> That mischief-making Time would never dare
> Play his ill-humored tricks upon us two,
> Strange, defiant lovers that we were.
> (lines 1–4)

The poem ends:

> And thus, with you believing me, I made
> My prophecies, rebellious, unafraid
> . . . .
> And that was foolish, wasn't it, my dear?
> (lines 11–14)

The poem basically claims that the power of art to immortalize an ideal love made so famous by Shakespeare is a farce, an illusion that misled the black speaker-poet to a greater sense of his poetic power and of love than was true. In effect, "Challenge" can be read as transforming the sonnet into a bourgeois blues poem, a point that Michael Manson demonstrates by suggesting that even the metrical structure of the poem invites into "Vestiges" that bluesy sound of the folk songs in the first three sections of the volume. But he is only partly right when he asserts that "'Challenge' thus humbly acknowledges class difference; and to white Americans, it stands as a reminder that if they are waiting for great universal, 'ageless and raceless' 'Art' from African Americans, then they will have to help create new social and economic conditions" (28). Though Manson is correct to suggest that white American expectations are misplaced on the art of a oppressed minority, I disagree with the implication that Brown yearns for universality in those terms. Brown is not arguing for an "ageless and raceless" art but for a mode of formalist poetics appropriate for his personal contradictory combination of mainstream culture and folk cultural knowledge. He imagines an art that was rooted in ethnic culture rather than in the ideologies of absolute difference and inferiority associated with "race" and with claims to the universal. Imagining an "ageless" and especially a "raceless" art can in practice mean a lack of cultural specificity, something that Brown as ethnographer and poet would reject. Instead the speaker is wondering if his attempt to immortalize the folk is as compromised as his attempt to immortalize love. Can his own persona be the end of the Southern Road? Would not that be accepting the supremacy of "ageless and raceless Art" along with white Americans? Would not the bourgeois poet be compromising his own self by writing folk cultural poetry? Clearly Brown's position as ethnographer is one of his ways out of this dilemma, as he claims the distance of participant-observer. Still, Brown confronts an essentialized notion of absolute difference to which, his poem implies, there is no solution. His love cheats on him, making the ideal of immortal love less appropriate to the blues. With his false vision of poetic selfhood, the speaker was thus too much invested in the ideal of an "ageless and raceless" art to recognize reality until he was forced to. In short, like Cullen's "Heritage," this poem renders the ambivalence of the bourgeois ethnic self as a defining component of that self. But Brown associates that ambivalence with the affirming existentialism of the blues. And that ambivalence can unite him to the community as a bourgeois person's version of the alienation and self-contradiction of the speaker in "Southern Road."

In other words, Brown actually questions both the bourgeois identity and the communal connections he, as a middle-class poet, seeks to embrace. Communal identity is not primarily the racist imposition that Mason seems to suggest, nor does Brown take it for granted that a bourgeois identity and its attendant poetics are ideal or the inevitable consequence of equality. Thus, in another sonnet, "Nous n'irons plus au bois," Brown admits the irony of his refusal to join bourgeois culture, undermining the sense that the volume implies that a communal, African American bourgeois culture is the end of the Southern Road. The addressee in the poem could be white or black: "I shall meet your friends, and chatter on / As trivially, as sillily as they" (lines 1–2). Brown clearly manipulates the sonnet to undermine its conventions and laments being trapped or strangled in the form in much the same way Cullen does. But Brown's poem also offers the alternative of the rural South and presumably of African American folk heroism:

When you reward me for my rank cowardice,
I shall call back, to fretting memory,
A hut, pine-circled, on a wild hillside,
And peace thrown lavishly away—*for this.*

(lines 11–14)

The individual subjectivity of bourgeois culture, no matter how communal or bluesy, is inadequate for social inclusion, but the myth of a happy rural life in a racist South is no more substantive. And the alternative of the individual blues voice is circumscribed by the social exclusion that constitutes it. Thus, the "vestiges" here are contradictory: the lingering yearning for a bourgeois poetic self and the lingering modes of cultural imperialism that necessitate the African American artist figure's alienation from himself or herself. Full reconciliation of these oppositions may be impossible, Brown implies, certainly as long as racism reigns. But valid and healing cultural expression is possible and will continue to validate the individual mind that creates it and the communal heritage from which that individual voice emerges. And this is the universal that already exists, the ageless art that is in no way raceless. Like Cullen's "Heritage" or "Yet Do I Marvel," Brown's "Vestiges" declares that bourgeois ambivalence is central to the process of self that makes for ethnic identity and ethnic poetics. That ambivalence is also what distinguishes the poet as innovative. The way art makes the self is what matters and will continue to matter, throughout oppression and beyond.

Southern Road is Brown's celebration of the psychic complexity and diversity manifest in black vernacular cultural forms in part by revealing both continuities and disruptions between those forms of vernacular cultural expression and the experience and forms of expression of the middle-class poet, both of which he wants to include as aspects of this communal path from southern deprivation to northern achievement and exploitation. Recognizing fissures in his own vision of black authenticity—namely his potential personal exclusion from that authentic expression—Brown finds himself foundering on the same problem with which Cullen wrestled in "Heritage," and this is one of the crowning glories of the Harlem Renaissance construction of the New Negro self. Taking on their varying versions of ambivalence about the meaning of black identity for the bourgeois poet and for bourgeois identity, all of these artists enact a contentious ethnic self-definition that led poets such as Hughes and Brown to their stirring innovations. Brown's volume about southern black life and cultural expression, itself a kind of blues expression resolving nothing, ends with his own mannered poetry, so even as Brown is criticizing the expectation that black poets write this way, he seems to be falling into the very trap he describes, no matter how powerfully he ironized the gesture. As such, the volume embraces the complications to African American selfhood first suggested by Du Bois and upon which Harlem Renaissance poetry elaborates in its construction of the relationship between poetic form and ethnically specific experience and expression. No matter how much we try to distinguish Brown's mannered poetry from Cullen's—and it is in fact quite different—that work in "Vestiges" engages in the same implication, namely that Brown is seeking a certain approval for his poetic gifts that may not be available exclusively through folk poetry. This paradox means enacting it and Brown's brave choice embraces its own "failure" as part of its affirmation. In all of its artistic and implied democratic glory, this is the New Negro self that it claims to be.

The best way to appreciate the ideals, achievement, and legacy of the poetry of the Harlem Renaissance, then, is to recognize the complicated conflicts between bourgeois and vernacular culture in the construction of African American selfhood, and the complex manipulation of this relationship in the creation of the poetic forms through which these poets represented, engaged in and attempted to resolve (indeed sometimes did resolve) these ambivalences. In that provisional resolution, these poets offered the artistic self-assertion that became a communal cultural affirmation, even if their explicit goal was the affirmation of the individual subject. And that collective affirmation became the foundation of social inclusion that was more substantive than assimilation because it located American values in individual distinction and communal heritage. Rather than make exorbitant claims either for the political effect or political failure of their work, scholars need to be more precise in defining the cultural agency of Harlem Renaissance art as this difficult pursuit of antihegemonic poetic formalism derived from the complexities of black selfhood and of black culture themselves. What mattered was the defiant African American imagination, the existential genius that unified the otherwise disparate and competing poetic strategies of this rich movement. So while art by itself may not be able to raise an entire people in world esteem, as James Weldon Johnson averred, any social effect it has emerges through its potential capacity to shape "mental attitudes" through the complex dynamics of formal mastery and innovation. And that shaping started with African Americans shaping their own minds through this New Negro poetics.

So, though many Harlem thinkers largely accept preexisting, Eurocentric ideals of "great art," they did not entirely give into bourgeois assimilationist desires, nor did Hughes and Brown entirely reject them. In both cases, formalism interacted with ethnic self-definition, in effect when not in intention, to render new meanings for poetic identity and therefore for ethnic identity that unified a disparate movement and motivated an entire tradition of ethnic self-definition in poetry. In these terms, both modes of expression—traditionalist and vernacular—were modes of cultural self-assertion that ultimately function on the same principles of aesthetic effect and cultural meaning, making both forms of expression parts of the beginning of a truly "racial" genius in African American poetry. Recognizing this ambivalence is thus not a critique of Harlem Renaissance self-definition but an acknowledgment of its complexity, its aesthetic difficulty, and its full political meaning and import, which is, in turn, a fuller, more complex appreciation of ethnic subjectivity itself. And this is, after all, the end to which Harlem Renaissance poets had pursued their quest for form, and it is their legacy.

4 "Weaponed Woman"
The Modernist Heroism
of Gwendolyn Brooks's Early Verse

Step forth in splendor, mortify our wolves.
Or we assume a sovereignty ourselves.

—Gwendolyn Brooks, "'God Works in a Mysterious Way'"

In the last two lines of "'God Works in a Mysterious Way,'" a poem published in her first volume, *A Street in Bronzeville* (1945), Gwendolyn Brooks identified the conception of personal agency and the ideal of a heroic "feminine" self-definition by which she characterized both the individual African American's and the African American community's difficult yet ultimately achieved cultural self-determination. These lines therefore characterize Brooks's complex modernist revision of the model of political resistance through artistic self-definition that is the defining characteristic of what I have been calling the bardic tradition and that makes her early work the most politically provocative of her career. As she suggested in this poem from her sequence of war sonnets, "Gay Chaps at the Bar," the defining agency of the imagination is its capacity to claim control over the ordering of experience from some "God" who has as yet failed to "step forth in splendor" to "mortify our wolves" of hunger, fear, and exclusion. Not just attributing this capacity to "soldiers" in their "war" against racism, though, Brooks claimed this sovereignty for ordinary African Americans and for herself as poet, implying that her virtuoso mastery of traditional form enacted in poetic texture the ordinary African American's negotiation of the racist discourses by which they are constructed and through which they must construct themselves. This ideal practice of self-definition became for Brooks the African American's primary mode of resistance to the social institutions such as the church and the institutional discourses of race that order reality implicitly in support of segregation and racist social hierarchy. In her first two volumes, *A Street in Bronzeville* (1945) and *Annie Allen* (1949), Brooks posited this pursuit of existential sovereignty as a more important resistance to racism than direct opposition or protest. Often locating this sovereignty in the domestic lives of black women, she implied that ordinary African Americans did not merely accept Eurocentric values. Rather, they profited from a necessary and self-assertive engagement with existing values and discourses. Exemplified by her most important women characters, Brooks's poetic and political ideal throughout her career consisted of this pursuit of individual sovereignty, making her early verse her greatest assertion of the need for African American cultural self-determination.

Though she is known primarily for her virtuoso use of Anglo-American poetic techniques in her first four books of verse and for being the first African American poet to win a Pulitzer Prize—both of which testify to her acceptance in the mainstream—Gwendolyn Brooks should be understood as a people's poet dedicated to the social and cultural health of black people. Her magnificently seamless integration of traditional poetics and African American vernacular language and cultural forms constituted a hybrid formalist artistry that did more than fulfill Brooks's early desire to persuade white Americans that African Americans were not "curios."[1] It also functioned as her sympathetic poetic enactment of what she saw to be the heroic existential self-definition of the ordinary African American people from the south Chicago neighborhood where she spent much of her life. What proved blacks were not curios, in other words, was hybridity, the unity of cultural traditions into one self-defining subjectivity whose dynamic pursuit of intellectual and cultural self-sufficiency was the most universal human experience. In this early verse, Brooks's third-person portraits and dramatic monologues depicted her characters' sense of themselves as the products of active intellectual practices that revised available cultural resources—the conventions and practices of both the oppressive Anglo-American culture and the African American past—into the shared language, rituals, values, and heritage that constituted African American ethnicity. And because her innovative formalist artistry was Brooks's version of this intellectual practice, her portrayal of this process of ethnicity had the effect of uniting the poet and her characters in their cooperative and simultaneous development of affirming identities. As in the verse of the entire bardic tradition, Brooks's artistry revealed ethnic identity to be in flux, but she also implied a modernist existentialism predicated on the poetic mind—exemplary of all minds—organizing the chaos of experience into sometimes fragmentary and momentary stays against confusion. Her formal virtuosity was thus more than a simple and self-defeating cultural assimilation. Traditional poetics became an aspect of African American cultural self-definition, just as ethnic cultural heritage became a defining component of poetic achievement. Finally, this combination persuasively suggested the fundamental interracial commonality of a socially constructed identity that, for Brooks, was the source of genuine interracial community. In this way, Brooks's verse asserted an ideal of social integration that was predicated on the ideal that African Americans enter the cultural mainstream as a community and on their own terms. These innovations were predicated on representing the active consciousnesses of women as exemplifying all humanity, an ideal that could produce alternative values affirming to a marginalized community.

This paradoxical affirmation of cultural self-determination as the means to social integration makes sense when understood as an implication of the dynamic, dialectical construction of what I have been calling bardic genius. Seen as constructing individual identity as an analogy of poetic genius, and poetic genius as a consequence of communal cultural selfhood, Brooks becomes a bardic poet who adapted to its fullest logic the portrayal of the defiant individual imagination that, as I discussed in chapter 3, characterized the Harlem Renaissance construction of a self-affirming New Negro identity. But where the New Negro poetics of the Harlem Renaissance constructed ethnic identity and poetic genius through the combination of romantic individualism and blues communalism in order to claim a cultural place in conventional Americanism, Brooks's vision redefined ethnic culture not as an expression of Americanism as much as an empowering alternative to it. This alternative validated the possible sovereignty of the mind over social and discursive circumstance and the democracy of a shared existential condition. And where Harlem Renaissance poets attributed this ideal primarily to exemplary political activists and artist figures, Brooks attributed it to all the black people in her neighborhood. Thus, though most scholars usually only attribute the mandate of cultural self-determination to the verse Brooks wrote after her famed 1967 conversion to Black Nationalism, the truth is that, when read in light of the idea of bardic agency I have generated in the last three chapters, Brooks's entire opus—but especially her first two volumes—asserts the ideal that African American cultural self-determination was central to any real justice. As scholar George Kent put it, Brooks's art enacted "existential tensions given particularism by styles of engagement, failure and celebration, created within black communities . . . still seeking to establish at-homeness in America" (30). Like the Afro-modernism that, according to Mark Sanders, Sterling Brown developed to refute racist discourses of African American cultural lack and absence, Brooks represented through the distinctive existential tensions of her community the complexity and, even more than Brown, the agency of the individual African American mind. In these terms, I conclude, Brooks's early work exemplifies her best political ideals, a vision of personal sovereignty culminated in many ways in the neglected prize-winning *Annie Allen*, a volume that is the defining work of Brooks's career.

Thus, I turn to this ideal of what I call a "feminine" sovereignty rather than the terms of "masculine" protest and political self-assertion common in literary study, because such a conception allows for a proper perspective on Brooks's early verse—its subtle resistance rather than didactic declaration and its emphasis on the often ordinary lives of women—without overestimating its difference from the work of her nationalist period until her death. My emphasis on Brooks's early work is not merely a reinforcement of the sometimes racist suggestion that her later work decreased in quality due to its more explicit political content, nor is it a brief for integration. Rather it is an attempt to recognize through Brooks's construction of a people's bardic genius that poetic genius is gendered and that it can enact a mode of self-assertion usually disparaged in the masculinist models of political activism so central to African American literary study. This gendered genius adds greater substance to the way in which ethnic genius challenges the liberal humanist ideal of the universal self. I call Brooks a "weaponed woman," then, because her version of bardic genius, by adapting traditional literary form and value to African American life, revises the conventional masculinist terms of political agency in African American literary and cultural study.

In her poem of that title, Brooks uses a variation of the traditional ballad stanza in order to represent how an ordinary woman exemplifies the ways in which the direct engagement with the social and cultural limits of African American life makes an individual heroic. For the described character, "life has been a baffled vehicle / and baffling," but, unlike the damsels in distress in many traditional ballads, this woman "fights and / has fought according to her lights / and the lenience of her whirling place," offering her "act" of living as an act of resistance.[2] Insightfully comparing Brooks to naturalist novelists such as E. P. Roe, Frank Norris, and Theodore Dreiser, Kenny J. Williams suggests that Brooks uses formal poetics as emblems of the "social control" and the undermining of communal values enacted by the deterministic environment—the lenience of one's whirling place—depicted in the naturalist novels: "While those who succumbed to the promises of the city were often pathetic, even the successful were not exempt from urban control" (50). In this case, Brooks revises the alternating rhyme scheme and regular tetrameter of most English ballads with unusual stress patterns in order to convey the character's baffled mind-set.

But Williams misses how those same formal characteristics imply active resistance to that environment. This representation of resistance is the defining component of Brooks's imagination and is my central emphasis in this chapter. By rhyming "and" with "and," the poem suggests that the character "fights" and "has fought" not with a traditional heroic weapon but with the "stiff frost of her face" and her "strong bag." The parallel rhyme of "stiff" and "if" in the second stanza asserts that the woman uses the cold dignity implied by "stiff / Frost of her face" and the economic independence of the "strong bag" as adequate defenses against the contingency (lines 6–7). And Brooks claims this same agency through her artistry, implying that her distinctive poetics, while acknowledging that circumstance, is simultaneously her own resistance to social circumstance and her representation of the shared existential condition of African American people.

This poem exemplifies how Brooks's revision of the traditional model of physical self-assertion of the traditional male heroic narrative also revises the model of direct political opposition by which many critics, such as Margaret Reid in *Black Protest Poetry,* define the antiracist meaning of African American poetry. If we accept the premise that direct opposition or vernacular cultural affirmation are the two primary modes of heroism for the poet, then it would be easy to agree with Arthur P. Davis that characters such as the "weaponed woman" are "unheroic" (100) or with D. H. Melhem that Brooks herself is unheroic and only becomes heroic in her later, more explicit protest poems. But Brooks complicates this emphasis on protest or grand stature, turning instead to the internal life of African Americans in relationship to social circumstances, suggesting that the mind is the character's and the poet's greatest weapon against racism as its discourses invade domestic spaces (including the mind) as well as public ones. This approach creates, for lack of a better term, a "feminine" heroism that acknowledges the fact that, as Mary Helen Washington suggests, stories about the internal lives of African American women have been excluded from African American literary history. As Washington wondered, is the neglect of the domestic and emotional lives of women in defining the African American tradition "because few critics could picture the questing figure, the powerful articulate voice in the tradition as a plain, dark-skinned housewife living in a kitchenette apartment on the south side of Chicago" (443)?

In her poetry, as in her novel *Maud Martha*, to which Washington refers, Brooks makes the traditional male questing figure into an ordinary man or woman who turns inward for that journey. The quest does not consist of changing external circumstances. It is the construction of an ideal similar to the ideal in the Anglo-Saxon tradition that heroism is not just the retainer's active loyalty to the lord and the military acts that result but is also "a feeling of personal integrity vital to the individual" (Andersson 577). In Brooks's art, this personal integrity consists of the capacity of her poor people potentially to overcome the alienation caused by poverty by having a moment of clarity about their relationship to society, a point that the weaponed woman garners from her control over her body and finances and that Brooks as a people's poet exemplifies (see Jameson). The result is that Brooks's distinctive existentialist artistry and formalist achievement construct a mode of antiracist self-definition that makes the individual mind the source of the antiracist agency of self-definition, a "sovereignty" that is largely underestimated in Brooks's early verse. The "weaponed woman" is an exemplary hero, then, not because anyone sees her defiance, necessarily, but because she achieves a (momentary) sense of wholeness, of personal integrity.

It is striking to me how the emphasis on cultural authenticity, vernacular poetics, and masculine models of heroism have obscured how fully Brooks uses poetic formalism as a central component of her validation of the possibility of personal integrity and a sovereign ethnic self-definition in the quasi-deterministic environment of urban poverty. It is even more striking that such bias has prevented the full appreciation of Brooks's central place in the African American tradition in defining the antiracist relationship between traditional poetic achievement and racist social and cultural discourses. That personal integrity, as Brooks portrays, is not based exclusively on African American folk culture but the interaction between will and all social circumstances, including the internalization of inimical aspects of mainstream culture and even the adaptation of Anglo-American culture that is allegedly opposed to African American cultural health. And this integrity is exemplified by Brooks's bardic self.

Instead of being politically dubious in the binary logic of African American literary study, her verse verifies what Homi Bhabba argued about postcolonial cultural identity in the dialectical logic of much poststructuralist and Marxist thought: "The 'right' to signify from the periphery of authorized power and privilege does not depend on the persistence of tradition; it is resourced by the power of tradition to be reinscribed through the conditions of contingency and contradictoriness that attend the lives of those who are 'in the minority'" (2). Though the African American cultural tradition certainly persists, Brooks's verse locates that integrity in contradiction and contingency derived in part from that tradition and that this evolving tradition creates in contradistinction to "authorized power and privilege." Brooks and her characters garner the "'right' to signify" from the dynamics of consciousness first and then from the language and cultural forms of the vernacular tradition, a cause-and-effect relationship that clarifies the fact that subjectivity is always simultaneously being constructed and constructing itself.

This process of cultural mutation, as Paul Gilroy would call it (2), incorporates Don Lee's observation that Brooks was "a black poet in the actual" whose work was "conditioned!" by "iambic pentameter, European sonnets and English ballads," but it also exceeds that characterization (13, 14). I concur with Gilroy's suggestions that such "conditioning" was in fact an inevitable part of the process by which African American identity was constituted both as a consequence of deprivation and as a pursuit of personal integrity in response. The fact that Brooks's work shows evidence of that conditioning should not obscure the fact that she also represents that conditioning in order to represent the internal lives by which people, including Brooks as the people's poet, resist that conditioning. Brooks's art offers apt representations of the contradictions that "attend the lives of those who are 'in the minority,'" including their own hybrid cultural selves and the sometimes minimal sovereignty they are able to derive from the claim of both a persistent folk tradition and a personal, existential version of the oppressive culture.

By approaching Brooks through this heroic existentialism and its implications of a revised heroic selfhood, it becomes clear that her practice in her first two volumes initiated a substantial shift in the African American poetic tradition away from the previously predominant romantic individualism and its associated bourgeois values that she is often implicitly and explicitly accused of reinforcing in this early work. Instead, her work constitutes what I will call a bardic modernism, a manipulation of the poetic self to reveal the contingent meaning of poetic value and cultural value and of social roles and to assert through that revelation possible social and cultural alternatives, at least in the individual imagination. Both the poet and the characters in Brooks's art enact a version of what Mark Sanders identified as Harlem Renaissance poet Sterling Brown's Afro-modernism, in which the poet and her characters refute the idea that "objectified blackness" was the antithesis to a cultured human identity through their own "social and psychic complexity," their ability to think and to imagine at all (1). Rather than allowing itself to be erased by racism or authenticity, this complex self refuted various manifestations of objectified blackness and justifies the complex formal structures of Brooks's verse as a manifestation of both those objectifying notions and the imaginative response. Her ballads are usually as much blues as British, her iambic pentameter as much vernacular bravado as traditional mastery, and her sonnets as much imaginative self-assertion as conditioned response, with each component of this virtuoso aesthetic undermining the falsely fixed ideological meaning of each in the larger culture. The combination transforms Brooks's integrationist ideals into persuasive ideals of the unifying power of aesthetic effect and the perception of shared human motivations that validates cultural difference as the necessary expression of those unifying ideals. The poet is one with the people as an exemplar of the sovereign power of the individual mind. In these terms, *Annie Allen* exemplifies how Brooks's virtuosity enacted an underestimated celebration of an innovative, anti-essentialist, antiracist feminine imagination through which the empowered African American individual—woman especially, exemplified by Brooks herself—becomes the defining practice of the cultural self-determination of the African American community.

In these terms, *A Street in Bronzeville*, Brooks's first volume, is perhaps her best, because it contains all of the elements of Brooks's representation of the racist modern condition that necessitates this existential heroism of African American people, that constitutes the bardic modernism of the poet herself, and that constructs a distinctive ethnic community from a common existential dilemma. Defining the neighborhood one person or locale at a time, the volume also defines the African American modern condition against which Brooks's Afro-modernist existential mind constitutes itself and articulates how that mind is the solution.

Brooks's "kitchenette building," the second poem in the volume, is her version of T. S. Eliot's modern wasteland, the economic and spiritual decay created by a racist system as it affects the mind and culture of poor blacks. Characterizing the "urban control" represented in Chicago Naturalism, the poem opens by characterizing the relationship between the emotional states of oppressed people and that material deprivation in order to anticipate the possibility of existential agency, as the collective speakers declare that "We are things of dry hours and the involuntary plan" and acknowledge that dreams cannot compare to economic necessity or the social responsibilities of gender roles within the family (line 1). First of all, the collective "we" of this speaker, along with the grayness, reveals the lack of individuality created by the "involuntary plan." Whether that plan is the blueprint of the confining building of the title or the sociocultural system of segregation that makes that building possible, these characters are so beholden to its dictates that they can only dedicate themselves to practical matters of existence. Having accepted the external world's conception of them as "gray things," these characters are more objects than subjects. They are the archetypal victims of economic deprivation and urban decay.

And the worst part of their alienating objectification is that there is no room for dreaming, whether through flights of fancy, introspection, or self-affirmation. This is the ultimate proof of their dehumanization. They wonder if the "white and violet" of dreams can "fight" with garbage in hallways or the closeness of the space in the kitchenette building. But the speculation about the power of dreams is cut off by the fact that the speakers acknowledge that they do not even let the dream in. Brooks uses "onion fumes" and "yesterday's garbage" to signify the diminished status of human ideals in a "fallen" modern world run by an "involuntary plan" of capitalism and racism, since those ideals cannot compete with the real and unavoidable personal, cultural, and historical detritus—rent, "feeding a wife," garbage—that circumscribed their impoverished existence. Similar to the status of the American dream in novelistic naturalism, as Williams suggested, the dream at the end of this poem—and all of the alternatives of artistic beauty and imagination more generally, such as "aria" and the "violet" associated with it—are rendered insubstantial. In fact, Brooks chose the colors "white and violet" "for their 'delicacy'" in order "to deal with [dreams] . . . as 'lovely lightsome things'" (quoted in Melhem 23). In William Hansell's words, these characters have "little time to reflect on their relationship to the larger society or even to their immediate community" (261). With their lives determined for them by the "involuntary plan," there is no inkling of the transcendence to which the romantic or Victorian poet historically aspired, leaving only the apparently defeated mind and will of characters like Eliot's J. Alfred Prufrock. This is a version of the capitalist alienation Frederic Jameson described as the inability of the "commoner" to see the system in which he operates, an inability that reinforces the conditions that prevent the seeing.

Brooks clearly rejects the idea that African Americans are completely dehumanized and shifts the emphasis of the poem from a protest of these social conditions to the validation of the fundamental and ultimately irrepressible humanity of these characters, who embrace as they resist their dreams. Even as the two middle stanzas of the poem make these deprived emotional and intellectual circumstances resolutely clear, they imply an alternative possibility of self-definition based upon the social understanding existing within the people themselves. Like many of Brooks's characters, the speaker(s) in "kitchenette building" enact(s) the psychic complexity of a marginalized people who use personal, even meager, resources to claim some place in the world. In this case, that complexity is even greater than the characters themselves realize, granting the readers insight into their fundamental humanity that makes the reader effectively part of "we."

> We wonder. But not well! not for a minute!
> Since Number Five is out of the bathroom now,
> We think of lukewarm water, hope to get in it.
> (lines 10–13)

The shortest sentence of the poem is also the most direct assertion that these characters are subjects, not objects: "We wonder." According to Brooks, "I wish to present a large variety of personalities against a mosaic of daily affairs, recognizing that the *grimiest* of these is likely to have a streak or two of sun" (quoted in Davis, "Gwendolyn Brooks" 100). In this case, the streak of sun is the fact that the collective speaker does entertain those "lovely lightsome things," that the lukewarm water hoped for, if achieved, is a diminished but actual dream and its realization. Moreover, the poem's formal properties includes fairly regular iambic pentameter, enjambment that defers or mutes the "masculine" rhyme—"fumes" with "rooms"—and that heightens the allegedly less substantial associations of "feminine" rhyme—"minute" with "in it." The poem's form thus implies the effects of the involuntary plan while also offering hints of a sustaining beauty—the rhyme itself—and a sense of self-defining response by which the "we" may survive. In short, through imaginative beauty, the dream does "survive" this poem. The characters are "aware of the emptiness of their lives [and] begin to question the meaning of things," as Hansell put it (265). This questioning is the foundation of Brooks's modernist heroism. This incipient political awareness gives greater weight to the fact that the reader is directly addressed and is therefore implicated in the struggle for the proper meaning of these characters' lives. These characters articulate their complex awareness of their modern condition, asking the reader to recognize how, by making do, the characters partially make themselves. They are not curios or objects, but ordinary people who deserve better.

In short, the imagination—dreams, wondering—is a defining resistance to the "involuntary plan" of the African American modern condition, especially for those without a great deal of social or economic power. Not only does this poem redefine the so-called "modern condition" for deprived African Americans—as Houston Baker put it in *Modernism and the Harlem Renaissance,* "Without food for thought, all modernist bets are off" (10)—it declares itself to be the source of and analogous to the social awareness necessary for racial self-assertion and interracial empathy that would resolve that black person's experience of modern cultural dislocations exacerbated by racism. If channeled properly by character, poet, and reader, that existential imagination ultimately helps to produce the power to resist the conditions that create such alienation. In this way, Brooks's modernist art is not about shoring fragments against ruin or reclaiming a lost Western tradition. Rather, it is the creation of a communal culture that provides an alternative to the fragmented Western culture that has long been inadequate for African American social and spiritual health. Not building Americanism through race values, this poet and her people are transforming Americanism into race values as a resolution of the modern condition.

In "The Sundays of Satin-Legs Smith," Brooks's oft-misunderstood mock epic, she makes clear how personal integrity is no mean feat. The poem opens,

Inamoratas, with an approbation,
Bestowed his title. Blessed his inclination.

He wakes, unwinds, elaborately: a cat
Tawny, reluctant, royal. He is fat
And fine this morning. Definite. Reimbursed.

He waits for a moment, he designs his reign,
That no performance may be plain or vain.
Then rises in a clear delirium.

He sheds, with his pajamas, shabby days.
And his desertedness, his intricate fear, the
Postponed resentments and prim precautions.
(lines 1–11)

This opening section embodies in its elaborate language—the ostensibly heroic blank verse, the occasional deferral of end-rhyme with assonance, for example—the extravagant imagination that it describes. Such formal quali-

ties broaden the contrast between dream life and actual life offered in "kitchenette building." In contrast to that poem, this poem's allusion to an epic
invocation suggests the possibility that these Sundays will be a powerful
defiance of social circumstance, a heroic pursuit enacted by an ideal hero.
Satin-Legs's "elaborate" gestures of designed extravagance reimburse him
more fully than lukewarm water could. But the extravagant language also enhances the antiheroism implied in the offer of a zoot-suiter as epic figure. In
fact, by narrating his life to an even more explicitly addressed reader, the poem
posits Satin-Legs as an object of scrutiny, not a subject, and implicitly criticizes the reader for rendering him as such even as it criticizes Smith for lacking integrity in his response. The poem ultimately condemns both the
reader's lack of understanding and Smith's lack of social awareness, implying
in the end that the poet's imagination and artistry constitute the affirming
alternative that could transform both character and reader.

On one hand, then, the values by which Smith defines himself are revised
notions of traditional beauty, alternatives to conventional values that the ignorant "reader" takes for granted as the ideal to which Satin-Legs should as-
pire. The poem therefore questions the very aesthetic values of traditional
artistry it also partially accepts, resisting the effects of what Addison Gayle
called the cultural strangulation of black people by the Western tradition by
dramatizing how that strangulation operates. The speaker, aware of the material and social limits that Satin-Legs faces, asks the addressed and ignorant
reader whether he or she would "deny him lavender / Or take away the
power of his pine" (lines 12–13). Given the meager resources Smith has for
creating his Sunday best, his use of pine for perfume instead of something
more expensive is to be preferred, even lauded. After sardonically suggesting such traditional alternatives as "a Really Good geranium" or "a bit of
gentle garden in the best / Of taste and straight tradition," the speaker concludes,

No! He has not a flower to his name.
Except a feather one, for his lapel.
Apart from that, if he should think of flowers
It is in terms of dandelions or death.
Ah, there is little hope. You might as well—
Unless you care to set the world a-boil
And do a lot of equalizing things,

Remove a little ermine, say, from kings,
Shake hands with paupers and appoint them men,
For instance—certainly you might as well
Leave him his lotion, lavender and oil.

(lines 32–42)

Were the world just, if economic and cultural luxury ("ermine") were not hoarded by "kings" but shared, then Satin-Legs would appreciate "finer" scents. But without such justice, "we" should leave Satin-Legs with what living he has. As a matter of course, he thinks of flowers and other forms of beauty only in direct relation to the social rituals he knows and which sustain him. But this character is not entirely dehumanized. The speaker describes Smith's Sundays with such phrases as "*his* title," "*his* reign," "*his* desertedness," "*his* intricate fear," "*his* bath," "*his* meticulous and serious love" for "the innards of *his* closet," and "*his* mirror" where he "*loves* himself" (emphasis added). Each of these moments of self-possession is a meaningful and potentially heroic contrast to the dispossession around him. As Hansell put it, "In a sense, the poem is one of the earliest suggestions that the acceptance of themselves by blacks must finally be their salvation, both politically and personally" (265). After all, if the "weaponed woman" can do "Rather Well" through her "strong bag," then Satin-Legs's clothing is merely a male alternative for this ideal of personal integrity. And the sexual exploits with which Satin-Legs ends his Sundays and which end the poem constitute his more intimate version of lukewarm water. Both practices defy the bourgeois cultural norms by which Satin-Legs would be found wanting in taste, revealing those norms to be matters of perspective rather than of universal value.

On the other hand, though, the poem reveals how Satin-Legs's self-possession is still too fully shaped by the values of the dominant culture to be effective resistance against his social and cultural deprivation or to be the foundation of unity even within the community. In fact, his is the mistake of which Brooks is accused in this early verse, which is to accept too fully external definitions of his life and possibilities, a mistake Brooks herself vilifies. Brooks is not nearly so accepting as her character or the addressed reader of those inimical values, as the contradictions in her portrayal suggest. For example, the poem criticizes Smith's preference for the blues over classical music because of how he allows the blues to reinforce his alienation despite its vocalization of the shared pain of his neighbors. On the one hand,

> Restaurant vendors
> Weep, or out of them rolls a restless glee.
> The Lonesome Blues, the Long-lost Blues, I Want A
> Big Fat Mama.
>
> (lines 103–6)

The speaker goes on to observe,

> Down these sore avenues
> Comes no Saint-Saens, no piquant elusive Grieg,
> And not Tchaikovsky's wayward eloquence
> And not the shapely tender drift of Brahms.
>
> (lines 106–9)

The speaker asks, "But could he love them?" Blues music is for both Brooks and Smith an emblem of his community's "drab" survival of the alienation created by externally imposed social limitations. But for Satin-Legs, these songs are isolated from their communal ritual in which the blues singer is believed to speak the pain of his or her audience, leaving them only to articulate loneliness and loveless sex (see Baker, *Blues, Ideology*).

Clearly Brooks is no blues poet, since she too seems to be disparaging of this aspect of the blues. Like the high modernist poets who are her models and rivals, she is distinguishing between the "higher" human emotions associated with classical music and the rawer, earthier sounds of the blues, analogously appropriate to this community as lukewarm water. Brooks prefers the "higher" emotions but recognizes that the classical music need not be the only mode capable of expressing those ideals. After all, according to the speaker of the poem,

> a man must bring
> To music what his mother spanked him for
> When he was two: bits of forgotten hate,
> Devotion.
>
> (lines 110–13)

As in the fragmented juxtaposition of much modernist poetry and visual art, Brooks's juxtaposition of these two kinds of music is actually the juxtaposition of two cultural traditions and sets of value, neither of which is ideal. Classical music is inappropriate for Satin-Legs's background but the blues as Satin-Legs understands them reinforces the cultural isolation and deprivation of the social situation (see Ellison). He accepts the blues only as songs of loneliness, a reading of them implied to be characteristic of bourgeois attitudes.

The problem is not with these cultural forms alone, then, but with the character's and the addressed reader's failure to recognize the need for an alternative interpretation of those cultural forms that would recognize the human emotional or existential impulses of both and that would therefore facilitate at least the cultural redistribution of the ermine of kings. In other words, both forms of music express fundamental human emotions equally and should be acknowledged as such. Unlike the "we" of "kitchenette building," whose hints of self-possession gain value by being shared, Satin-Legs's self-possession actually reinforces the social and cultural isolation imposed by injustice, a black ghetto-dweller's high-modernist alienation. So when Satin-Legs leaves home,

> Sounds about him smear,
> Become a unit. He hears and does not hear
> The alarm clock meddling in somebody's sleep;
> Children's governed Sunday happiness;
> The dry tone of a plane; a woman's oath;
> Consumption's spiritless expectoration.
>   (lines 81–86)

Absorbed in his own "desertedness" and "intricate fear," he shuts out the communal rituals of survival, including the blues, enacted by his neighbors, such as the "broken windows / hiding their shame with newsprint," the true make-do-ness of "ribbons decking wornness" the boy's "decentest patch," and the "temperate holiness arranged / Ably on asking faces" (lines 92–93, 97–98). Where the wonder of the "we" in "kitchenette building" is a limited but genuine imagining of an alternative, Smith's potentially existential self-creation is actually escapism that accepts the status quo, his inability to grasp the totality of his condition as caused by racist monopoly capitalism. In Melhem's words, "Smith filters both a white cultural and sociopolitical exhaustion, and a pre-Black Rebellion seeming quiescence" (20).

> The past of his ancestors lean against
> Him. Crowd him. Fog out his identity.

Hundreds of hungers mingle with his own,
Hundreds of voices advise so dexterously
He quite considers his reactions his,
Judges he walks most powerfully alone,
That everything is—simply what it is.
                    (lines 118–24)

All has deserted him. As Brooks put it in a 1984 interview, "I try to picture in 'The Sundays of Satin-Legs Smith' a young man who didn't even know he was a tool of the establishment, who didn't know his life was being run for him from birth straight to death" (Claudia Tate, "Gwendolyn Brooks" 42). Since he avoids the full self-examination necessary to understand his relationship to his community, Satin-Legs actually fails to accept himself and thus fails to validate the fundamental human emotions of his community's culture. And the addressed reader participates in this failure by failing to understand his reasons. From opposite sides of a cultural divide, the character and the reader reinforce the notion of the higher value of white culture, a practice that does indeed dehumanize Satin-Legs, despite the very real strength of his fundamental quest for self-fulfillment. An alternative is needed for this lack of affirmation.

Thus, this yearning for an alternative is not simply Brooks's disparagement of African American vernacular culture, as some have thought of this poem. Rather, this yearning dramatizes this character's failure and the failure of a society to provide for or allow everyone the resources and therefore the capacity to fulfill the "higher" emotions. Thus, Kent is only partly right when he declares, "Although technically the poem runs a contrast between white expectations and black reality, the reader's realization that all images of highest aspiration are in white terms is unsettling: Grieg, Tchaikovsky, 'the shapely, tender drift of Brahms'" (42). In offering this standard critique of Brooks's virtuosity, Kent does identify how ideals of justice and unity and cultural opportunity are offered in examples from Eurocentric bourgeois culture, and it *is* unsettling. But while Brooks does seem to accept aspects of bourgeois or European culture as an ideal, the juxtapositions of the poem undermine that preference, perhaps in ways that contradicted her own values. As Ann Folwell Stanford argues, "The text dismantles . . . and resists the notion of inherent value" (170). By acknowledging how the value of classical music is contingent upon social privilege, the poem refutes the universals it apparently accepts, linking them to white supremacy, not just to the economic deprivation that is the most explicit villain in the poem. Moreover, the relativity that Satin-Legs enacts in response—including his use of sexuality as transcendence—is no alternative. Even these forms of intimacy require proper self-recognition. The "decentest patch" is a more viable engagement with circumstance than the social withdrawal of zoot-suit extravagance because it is more realistic and functional, just as church is more meaningful not because of its doctrines, its claims to universality, but because it is communal. With these critiques, the poem challenges the "reader" in "The Sundays of Satin-Legs Smith" to participate in reconstructing a more egalitarian system of values by following the questioning of inherent value enacted by the poem. Reading the poem is the start of a new vision of social and cultural value and therefore of social possibility.

In other words, since Brooks's own imagination is fully engaged in how social values are largely determined by social context, privilege, and access, this poem reflects Brooks's own alternative, self-aware imagination, the "weaponed" existentialism that Smith pursues but does not achieve. First of all, as Brooks seems to know, verbal virtuosity in Standard English is as much an aspect of African American vernacular practices such as signifying as is informal language. As Stephen Henderson states, "There is a complex and rich and powerful and subtle linguistic heritage whose resources have scarcely been touched that [poets] draw upon." He gives this example: "Don Lee, for example, can use the word 'neoteric' without batting an eye and send us scurrying for our dictionaries. The word is not 'Black' but the casual way that he drops it on us—like 'Deal with that'—is an *elegant Black linguistic gesture*. . . . If one has heard the contrasting voices of Malcolm X and Martin Luther King, then further comment is superfluous" (33). What Henderson implies here about "neoteric" is that the style and context of the use of formal language can be an aspect of culturally distinctive language practices. Henry Louis Gates makes a similar point in emphasizing a distinctive black axis of "signification." For Gates, "signifyin(g)" is an adaptation of "white" words into a "Black linguistic gesture." This virtuoso use of "big words" goes well with the mock-epic examination and critique of the everyday effects of the ideologies of gender and race. Like Satin-Legs himself, then, Brooks wants to make sure no linguistic performance of hers is "plain or vain." Brooks's use of repetition and internal rhyme in lines such as "Sounds about him smear: / . . . He hears and does not hear" resembles the verbal virtuosity of the dozens—that street game of escalating stylish roasts—in which the creativity of the language is as important as the insult (Gates, *Signifying Monkey* 73). In fact, one can read the first half of the poem as a gentle game of the dozens with the reader, a subtle, elaborate, and elegant insult of the reader (and perhaps of his or her mama). In this "big-word" virtuosity, if you will, the changing registers of language and references to African American vernacular culture are subtle examples of Brooks doing high modernism with a black difference. As such, Brooks's own formal virtuosity revises the social practices of her communal alienation and makes her one with her community more fully than Satin-Legs is. Her version of self-possession in this elaborate and innovative poem is to be preferred.

And yet, despite her critique of Satin-Legs and the brilliantly ambivalent selfhood of "kitchenette building," Brooks does not claim to be uniquely capable of such social and imaginative awareness, of the self-possession she poetically denies to Satin-Legs. In poems such as "Negro Hero" and "Gay Chaps at the Bar," which are nearly as self-consciously artsy as "The Sundays of Satin-Legs Smith," Brooks depicts the heroism of African American World War II soldiers as having more to do with their redefinition of inherited values than with their military action. Here she makes this existentialism explicitly heroic. In the dramatic monologue "Negro Hero," the process of self-possession begins as follows:

I had to kick their law into their teeth in order to save them.
However I have heard that sometimes you have to deal
Devilishly with drowning men in order to swim them to shore.
Or they will haul themselves and you to the trash and the fish beneath.
(When I think of this, I do not worry about a few chipped teeth.)
(lines 1–6)

Told from the first person, the poem gives this "Dorie Miller" figure a voice and subjectivity that Satin-Legs, an object of discussion in the poem, does not have. Moreover, though this poem is more explicitly heroic, and not mock-epic, its language is more colloquial, locating that heroism in the ordinary rather than in the extravagant. Rather than the polysyllabic words and complex tension between the poet's voice and Satin-Legs's life, this poem operates through the internal monologue of a simple man in his simple, single-syllable words and homely images of trash and chipped teeth. Here is a more easily recognizable version of the vernacular virtuosity of "The Sundays of Satin-Legs Smith." Finally, even in this first stanza, in the midst of military action, the speaker's heroism derives from directly resisting externally imposed values, not from the violence in the service of a just cause. The greatest problem the speaker faces is not the gesture of grabbing the gun in the middle of an attack, in other words (though that is certainly dangerous!), but the effort to reconcile his actions to the racist expectations of his society. The speaker recognizes that in order for him to arm himself during the bombing at Pearl Harbor in the defense of democracy, personified as female, he had to ignore the reality that belied the ideal:

> for the sake of the dear smiling mouth and the stuttered promise I toyed
> with my life.
> I threw back!—I would not remember
> Entirely the knife.
>
> (lines 24–26)

He had to "remember" that the ideal was actually an alternative to the practice of his society in order to act in support of unifying social ideals.

In other words, the heroic in Brooks's verse is the means by which the African American existential consciousness and its social activism fills the vacuum created between the oppressive socially constructed values of the "reader" on one hand and the disempowering relativism of Satin-Legs on the other through the assertion of its own value. The speaker wonders: "Am I clean enough to kill for them?" Despite the ironies of the implicitly affirmative answer to this rhetorical question (his place *is* "in the galley still"), the speaker concludes:

> Naturally, the important thing is, I helped to save them, them and a part
> of their democracy.
> Even if I had to kick their law into their teeth in order to do that for them.
> And I am feeling well and settled in myself because I believe it was a good
> job.
>
> (lines 38–40)

Though his conception of democracy as "theirs" may be evidence of his being "conditioned" to white external definitions, the more important point is that the speaker has found some solace for his actions in his mind, as the repetition and revision of the first stanza in the last reveals. He wrestles with potential remorse for kicking the law in the teeth but is feeling "well and settled," a down-to-earth satisfaction more substantive than elaborate dress or a taste for classical music. Moreover, Brooks's understatement that those actions were "a good job" implies that it is more than a good job for a black soldier to affirm ideals of the society and to accept himself positively despite the national hypocrisy that makes his place in the galley still. Finally, democracy is portrayed as a state of mind and a consequence of the self-definition necessary for the nation's practice of these ideals, as even the poem's form exemplifies. The cyclical nature of the poem, created by the repetition of the first and last stanzas, suggests that this subtle progress will repeat itself and grow. In essence, in Brook's modernist art, the African American soldier's war is more with his own culture than with the nation's enemy, turning heroism inward to a "domestic" battlefield in order to move more fully into the social battlefield of a racist world. This implicit revision of the opposition of traditional feminine and masculine fields of action places the "domestic" or private and personal into its rightful place as the foundation of public political action. A war hero's heroics start in his mind.

In "Gay Chaps at the Bar," Brooks more fully implies that this war is won through this "feminine" self-acceptance of the "Negro Hero," because she implies that such self-possession is capable of changing external conditions. As such, Brooks's vision of military heroism clarifies the value she implies in her numerous poems about female self-definition to be discussed below. In this sonnet sequence, Brooks uses the sonnet's syllogistic structure—conducive to argument—to reveal the effects of war on love and to hint that the healing power of self-love extends beyond the individual mind into social activism. In "firstly inclined to take what it is told," the eighth sonnet of the series, for example, the speaker declares to the Christian Trinity a willingness to accept religion passively, a willingness that declines to skepticism in the next poem, "'God Works in a Mysterious Way,'" where the speaker observes that "the youthful eye cuts down its / Own dainty veiling. Or submits to winds" (lines 1–2). That "youthful eye" not only challenges its own fragile belief but is susceptible to other versions of belief or even to the "winds" of chaos themselves. Such a youthful eye, seeing through its religious training, must endure "the impudence / Of modern glare," namely the modern history—from the atrocities of segregation and lynching to the atrocities of Hitler's Germany—that appears unaware of God, convincing the speaker that perhaps he should be too (lines 4–5). Here again is the African American modern condition constituted as much by problems of meaning and lack of faith as by the social practices of racism. In order to reconcile himself to this chaotic context, the soldier needs the assurance of a new, self-affirming mode of meaning.

Not just an emblem of Brooks's mastery, then, the sonnet form becomes, like the ballad stanza in "weaponed woman," an emblem of the interaction between will and circumstance that constitutes the social agency of the existential imagination. In the entire sequence, Brooks uses off-rhyme for "an off-rhyme situation" in order to use existing structures to create new meanings beyond the satisfaction of the individual mind (Brooks, *Report from Part One* 156). The speaker of the poem requests that whatever divinity that may exists comes out of "Thy shadows" in order to prove itself more than "hate" or "atmosphere":

> Step forth in splendor, mortify our wolves.
> Or we assume a sovereignty ourselves.
>
> (lines 13–14)

These off-rhyme couplets, as Brooks called them, defy the common resolution potentially available in the final quatrain and couplet of the Shakespearean sonnet or the intricate closure of the Italian sonnet in deference to the "off-rhyme situation," leaving the possible self-assertion at the end as yet unresolved. But it is clear that an oppressive, misleading Christianity is discarded here and a new mind-set is begun. And if Christianity is read not just as religion but as a stand-in for all dominant discursive structures in society, then this growing self-awareness constitutes a powerful agency indeed.

For Brooks, this heroism is real, contradicting Williams's claim that "the reader knows the powerless people huddled together in an equally powerless place can never assume 'sovereignty'" (68). Not a matter of social power, this sovereignty is of the intellectual value of cultural expression and individual self-definition. Changing one's religious belief will of course change behavior, starting most simply with refusing to go to church. And given the Christian church's role both in the oppression of the slaves and in the emerging civil rights movement, this sovereignty is an alternative to an important cultural institution in race relations. Finally, since it is a "we" that will assume a sovereignty, that change of meaning has broad communal implications. The sonnet form reveals how even this new sovereignty must be invested in traditional ideals, as the speaker has not yet broken entirely free. In these terms, objections to Brooks's use of the form or to the idea that this sovereignty is real reveals the tendency in studies of African American culture to privilege conceptions of African Americans as victims rather than as agents. And while I acknowledge that this tendency depends upon an admirable desire to criticize the system that made them victims, I think Brooks would concur with my preference for recognizing the fact that African Americans are never entirely victims, that there are rays of sun, that fundamental humanity endures oppression and resists it. And this sovereignty is exactly the way to do so.

Brooks's characters are not primarily victims, then, but rather actors with agency more or less to manipulate the values and practices of their world within their individual and collective whirling places in ways that promise future change through social unity. This is the "feminine" nature of this heroism, a distinction I make not to reinscribe the preference for masculine ideals of heroism. Rather, I do so as an identifiable term for how Brooks seems deeply to admire the modest existentialism of ordinary people, no matter its social efficacy. But she does see social efficacy, especially in the lives of women. While scholars have commented frequently on Brooks's "black and tan" poems—her examination of color hierarchy within the black community— few have moved beyond the subject matter of gender to see how Brooks defines the internal lives of black women as her ultimate social norm and ideal. In "Sadie and Maud," for example, the alternative notion of heroism at the heart of Brooks's war poems becomes an unconventional sexuality through which the title character Sadie "assumed a sovereignty" herself. Using a fairly conventional ballad stanza, Brooks characterizes this sovereignty, comparing the two title characters' lives. Maud is more conventional and went to college, while "Sadie scraped life / with a fine-tooth comb" (lines 3–4). This poem poses two alternative notions of womanhood, neither of which is entirely conventional for the times. Neither woman marries. Maud attended college but not just for the sake of gaining a husband. Sadie does not stay at home to be domestic. And both experience the social cost of that unconventionality. Though an unconventional professional woman, Maud was sexually conventional and was therefore entirely unproductive since, in the end, she lives alone.

Meanwhile, Sadie's pursuit of full living and self-fulfillment is clearly a better choice than Maud's self-denial because it articulates a substantively alternative notion of sexuality related to the personal integrity of racial self-definition. Finding "every strand" of life with her comb, Sadie refused to be ruled by the social mores represented by her parents' and sister's shame about her behavior and her children out of wedlock. Undaunted, Sadie bore those two daughters as a measure of her self-assertive, self-authorizing vitality, since she "left as heritage / her fine-tooth comb" (lines 17–18). Not only does Sadie's sovereign approach lead to fulfillment, in other words, it potentially leads to social change, since her daughters will follow in her footsteps. Endowed with the same commitment to fulfillment as their mother, Sadie's daughters double her defiance of an inadequate, life-sapping conventional femininity. And as in "weaponed woman," Brooks uses the ballad form to emphasize the possibility that this story is part of oral history, a tale passed on from generation to generation to validate Sadie's choice. This revision includes the irregularity from stanza to stanza of rhythmic structure from five-syllable lines in the first stanza to seven- and eight-syllable lines in the third. This unconventional story is told unconventionally. And it will continue to be told, both as stories and as lived experience by Sadie's daughters. Self-fulfillment, like existential assertions of democracy, is a defiant act with a defiant legacy.

So, though few female characters in Brooks's Bronzeville are as openly and unambiguously defiant of social norms as Sadie, and though none of them have the public stage of Negro Hero, most of them seek and attain some degree of this sovereignty or personal integrity in defiance of conventional gender roles informed by the politics of race, especially the politics of beauty. Moreover, in the "Hattie Scott" sequence, Brooks provides a miniature version of the process of self-awareness by which she fulfills her ideals in the 1949 volume *Annie Allen* by adapting the traditional ballad to the blues reality of Hattie's life. Her ballads are blues poems here, adapting the blues attitude of stoic endurance through expression to the meditations of this blues woman and potential artist figure. In the first poem of the sequence, "the end of the day," Brooks establishes a tension between the domestic work that Hattie does for whites and the possibility of enjoyment, since her desire to escape her workplace keeps her from enjoying the view of the sunset available to her there. Like a good blues song, the catharsis is bittersweet: the workplace offers a better view of the sunset than her home has, but the oppressiveness of that workplace compromises its access to beauty. Her leaving is an act of survival and even muted resistance, even if it does turn her attention away from beauty. In "the date," though, the pursuit of fulfillment is more explicit, as the anticipation of good socializing creates an urgency to be relieved of the extra demands of her insensitive boss.

> Whatcha mean talking about cleanin' silver?
> It's eight o'clock now, you fool.
> I'm leavin'. Got somethin' interestin' on my mind.
> Don't mean night school.
>
> (lines 4–8)

Hattie is not actually chastising her boss. She is talking to herself. Again, Hattie's defiance is muted and internal, but it is the best she can offer. And it is genuine. It is a version of Ralph Ellison's famous definition of the blues, especially his sense that blues people transcend pain "not by the consolation of philosophy but by squeezing from it a near-tragic, near-comic lyricism" (78–79).

Though Brooks is certainly no blues poet, it is clear that she understands Ellison's idea of "fingering the jagged grain" of experience with the expectation of self-knowledge, solace, and, ideally, a sympathetic audience. Brooks was also aware of the necessity of revising the image of women in the blues in order for that affirmation to work for a woman singer. For example, in "Queen of the Blues," Brooks represents a blues singer who fails to understand how the men in her audience neglect her talent and see her only as the sexual object to which women are sometimes reduced in blues songs. On one hand, her dignity is compromised by not being acknowledged by her audience, but, on the other, she takes her status as queen seriously and resists the limited framing of her life enacted by those false expectations. That dignity is genuine, as is Hattie's, even if it is limited by social circumstances.

In "the battle," Brooks attributes to Hattie the fullest reach of this "feminine" blues in which Hattie's self-affirmation is validated by an implicit female community. It is an affirming version of the blues that Satin-Legs fails to recognize in general and that scholars such as Kent fail to recognize in Brooks's verse. In it, Hattie uses gossip to distinguish herself as a stronger woman than most by retelling a third-person version of a fairly typical blues scenario.

> Moe Belle Jackson's husband
> Whipped her good last night.
> Her landlady told my ma they had
> A knock-down-drag-out fight.
>
> I like to think
> Of how I'd of took a knife
> And slashed all of the quickenin'
> Out of his lowly life.
>
> (lines 1–8)

Evocative of a woman's community knitted together by conversation in a beauty parlor, this poem implies that Hattie takes this opportunity to get affirmation on an alternative notion of domesticity where a wife need not take such violence from a husband. Though the line "I like to think" suggests that perhaps Hattie might not be so bold after all, the fact that it is a line to itself also affirms her capacity for cognition—she likes to think, which is the foundation of existential agency. And one can imagine nods of assent from the listening women, both in support of Hattie's claim of strength and in her bitter acknowledgment of the unavoidable power of patriarchy. It is an implied call-and-response typical of African American vernacular culture such as the blues or church, where song leaders expect active participation from listeners.

Hattie concludes with an observation that she expects to be seconded:

> But if I know Moe Belle,
> Most like, she shed a tear,
> And this mornin' it was probably,
> "More grits, dear?"
> (lines 10–12)

This poem is clearly a protest of the constraints of conventional womanhood and domesticity, as those constraints sanction violence against women. It also implies a heroic female weapon of self-acceptance that would lead, if not to physical self-assertion against that violence, at least to the subversive act of leaving. Hattie has the power of mind to see another way of acting. As a result, it is possible that she will actually act differently. And it is an ideal that is shared.

In essence, then, Brooks's first volume defines a community unified by its individuals' attempts to define themselves in response to common circumstance and in common means, both of which are shared by the poet, who mutes her presence through dramatic monologues. What matters about black community is its place as a manifestation of the African American's pursuit of alternative values instead of the imposed values of a racist society. And the resistance to traditional gender roles, like Brooks's adaptation of traditional poetics, constitutes the genuine social agency of this otherwise exclusively internal, private agency. Existentialism in this context is the beginning of social activism, both for character and for poet.

Such ideals make *Annie Allen* the defining fulfillment of Brooks's feminine modernist heroism, clarifying a way of thinking about its critical acclaim that is not rooted in hints that Brooks sold out for it but rather in the blues existential consciousness of the African American woman. Its implicit narrative of female self-acceptance achieves all of Brooks's aims of ethnic self-definition, poetic distinction, and cross-racial identification. The volume traces Annie's maturing mind from traditional visions of romance in all of their passivity and their objectification of women to a mature womanhood characterized by self-awareness, self-sufficiency, and the self-assertion of raising children. Though in recent studies it is disparaged if it is mentioned at all, *Annie Allen* makes clear that, whatever the social or political circumstances, black womanhood can sustain itself and thus become a sustaining force in the black community. By the end of the volume, Annie's voice merges with that of the poet, explicitly granting Annie the narrative and imaginative capacities of the poet. Altogether, Brooks evokes clichéd notions of love, marriage, and motherhood to illustrate how Annie's romantic aspirations are thwarted by an oppressive society and then fulfilled more realistically through Annie's existential self-definition. And Brooks's own virtuosity is the ultimate proof of this fulfillment. Imagination is agency indeed, making Brooks a bardic peoples' poet.

The volume's "narrative" is broken into three broad sections, the first of which is called "Notes from the Childhood and the Girlhood," which traces Annie's lifelong problems back to the formation of her gender identity itself. Her sense of self shifts from the gender-neutral "childhood" to "girlhood" and is archetypal ("*the* Childhood and *the* Girlhood"). The volume's first poem, "the birth in a narrow room," implies how a rampant and self-absorbed creativity not unlike Satin-Legs Smith's gets filtered into the limiting parameters of traditional womanhood. It treats this gender identity as a personal analogue to the small domestic space of Annie's impoverished upbringing, which links it to the "involuntary plan" of racism. Gender identity is therefore as much a part of the deterministic environment of Brooks's realism as race. This point is not always discussed enough in studies of Brooks's work.

> Weeps out of western country something new.
> Blurred and stupendous. Wanted and unplanned.
>   Winks. Twines and weakly winks
> Upon the milk-glass fruit bowl, iron pot
> The bashful china child tipping forever
> Yellow apron and spilling pretty cherries.
>
>   (lines 1–6)

On the frontier of African American society, Annie's uniqueness is suggested but, since the uniqueness is but potential, the limiting circumstances of her birth are declared. On one hand, she is "wanted and unplanned," meaning she herself is part of the involuntary plan. "Twining" and "winking" are the actions of babies but they also suggest Annie's "blurred" and inadequate vision. The "bashful china child," according to Stanford, "more than simply hovering over Annie's life, [embodies] the 'illusory ideal' of beauty and the 'romantic presence' [that] are the very shapers and arbiters of Annie's identity and life choices" (284). In other words, Annie's gender identity is being determined right before her eyes. On the other hand, this yearning hopefulness and domestic heroism promise to grow into a greater vision of society. As Stanley Kunitz observes, the poem "is deftly inwoven, as by the series of fruit images . . . and, even more subtly, by the set of verbal dissolves (weeps, blurred, unplanned, winks . . . weakly winks, milk-glass) that anticipates and counterpoints the eventually achieved clarity of focus" (53). Thus, the poem, like much of the volume as a whole, places the reader in Annie's head as it moves from fuzziness and winking to clear focus.

As with Satin-Legs Smith, Annie's odd vision—her imagination—is a mode of coping with social deprivation and, like his, is potentially complicit in her oppression. It is at first a mode of escapism unlike the heroism that will later emerge and contributes to her acceptance of the passivity associated with the idealized but patriarchal gender identity she opposes to her mother's ideals. As a child, because she is imaginative, because she "prances nevertheless with gods and fairies," Annie will not notice that: "'I am not anything and I have got / Not anything, or anything to do!'" (lines 11, 9–10). On one hand, this is a powerful defense mechanism. In her mind, the tensions between homeliness and extravagance, reality and imagination, are quite balanced by her capacity to see gods and fairies in the vivid bugs and old jelly jars of her environment. On the other, it leads her to ignore practical reality, something of which her mother is absolutely aware, as is clear in "Maxie Allen," in which the point-counterpoint structure and jocular tone embodies the dialectical terms of possibility and restriction in the definition of black female selfhood. As Claudia Tate suggests, Brooks uses "conventional, formal satirical techniques" in this poem for "ridiculing aspects of Annie's life" as "the loose meter itself informs us that Brooks is censuring the poem's narrative content" ("Anger So Flat" 142). Its virtuosity is part of its critique of patriarchy. The first stanza reveals that

Maxie Allen always taught her
Stipendiary little daughter

To thank her Lord and lucky star
For eye that let her see so far.
                    (lines 1–4)

The rest of the stanza continues in this vein as the unimaginative mother urges her daughter to be thankful for Quaker Oats and for the ability to complain about poverty and for a healthy body. Like the speaker(s) in "kitchenette building," Annie's mother accepts diminished ideals and urges Annie to accept them in part for her own safety. The poem's light-hearted tone contrasts with the severity of the limitations of the mother's vision, especially when Maxie Allen points out that Annie can afford to dream:

you [Annie] don't have to go to bed . . .
With two dill pickles in the dark,
Nor prop what hardly calls you honey
And gives you only a little money.
                    (lines 28–31)

This necessary sacrifice operates in dialectical tension with the potentially heroic desire Annie has to pursue "somewhat of something other," though that undefined thing has trouble surviving the social demands of gender roles. Like Satin-Legs, the mother does not concern herself with yearning for more or challenging the systems—sociopolitical and discursive—that limit her. But the fact that Annie cannot identify her alternative to her mother's practicality is also a problem. The "narrative" of the volume reveals how patriarchy, like racial hierarchy, limits the kinds of dream fulfillment available to black women, eventually substituting limiting roles for that "something other." The contrast between structure and theme in the poem creates the dramatic irony that the reader knows more than either character of the impending danger of gender identity.

The rest of the volume's narrative portrays the full imposition of the "involuntary plan" of gender formation on Annie and the emergence of the heroic existential imagination that ultimately draws Brooks and Annie together into the one voice of Annie as a weaponed woman. This evolution is the central subject of "The Anniad," the second section of the volume and Brooks's highly innovative mock-epic, which represents Annie's coming-of-age as an epic journey toward the capacity to challenge the limiting discourses of patriarchy. As Stanford observes, "Instead of the patrilineal transfer of civilization" conventional in the epic, Brooks evokes that honored genre to depict a lineage of "frustrated domesticity," so that "the text rewrites the terms of cultural transmission and power relations" (277). The epic plot of this poem is Annie's internal journey toward awareness of the limitations of her romantic dreams she derived from and opposed to her mother's passive domesticity, even though the poem ends more with alienation than with self-possession. The poem opens:

> Think of sweet and chocolate,
> Left to folly or to fate,
> Whom the higher gods forgot,
> Whom the lower gods berate;
> Physical and underfed
> Fancying on a featherbed
> What was ever and is not.
>
> What is ever and is not.
> Pretty tatters blue and red,
> Buxom berries beyond rot,
> Western clouds and quarter-stars,
> Fairy-sweets of old guitars
> Littering the little head
> Light upon the featherbed.
>
> Think of ripe and rompabout,
> All her harvest buttoned in,
> All her ornaments untried;
> Waiting for the paladin
> Prosperous and ocean-eyed
> Who shall rub her secrets out
> And behold the hinted bride.
>
> Watching for the paladin
> Which no woman ever had,
> Paradisical and sad
> With a dimple in his chin
> And mountains in the mind;
> Ruralist and rather bad,
> Cosmopolitan and kind.
>
> (lines 1–28)

Brooks drops the subjects from compressed clauses to reveal the passivity of her female epic hero. Despite the weighty possibilities of the epic and of Brooks's ambitious word magic, in other words, Annie's head is "light" on the featherbed and her sensuality is all "buttoned in," as social conventionality and gendered passivity compromise vitality. Rather than opening with an epic invocation, then, this mock-epic asserts the ordinariness and folly of Annie's situation, an opening deflation of epic possibilities. Whatever higher gods there are—perhaps genuine deities—ignore Annie while the lower gods—perhaps empowered humans such as her mother—berate her for her passivity and her dreams. Moreover, Annie is objectified here in much the same way Satin-Legs was, and her objectified state is meant to be an object lesson for the reader. As in the "pretty cherries" in "the birth in a narrow room," Annie, in her false idealism, pictures "Buxom berries beyond rot," a vision that hints at notions of domestic beauty similar to those in the earlier poem. Imagining that the beauties of her childhood do not change, Annie implies that art is the static monument to truth and beauty that is Keats's Grecian urn. But what the rest of the poem suggests is that such static monuments deceive, because they are based on the self-defeating gender norms against which the volume argues.

The danger in traditional notions of physical and poetic beauty is that these abstractions of beauty are tied to a specific sociocultural history and that accepting them means accepting associated notions of white supremacy and patriarchy that compromise the capacity of African American women to achieve self-possession. Because Annie simply waits for her impossible, self-contradictory paladin ("Ruralist and rather bad, / Cosmopolitan and kind," "Who shall rub her secrets out / And behold the hinted bride"), she lets the ideals of the oppressive external world determine her sense of self:

> Think of thaumaturgic lass
> Looking in her looking-glass
> At the unembroidered brown;
> Printing bastard roses there;
> Then emotionally aware
> of the black and boisterous hair,
> Taming all that anger down.
>   (lines 29–35)

As Stanford observes, these lines posit the "bastard roses" as more than sloppy, overdone makeup. It recalls the flowers and classical music and the associated bourgeois and normative cultural values of the addressed reader in "The Sundays of Satin-Legs Smith." Such ideals "simply do not belong in Annie's world. They are illegitimate signifiers of an appropriated, culturally determined, and impossible notion of beauty" (289). Accepting these illegitimate and impossible notions of straight hair and light skin, Annie attempts to tame the "anger" of her nappy hair into Anglo straightness. This practice is the archetype of the self-hatred African Americans develop by too completely internalizing dominant cultural values. Where Hattie Scott's sense of beauty, while similarly beholden to Anglo-Saxon models, emerges from a sense of pride, Annie's represents self-sacrifice to a patriarchal notion that is entirely abstract and therefore all the more impossible and self-defeating. Trying to fit into the narrative of damsels and knights, she must also fit into those notions of beauty. As in Satin-Legs's case, Annie must ignore a black reality in order to fulfill her imaginative aspirations, and, as the poem's form embodies, she wholeheartedly and passively dresses her life up in them.

The same can be said of Annie's conventional vision of masculinity, a version pervasive in the poor black community of Bronzeville as Brooks represents it and central to the "involuntary plan" of racism and poverty. Annie's paladin is transformed in her imagination (and his) into an ideal he cannot fulfill, and Annie's marriage to him thus illuminates the irreconcilable tensions between her faulty imagination (and his) and her reality. The narrator notes of Annie's "tan man's" arrival, "How he postures at his height; / Unfamiliar, to be sure, with celestial furniture" (lines 50–52). Yet, false as he may be—his height a posture merely, based on being male rather than on knowing higher ideals—Annie allows him to be a "Narrow master" who "mastercalls" as "the godhead glitters now / Cavalierly in his brow" (lines 43–44). But that "godhead" is obliterated by the reality of war, both as actual conflict and as metaphor for existential struggle. After the military draft "Names him. Tames him. Takes him off," the tan man returns home disempowered:

With his helmet's final doff
Soldier lifts his power off.
Soldier bare and chilly then
Wants his power back again.
No confection languider
Before quick-feast quick-famish Men
Than the candy crowns-that-were.

                    (lines 126–33)

To recover the remembered masculinity that was an imaginative projection paradoxically validated by the horrific violence of the war, the "tan man" finds a mistress, a confection rather than the sustaining nourishment of self-fulfillment. The sense of masculinity accepted by Annie and her husband depends on conquest rendered impossible by racial injustice and by the fact that the sanctioned violence of war was but a temporary solace. In addition to destroying himself (he dies of disease), his infidelity destroys Annie's romantic picture of her family and her sense of being desired.

But this destruction is the prelude to Annie's transformation, a transformation that posits alternative values and a possibly alternative imagination, an existential selfhood and its matrilineage that, to reiterate, is exemplified by the virtuosity of this poem. This destruction of the family is the poem's equivalent of an epic trip to the underworld, a dark moment leading to transformation. Annie emerges the wiser. As it was for Sadie, single motherhood becomes Annie's alternative, though it too starts of as an ambivalent creativity. Once Annie loses her paladin,

> "Then incline to children-dear!
> Pull the halt magnificence near,
> Sniff the perfumes, ribbonize
> Gay bouquet most satinly;
> Hoard it, for a planned surprise
> When the desert terrifies."
> (lines 226–23)

Here Annie may replicate the same domestic lineage started by her own mother, forcing her children into the false ideals she was unable to achieve. But the concluding lines of the poem clarify how this end is a new beginning: "Think of tweaked and twenty-four. / Fuchsias gone or gripped or gray, / All hay-colored that was green," and "Think of almost thoroughly / Derelict and dim and done," Annie, again with no subject in her clauses, sits "Hugging old and Sunday sun. / Kissing in her kitchenette / The minuets of memory" (lines 288–90, 295–96, 299–301). This deflation of Annie at the end of "The Anniad" represents more the deflation of the conventional dreams available to Annie and their cost to her. The reader is to imagine the lost vitality to be in part a loss of the naïveté that led Annie to buy into oppressive values in the first place. The fuchsias that are gone refer to how Annie sees the world—it has lost its luster but she has not. Though beaten and "*almost* thoroughly / Derelict and dim and done [emphasis added]," the minuets of memory dance toward an imaginative legacy, which, for Annie, is her children. And there is also Brooks's poem.

Brooks's own virtuosity becomes the model by which to understand the possibilities of Annie's imagination as it is validated by the end of the volume. The poem does not "reproduce" ambivalence about female power, as Stanford states and others imply. It is, instead, a critique of a particular kind of creativity, one that is circumscribed within the patriarchy that makes all blacks into men and all women into white damsels. Stanford is only partly right to conclude that "'The Anniad' resists male creative presence and represents female creativity as at best a thwarted enterprise" (287). First, Brooks literally rewrites the title of the *Aeneid* to reflect the epic story of her ordinary black woman character, a gesture that genuinely resists or rewrites "male creative presence." Moreover, as in "The Sundays of Satin-Legs Smith," Brooks uses a big-word virtuosity that can and should be associated with African American vernacular cultural language practice. The poet's language is purposefully not vernacular, but the wordplay participates in that self-defining tradition. Finally, given her direct address to the reader, Brooks does not want Annie's imagination to be entirely representative of all women. As in Satin-Legs's case, Brooks's speaker is schooling the reader on what can happen to women due to the emotional and intellectual deprivations caused by racism. But it has not happened to Brooks, so that female creativity is not thwarted. And as the rest of the volume demonstrates, Annie largely recovers. Conventional female identity may thwart its own associated fantasies, but the imagination itself is enduring. Annie's creativity becomes resistance, both within and against the terms of its own making.

In the next section, "The Womanhood," Annie's role as mother becomes a complicated but ultimately affirming outlet for her creativity. And since it shapes both Annie and her children, it is implied to be a social agency. In the process, Brooks defines womanhood in terms of the existential self-definition that is also central to ethnic identity. The sonnet sequence "Children of the Poor" subtly brings Annie's imagination closer to Brooks's own. Left with the existential question of how to create new values out of the vacuum created by a lost husband and lost illusions, Annie comes to recognize that she must pursue self-fulfillment through values appropriate to her individual self-definition, not ones appropriate to conventionality. But though she may feel unequipped to face that existential vacuum (after all, Annie does say she lacks "access to my proper stone" [line 10]), the realistic attitude she has adopted is an improvement over the "thwarted" creativity of the opening poems in the volume. Moreover, the artistry of the sonnets themselves belies her insecurity. As in "Gay Chaps at the Bar," Brooks uses the sonnet's syllogistic structure to exemplify the tensions in Annie's psyche as Brooks "thwart[s] the expected resolution of the sonnets' dilemmas . . . [and] heighten[s] the sense of the mother's frustration and her inability to provide meaningful answers to her children" (Gary Smith 49). The formal coherence of the poems reveals what Annie's mind and will can make of the dilemma of single motherhood.

For example, in the second sonnet of the sequence, "And shall I prime my children, pray, to pray?," the speaker—presumably Annie as mother—begins to fight by reshaping religious meaning for her children. She resolves to

> revise the psalm
> If that should frighten you: sew up belief
> If that should tear: turn, singularly calm,
> At forehead and at fingers rather wise,
> Holding the bandage ready for your eyes.
>
> (10–14)

For her children, she will do what is necessary to heal the pain of a new, less glamorized or glorified vision of the world. That healing will be her protection against the "modern glare." And while the protective gesture can be read as Annie imposing delusion on her children, the most important implication is that new meanings might result. In the process of being "deaf to music and to beauty blind" (line 11) in "First fight. Then fiddle," the mother revises the psalm, a song of ultimate meaning. In fact, the music *is* the fight. Sewing up the psalm is changing it. And changing the psalm is changing cultural meaning. Though hers is hardly as defiant as the soldiers' in "Gay Chaps at the Bar," Annie is here assuming a sovereignty herself. In essence, what Annie passes on is not any particular meaning but the commitment to making it. The last poems of the volume—many of them arguably attributable to the mature Annie's voice—use free-verse rather than metered verse and largely irregular forms to assert and to enact the freer mind-set Annie has largely achieved.

In fact, Annie's voice is so close to Brooks's in this section that she offers the same social critiques as Brooks does. And while that critique is predicated on the ideals of integration that Lee rightly calls conditioned, that conditioning remains part of the poem's antiracist meaning. In "XI," a poem that opens, "One Wants a Teller in a time like this," Annie yearns for someone to say that "*Behold / Love's true, and triumphs; and God's actual* [original italics]" (line 15), though that someone is herself. The poem is conditional, heightened by the italicized advice from the Teller who is so hypothetical that the ending advice has no quotation marks. There is no actual speaker other than Annie expressing the yearning for the advice that she herself is giving. In fact, she also points out how such a "Teller" can be misleading. Annie seems implicitly to be acknowledging what Brooks knows: without such a "Teller," "we" are left to our own devices, an assertion of "our" "sovereignty." In other words, Annie realizes that she must be the one who defines her existence. And since this poem, like most of the poems in this last section, is written in free verse, it is clearly arguable that Annie's imagination has been liberated from the constraints of the formalism associated with traditional gender roles, Annie's insecurity notwithstanding. Thus, the section includes poems in which one of Annie's children always keeps reaching for something other even though it causes him pain; in which Cousin Vit's funeral is a validation of her unconventional being that extends even after her death; and in which, as the volume ends, the combined voice of Annie and Brooks criticizes the careful men of the Civil Rights Movement for their gradualism. The poem declares the need to act, to "wizard" a direction out of the chaos of the changes in that era. Even more than in *A Street in Bronzeville,* then, Brooks becomes one with her character. And in that oneness, the reader is made to be aware of the African American woman's heroic existential yearnings and to be persuaded to participate in her liberation to be an existential individual. Without Annie losing her distinctiveness as a character, Brooks has made herself one with both her black (female) community and her implied reader.

One last point needs to be made. The ideal effect or social agency of these innovations is an assertion of commonality with white readers, through this validation of ethnic and gender difference, but that assertion has been read too simply and inaccurately as self-deprecation, a compromise of her affirmation. In "A Bronzeville Mother Loiters in Mississippi: Meanwhile A Mississippi Mother Burns Bacon," from her 1960 volume *The Bean Eaters,* for example, the agency of Brooks's claim to commonality at the heart of difference is quite powerfully clear, as is the misreading of it. Writing from the perspective of a white woman and mother, Brooks clarifies how female self-definition is a substance of Brooks's political commentary and of an ideal of the antiracist poetic effect necessary for interracial community. By rewriting the story of the lynching of Emmett Till as a dysfunctional ballad, Brooks implies the experience and social status of motherhood can unite a black and a white woman despite the problems of race.

> From the first it had been like a
> Ballad. It had the beat inevitable. It had the blood.
> A wildness cut up, and tied in little bunches,
> Like the four-line stanzas of the ballads she had never quite
> Understood—the ballads they had set her to, in school.
>
> (lines 1–5)

The poem's irregular line lengths symbolize the ragged ways in which experience defies the controlled "little bunches" of lines characteristic of the narrative, noncontemplative ballad stanza, since she does not entirely fit into the role of "the milk-white maid" nor does the teenaged black boy who died seem quite like the "Dark Villain" and, as the poem proceeds, her husband seems less and less like the "Fine Prince."

Though the Mississippi mother had felt like her story had been a ballad, placing herself, her husband, and the lynched boy in the archetypal roles signaled by Brooks's "emphatic capitalization" (Melhem 210), she came to realize that, "from the first," her life did not conform to the ballad, the violence of this awareness being hinted at by the burning bacon. She recognizes that life had been falsely but powerfully "set to" this patriarchal narrative. But in this case, "although the pattern prevailed, / The breaks were everywhere" (lines 48–49). Worse, she realizes that her self-worth and worth to others has been determined by this false narrative. Now, the mother begins to fear that "sometimes she fancied he looked at her as though / Measuring her. As if he considered, Had she been worth it?" (lines 52–53). She realized that "He must never conclude / That she had not been worth it" (lines 57–58). Just as Annie did not, in the end, measure up to the military power her "tan man" had lost, the white mother here may not somehow measure up to what her husband needs in order to cope with his horrific actions, once justified by heroic manliness. The old stories were not working for him either. So, as the images of inadequate domesticity, such as the burnt bacon or her husband's slapping of her child, pile up around her, and as the story she constructed falls down around her, she realizes that her husband is a murderer, that she is subject to his assessments and his power and that, like Annie, she has been conditioned to cooperate in that murder and in her own subjugation. And as her husband slaps their child, she realizes that it takes violence to maintain these false narratives.

Brooks's strategy in this representation has led to a characteristic misstatement of how this powerful existentialism can validate both commonality and difference, ethnic culture and female community, without sacrificing an awareness of social circumstance and without dulling the incisiveness of social critique. Acknowledging one's place in a societal narrative or ideology is a substantial component of political consciousness, whether for antiracist struggle or feminist commentary. And yet Kent, for example, argues that "the black observer [in many of Brooks's poems] becomes . . . too oblivious of the immediately historical pressures in a jet-speed trip to the universal" and concludes that, as a result, "'A Bronzeville Mother . . .' [*sic*] has pleased many because of the poet's stance of considering a white woman, who was the source of the lynching of an early adolescent black boy, simply as a mother. [But] in doing so, the poet ignores the grotesque historical conditions that the heroine would have to work through before exemplifying the humanity with which she is endowed" (43).

In this assessment, Kent assumes that motherhood cannot be the means through which a white woman can realize the horrors of sexism and racism, including her own biases, and overlooks altogether how the very process and formal structure of the poem are meant to embody her engagement with those "grotesque historical conditions" he says Brooks ignores. Kent also assumes that racism trumps any capacity for identification between blacks and whites, even though gender identity and the oppressive character of patriarchy and misogyny provide similar kinds of motivation for unity as racism does. But since Brooks sees more points of identification than race, her work is actually a more sophisticated analysis of social interaction and historical conditions than Kent's. She only illuminates a common human experience of disillusionment and the common necessity of finding a new way of understanding self and world, locating the two sometimes in the minds and lives of poor blacks and sometimes in the lives of women. The white mother has not in fact transcended her own racism. She has only recognized her place in a patriarchal narrative not of her own making and the need to claim some personal integrity in response. And Brooks has brought the reader to this realization by becoming "one" with the white mother. That identification is a genuine antiracist ideal, even if it is not political opposition or nationalist affirmation. And brilliantly, the poem leaves open the extent to which the white mother will claim the integrity that Brooks as poet clearly has.

By recognizing this existential implication of Brooks's formalism, we can recognize the realistic representation of African American self-definition in the naturalistic context of Brooks's Bronzeville and the politically sound and artistically brilliant representation of the process of ethnic self-definition as the foundation of interracial unity. Formalist artistry in Brooks's poems becomes the emblem of the most fundamental component of human life for Brooks—the existential imagination. The work she produced in this early part of her career did reveal how her tastes and values were "conditioned" by her time, including her acceptance of the mainstream principles of social integration that implied the erasure of ethnic culture. But the poetry does something different, creating a dynamic hybrid conception of the process of ethnic self-definition that she made central to the African American poetic tradition following the Harlem Renaissance construction of the New Negro poetic self. For Brooks, this created a domestic or nontraditional heroism that validated the life of an ordinary woman named Annie and that validated Brooks's own art as the centerpiece of this pursuit both of commonality and of ethnic distinction. Brooks writes poetic formalism in her own terms, and while the legacy of black nationalism has rightly led us to be skeptical of the capacity of the African American poet to reclaim that tradition, such skepticism need not lead to the unfortunate dismissal of the complex political significance of Brooks's mastery. Not a "jet-speed" trip to the universal, her work is a representation of the difficult realization of the universal in the oppressed individual as the universality of that pursuit of personal integrity gets constructed and expressed in ethnic culture.

Thus, the heart of Brooks's political achievement is visible in her early work, usually valued only for its literary virtuosity. Within the representation of the characters in that early formalism, Brooks provides a substantive vision of the personal integrity of individual African Americans in the face of overwhelming deprivation. And since Brooks's own virtuosity is her emblem for this integrity, it is more than innovation for its own sake. The effect is an affirmation of all African Americans' capacity to redefine cultural values in their minds. And when those individuals unite their existential imagination into a communal revision, then social institutions must also change. It is not only in the lives of men that resistance happens, nor is it only in the revision of social conditions. Changing a mind can change a world, and this ideal is what makes Brooks and her character Annie Allen into weaponed women. Given the longstanding influence of Brooks's verse, her feminine existential heroism was a mode of heroism indeed.

5 "Our Souls' Strict Meaning"
Robert Hayden's Spiritual History

These are the vital flesh and blood
Of any strength we have; these are the soil
From which our souls' strict meaning came.

—Robert Hayden, "'We Have Not Forgotten'"

ike that of most African American formalist poets before the Black Arts Movement of the late 1960s, Robert Hayden's poetic career is defined by a beautiful paradox: his well-known resistance to political obligation in poetry, his resolute integrationism, and his even more resolute aestheticism all functioned in his poetry as a model of communal ethnic self-definition and antiracist social activism. Despite his often eloquent and persuasive demurs, and contrary to the numerous critics who have accepted or rejected those comments rather than read the poetry carefully, Hayden is a "political" poet in the broadest sense of the term. His most famous and most important poems, most of which involve African American characters and/or African American history, define the relationship between the individual self and the course of history as mutually informing processes of positive and affirming change motivated by transcendent spiritual values. Those famous poems thereby implicitly made African American ethnic self-definition into a prime mover in history in part by being a microcosm of that history and in part by being the defining symbol that Hayden used to motivate readers to practices of social justice. For Hayden, the politics of poetry derived from a symbolic spiritual epistemology rather than didactic protest, a transcendent experience of enduring ideals rather than calls for social activism. In a sense, transcendence became activism for Hayden. This paradoxical politics was produced by Hayden's use of symbolism to verify in the historical reality of marginalized people the ideals of Baha'i spirituality, to which he converted in 1946, including the ideal of a divinely ordained progress of history. Throughout his career, Hayden implicitly claimed that spiritual growth was the framing logic of even the tragedies of African American history, making spirituality also therefore the source and frame of positive individual self-definition for ordinary African Americans and African American freedom fighters. And history garnered its sociopolitical meaning from the spiritual transcendence of individuals who move it and in the poetry of poets who recognize that spiritual meaning. Like transcendence, symbolic poetry becomes activism. Compared to religious prophets and freedom fighters, Hayden's poetic self-concept became the defining model of ethnic difference and historical change.

So even though Hayden is fairly well known for his claim to be "a poet who happens to be Negro" rather than a "Negro poet," and consistently expressed his preference for "common humanity" over the "phase of ethnicity" he understood Black Nationalist poetics to be, his verse asserted a socially substantive and culturally distinctive African American poetic genius as a symbol and manifestation of enduring and lived antiracist values. In this way, rather than opposing ethnicity and common humanity, as most scholars and Hayden himself seemed to think his poetry did, Hayden's verse actually made them inextricable in the evolution of individual spiritual and social self-awareness. Thus I derive the title of this chapter from "'We Have Not Forgotten,'" an otherwise unknown poem from Hayden's first volume, the politically explicit *Heart-Shape in the Dust* (1940), a poem that anticipates the symbolism of spiritual self-knowledge by which Hayden's best poetry remakes the conception of an "African American poet" into a defining manifestation of human commonality. In the poem, Hayden's speaker defines his soul's meaning as

> the prayers you prayed,
> Black fathers, O black mothers, kneeling in
> The cabin-gloom, debased

and as the "springtime pageantries of faith"—the self-affirming effects of devotion—that came out of those prayers.[1] In this vision, prayer becomes a mode of self-defining, politically meaningful expression for the speaker's ancestors that now motivates this speaker to a comparable act of self-definition in poetry. The poem is thus very much like a prayer. Most of Hayden's poems similarly assert that this "vital flesh and blood" of our "souls' strict meaning," as this speaker put it, transforms individual identity into a symbolic and actual point of identification through which "we"—African Americans past and present and readers of poetry at all points in history—can unite in spirituality, cultural heritage, and social activism. This spiritually transcendent self becomes "the roots of all our dreams of freedom's wide / And legendary spring" (lines 10–11). This unity of past and present, spirituality and history, becomes part of a trajectory of the increasing spiritual self-knowledge in the poetic self that brings about modes of expression that unify the self to its history and community and that conceptually parallels and envisions genuine social unity. Thus, Hayden's anti-ideological spiritual self was a historically situated ethnic self created from memory and heritage whose mind enacted the dialectal process by which religious belief transformed aesthetic beauty and the poet's ethnic self into the primary social manifestation of spiritual ideals. In this way, poetry and political resistance came from the same source—the historical process of spirituality that guided the spiritual process of history. By extension, the humane values of common humanity and the specifics of ethnicity, including oppression and resistance, gave antiracist meaning to one another.

This defining paradox of Hayden's career has been misunderstood in the terms of social integration versus nationalism, or the so-called universal versus the ethnic, that have dominated studies of Hayden since he first came to international prominence in 1966, when he won an award for his 1962 volume *A Ballad of Remembrance.* Since Hayden came to prominence at the same time as black militancy in art, his resistance to that ideological vision of poetry— whatever its genuine merits—was distorted by that lens to be a rejection of ethnic selfhood and social justice. But this practice of constructing artistic selfhood from a combination of spiritual idealism and political pragmatism, inimical racial ideology and ethnic cultural heritage, reconciles what even Hayden opposed. Whether he is called a "black poet" or not, in other words, the speaker in "'We Have Not Forgotten'" derives his claim to voice from a connection to his ethnic past. He thereby fashions his poetic expression as the extension of that communal past while offering his (admittedly clichéd) mastery of romantic pantheism—freedom as a kind of God dwelling in a spring— as validation of his individual prayer and his distinctive poetic vision. This combination implies that verse was the concrete historical manifestation of a historically genuine but conceptually abstracted ideal personhood, an ideal that was validated as an alternative to the racial categorization it evoked and that was exemplified by the spiritually and artistically self-aware poet. And, in Hayden's case, it also implied—somewhat against Hayden's will—how ethnic cultural heritage and the lived values of that past were for the African American poet the necessary historical embodiment of the "universal" human self. Hayden's ideal of the poet depended upon this spiritual identity as common humanity and is "political" in the broadest and often the most meaningful sense of the term, then, because it acknowledges through artistry the fact that the individual subject or "self" is a construction situated in specific social and historical circumstances whose constitution enacts conflicts in social ideologies that could motivate awareness of alternative and, in Hayden's case, transcendent ideals. And even if one believes in the self as a transcendent spiritual entity, as Hayden did, that entity could only be understood as it was expressed in culture, especially in poetry. This truism is the defining anxiety and beauty of Hayden's symbolism.

Hayden's contribution to American letters throughout his career consists of a vision of poetic meaning predicated on a process of self-knowledge that rejected the static categories of race politics and other social ideologies through the tension between those ideals and the attempt to conceptualize a self transcendent of those ideologies. Readers of Hayden's verse need to move outside of the binary terms of the literary debates sparked by his resistance to the Black Nationalist militancy of the late 1960s in order to see how substantively he fulfilled the principles of self-worth and communal cultural affirmation central to those ideals through this symbolism of process. Hayden's vision is more persuasive than the idea in African American cultural study, derived from the nationalists who criticized him, that the pursuit of individuality central to spiritual self-knowledge in Hayden's verse is an expression of the worst implications of bourgeois individualism, an association that led Stephen Henderson to assert of Hayden that "sometimes a[n African American] poet in his effort at [individual] self-revelation moves outside of the immediate concerns of the Black Community" (26). In Hayden's verse, individual self-revelation was actually predicated on African American history and thus could not move outside of the immediate concerns of the Black Community, especially since the individuation that Hayden represents was construed in his verse as a manifestation of the values that make freedom fighting and communal affirmation possible. This necessary historicism in his poetry is also therefore more complex than the disrespect of African American ethnic cultural difference implicit in the claim made by such otherwise perceptive critics as Louis Turco, who, in his argument against critics such as Henderson, declared that Hayden's verse transcended the "merely ethnic" (180). But the ethnic was not for Hayden, as it was for both Henderson and Turco, hermetic and absolute difference and thus does not conform to Turco's limited critique of the excesses of Black Nationalism. Instead, ethnicity in Hayden's verse was the historical manifestation of the ideals that Hayden believed transcended ethnicity. Through ethnicity, Hayden's verse enacts a symbolist epistemology in which the constitution of the poetic self exemplifies politically liberating and socially unifying principles. The poetic mind became an ideal spiritual and human mind.

I call the social meaning of Hayden's spiritual vision his "spiritual history," therefore, because this ideal of imaginative genius offered a parallel between the personal and the historical that not only identified the ideal spiritual meaning of personal and communal history, it also suggested that art could speak that spiritual meaning into existence. This component of Hayden's verse is perhaps the most neglected and also the most "political." An extension of W. H. Auden's assertion that the poet must lead the reader to solve for x as in algebra, an assertion Hayden claimed to have embraced in a poetry workshop with that famous poet, Hayden's verse encounters and resolves his struggle to resist losing fact at the expense of the ideal or submerging the ideal to the travesties of history (Williams, "Covenant of Timelessness with Time," 731–49). Hayden's verse sought to convey to the reader (and prove to the poet himself) the idea that the African American spiritual self was the ultimate fact and the ultimate symbol, an ideal closer to Walt Whitman's belief in physical sensuality as spiritual connection and democratic ideal than to the call to didacticism characteristic of the nationalism that still haunts studies of Hayden's verse. As in Whitman's "Song of Myself," Hayden's verse, especially in *Angle of Ascent* (1975), presents the journey of the poet as a model both of the reader's journey and of the journey of history, each journey reflecting the other and all three divinely motivated toward justice and unity.

John Hatcher suggests this possibility of a spiritual narrative in *Angle of Ascent*, likening his work to the Baha'i faith's central doctrine of "progressive revelation," the principle that there is only one divine being that all of the world's major religions were worshipping with greater and greater articulations of spiritual truth (*From the Auroral Darkness,* 1984). But just as Sterling Brown complicated Walt Whitman's "open road," as Mark Sanders argued and as I discussed in the third chapter, Hayden complicated this ideal by suggesting that this historical progress depended less on a dubious identification with all people predicated on white privilege and more fully on the historical individual's location of himself or herself simultaneously in spirituality and in history (38). This vision also therefore revealed that the complex internal lives of African American people, exemplified by the poet and other artist figures in both Brown's and Hayden's work, was the poetry's most substantive challenge to racism.

In these terms, Hayden is best understood as practicing a symbolist poetic version of the ethnic poetic self-fashioning I defined in chapter 1. Its activism was its validation of individual self-definition, especially for socially marginalized people, as a prime resistance to injustice, an abstracted construction of the imagination formalized and made concrete in history as much by its embodiment in poetic form as by the evidence of its existence in spiritually motivated acts of resistance recorded in traditional histories. Hayden's poetics of political transcendence should thus be seen not as misguided rejection of the didactic religious and political tradition in African American poetry (what Fahamisha Patricia Brown called "the poetry of preachment") but as an extension of them through the symbolist poetics described so well by fellow symbolist Hart Crane (Brown 45–63). In Crane's words, "It may not be possible to say that there is, strictly speaking, any 'absolute' experience. But it seems evident that certain aesthetic experience . . . can be called absolute, inasmuch as it approximates a formally convincing statement of a conception or apprehension of life that gains our unquestioning assent, and under the conditions of which our imagination is unable to suggest a further detail consistent with the design of the aesthetic whole" (Gelpi 397). Like Crane's "formally convincing statement," Hayden's symbolic history of the individual soul in a given poem enacts the unity that it is supposed to reflect, seeking to construct in aesthetic form what too many scholars of African American culture take for granted as an absolute and absolutely extant ethnic self. But despite its resistance to assuming the existence of ready-made blackness, Hayden's aesthetic absolute still seeks to validate the African American social self by construing the poetic imagination itself as the defining enactment of the social and spiritual principles of selfhood, spirituality, freedom, and equality it seeks to instantiate in poetic form and that derives from the African American expressive tradition.

Extending that tradition starting with slave poet Phillis Wheatley, Hayden imagines a pre-political self whose existence ideally unified people despite socially constructed and enforced differences. But, unlike for Wheatley, this self for Hayden may have only existed in art, even as its existence in art in the formally convincing statement implied and even validated its existence in the (spiritual) world. In other words, poetry made rather than reflected this ideal ethnic self. Like the speaker in "'We Have Not Forgotten,'" Hayden's most important characters throughout his career validated in their very represented existence the possibility that individual self-knowledge constituted historical knowledge and that literary beauty constituted ideal social perception. What the poetry reflects, then, is as much the existential meaning-making processes of the poetic mind and of the production of poetic beauty as the social reality of black people. While this symbolist practice was a removal from politics for its originators, such as Baudelaire, it functioned in Hayden's attention to history as the capacity to "derange" the mind, as Baudelaire put it, for the sake of changing rather than withdrawing from politics. It is a symbolism dedicated to the cause of social self-definition and the recognition of spiritual absolute potentially enacted by the aesthetic absolute, a process capable of motivating social activism in the reader.

Thus, despite the suspicion with which many African American critics have treated it, this paradoxically symbolic historicizing of the individual operates as an extension of the African American expressive tradition predicated on validating African American emotional life. Hayden's spiritual symbolism functions in its communal address in much the same way as the blues, as defined by scholars such as Houston Baker. According to Baker's persuasive conception in *Blues, Ideology and Afro-American Literature*, "The material conditions of slavery in the United States and the rhythms of Afro-American blues combined and emerged . . . as an ancestral matrix that has produced a forceful and indigenous creativity" that is the blues (2). Given this matrix of material conditions and the expressive imagination, the blues (and the blues-oriented critic) garners the capacity to resolve "antinomies" of racism "in the office of adequate cultural understanding" (6). Baker concludes, "The [blues] singers [or poets] are always at this intersection, this crossing, codifying force, providing resonance for experience's multiplicities. . . . Hence they may be conceived as translators" (7). In characterizing this "matrix" of history, heritage and consciousness, Baker is not thinking in terms of symbolism, but these terms aptly characterize the symbolic function of poet and character in Hayden's symbolist "absolute." While Hayden is not a blues poet, then, his conception of spiritual history similarly encodes both material conditions and indigenous creativity in poetic form and in the poet's represented consciousness. Hayden's poetic self-fashioning is thus arguably a spiritually affirming and optimistic extension of or parallel to the blues tradition, a liberating spiritual vision not unlike that which Martin Luther King Jr. made so famous in his "I Have a Dream" speech, in which living up to American ideals made the "content" of one's character the ultimate meaning of the color of one's skin. In these terms, Hayden's poet is a translator whose mind, as recorded in the poem through the minds of characters, serves as the crossroads of meaning that Baker describes, a complex, ideally absolute formal statement that, in its complexity and self-contained wholeness, ideally resolves the antinomies of racism into the unified whole of the spiritual self and its matrixlike manifestation of social values. And it does so without the sometimes somber existentialism of the blues because, for Hayden, this aesthetic absolute was transforming.

Thus, like his contemporary Gwendolyn Brooks, whose work I discussed in the last chapter, Hayden's formalism was what I call a bardic modernism rather than political assimilationism, an African American poet's resolution of the loss of the so-called old certainties by representing how they were never lost in the first place. Instead, they were affirmed by the self-constitution of the African American community as exemplified by historical and artist figures. Instead of the traditional modernist formal fragmentation, then, Hayden's "absolute" was an ideal aesthetic unity meant in its unity to destabilize conceptions of absolute racial difference and authentic ethnicity. It did so by defining and even "enacting" the lived experience of black people as that experience revealed the existential creation of affirming social meaning. But contrary to Brooks's social emphasis, by which I defined bardic modernism, Hayden's version was explicitly epistemological. Rather than representing individual characters transforming themselves in the narrow social space of isolated poverty, Hayden's verse represents the possibility of a new way of perceiving the whole of phenomenal and spiritual realities derived from the distinctive African American perspective on history, a way of perceiving that would lead people to enact spiritual values. As Hayden put it, "I do know that I'm always trying to get at the truth, the reality behind appearances, and from this has come one of my favorite themes. I want to know what things are, how they work, what a given process is and so on" (quoted in Gendron 16). Hayden's spiritual history is thus about the process of making spiritual meaning out of historical fact, both by reading it through poetry and by living the values read there. With the hint given in the symbol of the "angle of ascent," it becomes clear that Hayden's entire career can be read persuasively as an evolution towards this vision of historical, social and spiritual wholeness derived from the meaning-making function of innovative, self-referential, and fully achieved symbolic verse. Exemplified in *Angle of Ascent* by Hayden's own spiritual history, this vision is his remarkable answer to the binary logic of racial understanding and to the possibility that poetry could be a persuasive means to liberation so central to this tradition.

Thus, though Hayden was not nearly the symbolist or aesthete at the beginning of his career that he was at the end, his entire body of work is predicated on illuminating the power of the individual mind and of African American poetic genius to motivate social change by understanding new, socially just, ultimately transcendent meanings of social identities. As a result, though Hayden sought to destroy all copies of his first volume, *Heart-Shape in the Dust,* the volume reveals how the political didacticism and naïve romanticism that Hayden wanted to forget are crucial for understanding his full achievement by which he preferred to be remembered. Raised in poverty in and around Detroit, Michigan, before, during, and just after the Great Depression, Hayden was a prime candidate, as were many African American intellectuals of the time, for socialist ideals. Once he became a published writer, Hayden involved himself with leftist organizations—especially the writer's groups—producing plays and poems that called for socialist action in response to the alleged failure of capitalism. But even at their most radical, his political ideals were often characterized in his verse as an aspect of the poet's self and were related quite directly to Hayden's conceptions of the poetic beauty that made spiritual history possible and valid. Following Harlem Renaissance poets such as Claude McKay and Countee Cullen, for example, the latter of whom Hayden read "with baited breath," Hayden places the individual poetic self at the heart of proletarian protest in verse, setting the stage for the later positing of his own career as an ideal of ethnic self-definition through spiritual transformation. In this first volume, then, following his Harlem Renaissance models, Hayden adapted to African American life and to his socialist ideals the romantic conception of poetic genius as the defiant imagination struggling "against all limitation." Combining this "New Negro" ideal of political liberation through individual romantic genius—as I characterized it in chapter 3—with the calls to action of the WPA proletarian writers, Hayden began to associate the poet's political ideals with the ideals of poetic beauty and meaning (Hatcher 95, 3, 64–66). His political ideals did change in meaningful ways, but this ideal balance remained his primary aesthetic and political priority in poetry.

In "To A Young Negro Poet," for example, Hayden asserts the centrality of beauty to the poet's role as the keeper of memory and the motivator of political activism. That beauty should inspire equally beautiful and liberating social action.

Make me a song, O dark singer,
With the sunlight and the moonlight in it,
The wind's sound and the rain's sound
And the sound of slow midnight bells
In wind and rain and leaves.

(lines 1–5)

This first stanza of the poem, about romantic beauty conventionally understood, is the poem's thesis. Though it lacks the turn inward to the consciousness of the speaker of Hayden's later symbolist introspection, it does characterize the mind of the dark singer, who must take as his or her model the
beauty of nature. This romanticism echoes many other poems in his volume,
including his homage to Keats's "La Belle Dame San Merci," "'He Is Fore-
doomed,'" which reads in part,

And the longing for that angel turned to ghost,
    By cold caresses bruised to the bone,
He shall lay siege to heaven and be lost
    To earth.

(lines 9–12)

In the almost stereotypical understanding of romanticism, nature in its harmony is a model for the harmony of human consciousness, potentially even
being the locus of an indwelling divinity that is the substance of beauty. Sunlight and moonlight suggest nurturing warmth and a light in the darkness
while the sounds of the wind suggest a song in nature as beautiful as the
human-made noise of the bells. The longing for an angel becomes the traditional romantic concern with the inability of the poet or of poetic language to
convey this ideal.

When attributed to the young Negro artist, these clichéd romantic principles become the foundation of the effects by which verse conveys it political
ideals. The second stanza of "To a Young Negro Artist" enriches this portrait
of the African American romantic poetic genius by offering the antithesis
about the romantic nature of race pride and political unity to the thesis of
romantic beauty.

Make me a song, O dark singer,
Brimming with the laughter of honest men

And the beauty and laughter of valiant women;
A song with the heart-beat
Of inarticulate millions in it.

(lines 6–10)

As in "'We Have Not Forgotten,'" the poet should speak for the "inarticulate millions" of his race by declaring their heartbeat to be his own, conveying to the reader the beauty of people and of their shared culture and bloodlines through the beauty of poetic achievement. This conception of the political role of the poet was made more explicitly about social activism in poems such as "Speech":

Hear me, white brothers,
Black brothers hear me:

I have seen the hand
Holding the blowtorch
To the dark, anguish-twisted body;
I have seen the hand
Giving the high-sign
To fire on the white pickets;
And it was the same hand,
Brothers listen to me,
It was the same hand.

(lines 1–11)

Taking as his text the socialist's argument against nationalisms of all kinds, Hayden's poet has a prophetic vision that identifies the same, presumably capitalist, "hand" lynching and burning African Americans on one hand and breaking the strikes of white workers on the other. In both poems, the honesty and valiance of the people implies their place in a socialist revolution, and the poet's task is to articulate their hearts and, therefore, their political interests. In this case, their hearts may lead them to fall into racial animosity rather than see the social and political clout of a truer interracial unity. The poet will guide the reader well.

In "For a Young Artist," romanticism and the political are then united in the poem's attempted synthesis in its third stanza.

Make me a song, O dark singer,
With hope and the new tomorrow in it,

Bright as the moon, the sun,
Brighter than wind-swept harps of rain
Glittering in a summer morning's sun.

(lines 11–15)

In this stanza, the "hope and the new tomorrow" of the last stanza links the "midnight bells" of the first stanza to the laughter of the people. The morning sun signals the possible new day available both in the people and in the poet's celebration of them, the combination of which may lead to the unity called for in "Speech." As Hayden put it in "Dedication," for example, the poet must "gather unto your heart / the living poems of [the people's] faces," must "Clasp their hands, O poet, touch their hands / and know the ultimate *meaning* of your own [emphasis added]" (lines 1–2, 7–8). Similarly, "Essay on Beauty" declares,

There is no more blood-burning loveliness to me
Than slaves at Valley Forge fighting for liberty,
Than Toussaint's freedom-dream, the Douglass memory.

(lines 4–6)

"Dedication" concludes by associating Hayden's leftist politics with a mandate to beauty: "Let their long sorrows leap like furies in your song. / Their spilled blood become the song's Mystic Rose" (lines 13–14). In the abstractions of the apprentice romantic poet, then, Hayden validates the hope of social justice as the primary antecedent for the nature imagery of the poem. Social unity and justice constitute the ultimate beauty for the "young Negro poet," since the beauty of the people and the beauty of nature are the same.

What makes *Heart-Shape in the Dust* worth our attention despite its flaws in technique and conception, then, is the way in which its very flawed political and poetic conventionality rewrites the meaning of race, especially its binary logic, through an emerging definition of symbolic poetic beauty. "Sunflowers: Beaubien Street" is probably the most accomplished poem in the volume, because it offers a version of the dialectical symbolism of spiritual process that is Hayden's defining achievement.

The Negroes here, dark votaries of the sun,
Have planted sunflowers round door and wall,
Hot-smelling, vivid as an August noon.

Thickets of yellow fire, they hold in thrall
The cruel, sweet remembrance of Down Home.

(lines 1–5)

As in "To A Young Negro Poet" and "Dedication," the personal past of the speaker, in this case derived specifically from Hayden's own childhood, is tied directly to the collective historical pasts of other African Americans. Sunflowers in a Detroit neighborhood embody the memories of a southern past of slave and sharecropping labor, almost like a collective racial unconscious into which the speaker includes his memory of his neighborhood. These sunflowers link the speaker, who did not experience the South, to memories of his parents and his ancestors, creating an emblem of cultural heritage and imaginative self-assertion upon which the poet models his voice.

Thus, this beauty embodies both the ideal and the real, the spiritual (in its broadest, nonreligious sense) and the historical, in a possible balance that speaks to and perhaps even creates an affirming ethnic identity. In other words, the beauty of the sunflowers represents both the degraded condition of these ghetto dwellers and their emotional survival as an emblem of this condition throughout the entire history of blacks in the United States. Though not roses or other such classical images of beauty, these sunflowers declare the desire for beauty among blacks, becoming in effect the symbolic substance of black humanity. This worship, if you will, of the psychic or cultural wholeness symbolized by the sunflowers makes beauty the characters' best and most consistent defense against the horrors of "Down Home." It helps them endure the deprivations of a poor Detroit neighborhood.

O sunwhirled, tropic tambourines
That play sad juba songs in dooryard loam,
Recalling chain-gang heat and shimmering pines;
O sunward cry of dark ones mute within
The crumbling shacks: bright image of their will
To reach through prayer, through long belief the sun
Fixed in the heavens like Ezekiel's Wheel.

Here phonographs of poverty repeat
An endless blues-chorale of torsioning despair—
And yet these dark ones find mere living sweet
And set this solid brightness on bitter air.

(lines 6–16)

Compared to Ezekiel's wheel, the sun becomes both the religious embodiment of the ideal of heavenly glory and an analogue to "their will" to freedom. The steadfastness of prayer matches the fixed place of Ezekiel's wheel, and though the pain of the memories is as "torsioning" as the despair of the blues, those memories, those symbols of a lost past, help allow these people to find "mere living sweet" because those memories are religious in nature. And the poem functions like the sunflowers, recalling the beauty of memory and of pain and revitalizing it for the audience in the same way the sunflowers did for this community. The poet's role is as much the affirmation of a common human desire and capacity for creating beauty as it is the cultural affirmation and political motivation of black people, since each is a central aspect of the other. And the association of his art with the spiritual value of the sunflowers enacts the dialectic between art and politics that is so central to Hayden's career.

None of these poems appears in *Angle of Ascent,* but they clearly anticipate the central role of beauty as a model of the historical transforming power of the individual spiritual self and are clear forerunners to the verse of what scholar Robert Chrisman aptly called Hayden's "transitional period" (132–33), the work between *Heart-Shape in the Dust* and Hayden's award-winning 1962 volume, *A Ballad of Remembrance,* the volume that initiated his greatest fame. By 1948, when Hayden published his next slim volume, he had converted to the Baha'i faith, had moved to the South to teach at Fisk University, was enraged by segregation, and was overwhelmed with teaching responsibilities that limited his productivity. Nonetheless, the next three volumes—*The Lion and the Archer* (1948), *Figure of Time* (1955), and *A Ballad of Remembrance* (1962)—reveal his broadening sense of how the poetic self and poetic meaning were potentially absolute embodiments of the spiritual ideals that constituted the meaning of history and social justice. Moreover, Hayden had moved from proletarian artist circles into the University of Michigan graduate program where, in part in study with W. H. Auden and in part through his Spanish major, Hayden was exposed to surrealist poetry and painting. Those influences are central to what Hayden called his "baroque" period, in which he pursued the complexity of metaphor and the interaction between the presumed objectivity of poetic form and the subjectivity of both the reader and the poetic speaker that made such poetic form a necessary expressive channel for the baffling and potentially alienating dynamics of the mind. It also reveals the tempering of Hayden's socialism but the extension and complication of his commitment to unity through beauty. His best work in these volumes, some of which were included in *Angle of Ascent,* suggest how this emerging aes-

realities which are being united [in an image], the stronger will be the image and the more emotional power and poetic truth it will have" (Chrisman 139–40). In his work of this era, Hayden began to yoke mind and world, history and ideal through "distant" and yet "true" metaphoric or symbolic connections. And as the poems of these "transitional" volumes show, this new dialectical approach juxtaposes these two cultural traditions—African American populism and surrealist art—as part of an ideal unity that is central to the hybrid ethnic self at the heart of Hayden's verse and that places him squarely in this bardic tradition.

As a result, Hayden's six poems in *The Lion and the Archer* are primarily an *ars poetica* for this new, subtler, and slightly less radical vision of the social unity available in the world and the motivation to pursue that unity available in poetic beauty. For example, in "The Lion," the last poem in the volume, Hayden tempers the idealist vision of poetic power that substantiates his former proletarian political vision. "The Lion" concludes:

> I see when I enter the cage
> a beast of Revelation,
>   a captive prophet-king
> in byzantine disguise;
>   my soul in exultation
> Holy Holy cries, as he leaps through turning fire:
>
>   As he leaps through circles of fire,
> gold shadow of my will,
>   dire beauty that creates
> and tethers my desire,
>   my soul, the archer said,
> exults and Holy cries. And Holy cries, the archer said.[2]

Unlike the objective bard spokesman in *Heart-Shape in the Dust,* a speaker who believes in a direct relationship between his will, his words, and the world, Hayden's speaker here engages with the imagination as a mode of individual, self-authorized self-examination aware of its dubious connection to the material world. Inviting the reader into the poet's mind rather than directing the reader's attention to systematic injustice, Hayden explores whether or not the imaginative faculty that is the lion can be tamed by the will. He wonders whether or not that imagination is a threat to sanity that the speaker wishes to kill to prevent the self-indulgent, potentially apolitical, performance for which he ultimately opts. He offers a symbolist belief that any aesthetic performance deriving from those internal dynamics of the mind may only be the expression of that one mind, not necessarily a prophecy of social justice applicable to all. This concern with the potential limitations of individual vision complicates the simplistic epistemological thinking of the romantic protest of his preceding volume. Though didactic protest is stirring and clear, it often reduces the complexity both of social reality and of art. After all, the lion is but a "gold shadow" of the will and may therefore be unable to fulfill the dictates of the will, this character's self-satisfaction notwithstanding. The potential futility of art here is quite a distinction from Hayden's former unquestioned belief in the poet's voice as commensurate with the will of his people and the (clichéd) poetic image as entirely commensurate with the emotional or political reality it purports to represent. This greater savvy about the process of signification and the dynamics of the imagination also suggests the withdrawal from politics for which his readers criticize him. And the self-consciousness is indeed a withdrawal from the vision of the bardic poet as exhorter. Nonetheless, even in tempering Hayden's sense of the capacity of poetic genius to align itself with social activism, the poem implies that the process of meaning making in the dance of the intellect itself is potentially holy, especially when offered not in self-indulgence, but in resistance to realities that should not be ignored.

Two other poems in the volume—"Magnolias in Snow" and "Eine Kleine Nachtmusik"—clarify how these dynamic workings of the mind can and do respond to social realities through the humane values captured by this record of the poet-speaker's mind. "Magnolias in Snow" shows how snow on southern trees can become an emblem of the human process of making meaning as it is sometimes warped and can sometimes be transformed. The snow on the magnolias "alters and elaborates perspectives" and

> confuses South with North and would deceive
> me into what egregious error
> but for these trees that keep their summer-green
> and like a certain hue of speech mean South.
> (lines 1–5)

After all, Hayden writes, "Magnolias stand for South, as every copy- / reader knows, and snow means North to me" (lines 6–7). This stanza asserts that clichéd artistry is as arbitrary and confining in its meaning as the arbitrary social stratifications of racism and segregation. The poem suggests that the un-usual, even misplaced, snow could lead to transgression of social custom. A kind of "natural" deconstruction, this alternative "meaning" to what every copyreader, poet, and southerner knows, could ideally motivate the revolu-tionary action of revising accepted conceptions of meaning simply by being beautiful. In resisting the social transgression the snow suggests, the speaker also recognizes that his acceptance of what magnolias mean in the normaliz-ing discourses of "copyreaders" is tantamount to his accepting the racist so-cial order. Thus, implicitly, the ranting of the didactic political poet, in his or her inattention to the subtle paradoxes of beauty, can no more change the so-cial realm than ignoring or even accepting the arbitrariness of the difference between North and South. Overly rigid notions of meaning, in other words—whether from the activist or the racist—are the underlying basis of the social status quo, notions that beauty itself, if noticed carefully, can challenge and counteract. (Even the poem's accentual structure—ten syllables of irregular metrical pattern—resist the rigid formalism of Hayden's rhetorical verse.) After all, what is the true meaning of these regions of the country if the sym-bols for the two—snow and magnolias respectively—can meet in reality where they usually do not in art or mind? The beautiful contradiction be-tween snow as North and magnolias as South raises awareness of the process of meaning making and hints at how one can (perhaps) participate actively.

There are dangerous consequences to these epistemological musings that the speaker eschews here for his own safety, but which the activist imagination nonetheless takes up. Could art lead to the breakdown of the opposition be-tween North and South, change and stasis, active and passive thought, segre-gation and integration? Beauty is both consolation and possibility, just as Crane implied.

> But still, snow-shine upon magnolia leaves
> that wither into shapes of abstract sculpture
> when brought inside for garnishment,
> does compensate for things I must forgo
> if I would safely walk beneath these trees.
>
> (lines 11–15)

First of all, art allows the speaker to endure the horrible contradictions of the segregated South, to which Hayden had been exposed for only five years, since his move in 1943 to teach at Fisk University, where he would teach for much of the rest of his life. The beauty of things distinctly southern, as they shift in form, allows the speaker to have compensation for the social horrors those same beauties falsely and paradoxically represent. Secondly, though, the sustaining beauty of the transformed magnolia leaf reveals, like the snow in the South, the complex and multifaceted nature of beauty itself, something that can serve as a model for social interaction: "O south, how beautiful is change." Material reality is not only indifferent to human meaning—especially social organization—but sometimes defiant of it. Also, the changes in the beauty of the leaf remind the speaker and, potentially, the South, that change is an aspect of beauty. In other words, Hayden's symbolism emphasizes the symbol as a process, a shift in the meaning of accepted associations that should motivate revisions in social organization. Change is more beautiful than the complacencies by which certain clichés and social practices are maintained and is therefore a "revolutionary" implication of traditional literary value.

"Eine Kleine Nachtmusik" makes almost the same point, except that it moves from focusing on the personal, individual mind of an African American southern speaker to showing how the artist as symbolic figure is the most enduring symbol of humane values and ideals in all of human history. The poem also represents one of Hayden's earliest attempts to create a multicultural art commensurate with a hybrid African American poetic self that always resides beneath or behind whatever poetic speaker or character is in the foreground in Hayden's poems. The poem discusses the horrors of war in Europe and juxtaposes that to the hope and the futility of the artist-figure Anton, who "hunches in a cold-starred room and reads and hears / the clawfoot sarabande, the knucklebone passacaglia coming close," and who "aching reads re-reads the dimming lines, / Warms his fingers at the candleshine and turns the page" (lines 9–10, 15–16). In the second stanza of the poem, Anton is the alternative to what, in the first stanza, are the consequences of war:

The siren cries that ran like mad and naked screaming women
with hair ablaze all over Europe, that like ventriloquists
made steel and stone speak out in the wild idiom of the damned—
oh now they have ceased but have created a groaning aftersilence.

(lines 1–4)

In that silence, "only the dead are relaxed and warm" (line 8). The silent aftermath of war leaves space for potential nihilism or for the same corrupt values that led to the war in the first place. Cultural traditions and moral values are as destroyed as the buildings of Europe. Steel and stone "spoke" only the reverberations of bombs and violence, because they had no language of their own as sculpture would have. By contrast, the subtle sound of turning the page implies a possible expression that the silent Anton offers, though the power is clearly dubious compared to the loud cacophony and even louder silence of war and its aftermath.

The implied intellectual acts of the artist figure represent the validation of the integrity of the artist and of art and imply that such integrity potentially preserves and conveys the truer and more enduring values that survive war and that might even be able to prevent it. It is, in other words, a model for all human integrity and is an alternative to the social and epistemological violence of war. As the march of the war encloses Anton, it sounds like music to the frozen, ignored poet warmed only by the light of his reading. The artist's or student's irrelevance is a clear implication here but the title, "Eine Kleine Nachtmusik," sets up an ironic contrast between the Mozart serenade of the same name and the discord of war, especially since such an interaction between peace and violence, like the interaction between verbal and nonverbal arts, embodies the alternative meanings that can sustain and endure the contradictions of social life. The poem concludes with a dubious but firm affirmation of the commitment to beauty and implies, to my eye and ear, that eventual necessary and empowering act of Anton the artist:

Now as skin-and-bones Europe hurts all over from the swastika's
hexantanz: oh think of Anton, Anton brittle, Anton crystalline;
think what the winter moon, the leper beauty of a Gothic tale, must see:
the ice-azure likeness of a young man reading, carved most craftily.

(lines 21–24)

Europe has starved and is in pain due to the evils of Nazism. The winter moon, eventually ushering a new season, sees in Anton a version of its own "leper beauty," its own bare, misunderstood radiance, borrowed in part from another sun but still giving sufficient shine. This association is especially powerful since the moon functions in Baha'i symbology as a figure for the religious prophet who reflects the light of the sun as God. So too will Anton give sufficient if borrowed shine, at least as an image of an ideal if not the practice of that ideal himself. The fact that the image is craftily carved alludes to the self-critical, self-mocking skepticism of "The Lion," but like that poem, this poem declares that the art will endure, as will the impulse to art, which is the crucial point. Images may not be the ideal, and the artist as an image of an ideal indeed suggests a deconstructing distance between that possibility and the social reality. But that image still reflects what it cannot name. Thus, the discord of war, in the end, will not (hopefully) stifle the music of the student, the poet, the humanist, though clearly that humanist cannot afford to be as entirely oblivious to war as Anton is. And clearly the life of the European mind has much to teach the African American poet, so Hayden's recourse to that model is not a disparagement of his own heritage. It is an embrace of a remarkably broad one.

Thus, this baroque artistry can function as a very substantive engagement in African American history, adapting a European mode of artistic juxtaposition to the protest of social reality more persuasive than the didacticism of Hayden's first volume. In these terms, Hayden's aestheticism is constructed as the enactment of just values, as in the more substantive image of the "leper moon's" borrowed shine. For example, in "Figure" from *Figure of Time* (1955), Hayden suggests how, paradoxically, the "beauty" of a lynching reveals the complex compromise of social ideals that led to the lynching. And it reveals how those same values should render obsolete the dehumanization and the "othering" of black people that make this horrific act possible. It therefore protests what made the lynching possible and identifies the values that will prevent it in the future, broadening the meaning of this protest in much the same way "Eine Kleine Nachtmusik" does.

Figure

He would slump to his knees, now that his agonies
are accomplished, would fall but for the chain that binds
    him to the tall columnar tree.

His head hangs heavily away to one side, we
cannot see his face. The dead weight of
    the quelled head has pulled

the haltering chain tight. A clothesline nooses
both wrists, forcing his arms in an arrowing angle
    out behind him. Stripes

of blood like tribal markings run from the naked
shoulder to naked waist. We observe that his jeans are
    torn at the groin;

that the lower links of the chain cut deeply into
the small of his back and counter the sag, the downthrust.
    And we observe the chain—

the kind that a farmer might have had use for or a man with
a vicious dog. We have seen its like in hardware
    stores; it is cheap but strong

and it serves and except for the doubled length of its lashing
him to the blighted tree, he would slump to his knees, in
    total subsidence fall.

He is scythe in daylight's clutch. Is gnomon.
Is a metaphor of a place, a time. Is our
    Time geometrized.

If one key component of any definition of modernism is an expansion of the
notion of the beautiful either to broaden it or to question it or both, then
beautifying a lynching certainly qualifies as a version of Hayden's bardic modernism. Validating an implicit poetic self analogous to the cold distance of
Anton, this symbolic depiction offers no outrage or accusation common to
protest verse, including Hayden's own, but rather a quasi-objective deline-
ation of the "beautiful" details of the lynched man's attitude. This dispassionate approach allows for a more powerful redefinition of the *meaning* of lynching because we can see that everyday tools, embodiments of various cultural
values, can be used in acts of horror. Moreover, those same tools of violence
that killed the man also hold him up. Instead of asserting that lynching is
wrong, which most people already know, the poem analyzes the potential
human motivations, the snapshot of societal values the poem embodies, suggesting more fully the complex cultural ideals, history, and practices that lead
to the lynching and that can lead to alternatives. This approach more com-
prehensively implicates the reader in this horrific act and its aftermath. The
poetic bard here is still teaching about justice and the meaning of the inarticulate millions, but it is the recognition of the process of meaning and the manifestation of ideals in concrete reality that makes this a better poem, if not
always a more persuasive protest.
    The chain is particularly important for understanding the complicated tri-
umph of the poem. On the one hand, the chain is the centerpiece of the violence, recalling slavery's shackles and the "stripes of blood" as "tribal markings" that recall simultaneously an African past and the "savagery" associated

with that past that has been more fully enacted by the whites who did the lynching. It attributes that savagery more to whites than to blacks. But the chain is also an image of connection, union, as in chains of evidence and of command, making it an emblem also of the interconnected nature of survival, proof, and meaning. Lynching can thus be seen as the weakest link in the "chain" of values that holds the society together. The values and mechanics of the racial horrors of the time are as characteristic of American society as the violence, lack of concern, scapegoating, and passive acceptance that make lynching possible. As the poem reveals the values extant in society, it implicitly proposes alternative values, a better possible foundation for the existing human unity represented in the negative here, by which our society ideally could live in harmony. If we can but recognize the centrality of those values, and the inextricable connections among all people, perhaps such horrors can be revised. And as with Anton, it is the dispassionate but meaningful art, in its illustration *and* enactment or embodiment of those ideals, that makes perception of these values possible. Here, beauty and politics are more fully one than they had been in any of the earlier work in Hayden's career. Though not a socialist call to action, it is a way to identify the centrality of racism to our society and an assertion of the need for alternatives for justice to be achieved. And while I always cringe a little at the suggestion that racism hurts white perpetrators as much as black victims, I also celebrate how Hayden's bardic self becomes an embodiment of just such an angle of vision, a capacity to perceive the deepest truths of human unity that should lead to acts that would prevent the lynching. This approach may allow callous people to exonerate themselves more easily than the accusations of protest, but it also, when understood fully, offers a broader sense of accountability to all who read. And, to reiterate, it makes for better poetry, certainly in Hayden's poetic career if not in general principle.

These ideals make Hayden's most important volume, *Angle of Ascent*, a powerful answer to Hayden's own commitment to revealing human unity and to the misguided and simplistic critiques of scholars who overestimate his assimilationism, either by nationalist or by traditionalist standards. The volume makes even more resolute Hayden's ideal that an underlying human unity is the most fundamental component of justice and that living such ideals, including in the process of perception that motivates and is recorded in poetry, is the only way to make those values manifest. By placing all of these poems in reverse chronological order in *Angle of Ascent*, Hayden declares to the reader that the angle of ascent is as much a reach back to the meaning of the past as a projection into the future. And since the volume begins with new poems on personal family history and ends with Hayden's oldest poems in the volume, his most famous poems on African American history, the collection's narrative provides two cycles of symbolic meaning. First, it parallels Hayden's personal meaning with the meaning of African American history. Second, it suggests that the angle of ascent both starts and ends in Hayden's oldest poems. The result is that the volume moves beyond the portrait of a single unified consciousness (Hayden himself) that experiences a psychic descent from the poetic retrospective in the first section of the volume into the personal and historical tribulations of the middle two sections and then into "epiphany and consolation" through a "mystical encounter" with Baha'u'llah, the Baha'i prophet in the last section, an epiphany confirmed in that section's famous history poems (Hatcher 181). Instead (or in addition), the volume is a portrait of the artist as a portrait of African American history and spiritual transformation, concluding that Hayden's ultimate achievement is his self-definition as a young and emerging idealist whose art could motivate social justice. In this way, the lived values of the poet become the lived values of history, making Hayden's conception of himself in many ways a richer ethnic self-affirmation than nationalism and its legacy will allow.

Thus, the volume's brilliantly chosen title, the symbol of the volume's "narrative," comes from the last stanza of the poem "For a Young Artist" in the volume's first section, a study of artistic motivation that asserts the mysterious process of meaning that much of the rest of the volume suggests is the spiritual validation of Hayden's commitment to living values of unity.

> In the dark, his heavy wings
> open and shut stiffly spread
>   like a wooden butterfly's.
>
> He leaps, board wings clum-
> sily flapping, big sex
>   flopping, falls.
>
> The hawk-hunted fowl
> flutter and squawk;
>   panic squeals in the sty.
>
> He strains, an awk-
> ward patsy, sweating strains
>   leaping falling. Then—

> silken rustling in the air,
> the angle of ascent
> achieved.[3]

Both Fetrow (126–27) and Pontheolla Williams rightly point out the autobiographical character of the poem, and Wilburn Williams aptly analyzes its portrayal of the artist as "inviolate" in his "unwavering quest" (151, 152), but all three miss how, by manipulating traditional associations of artistry with flight, Hayden incorporates negative conceptions of creativity and the stereotypes of the male artist's effeminacy in order to characterize the trials of the artist in the face of an anxious and uncomprehending society. What matters as much as the unwavering quest, in other words, is the process of transformation, the implicit growth of self-knowledge from pain and insight that leads to flight, and that is in itself resistance to the ideology of society that renders art difficult and the artist useless or outcast. It is not necessarily the case that this poem is a rewriting of "To a Young Negro Artist" *from Heart-Shape in the Dust,* but this objective portrait of the artist is a measure of the distance Hayden was from that stirring but abstracted conception of the poet. Here the narrative of poetic transformation is predicated on a mystery of consciousness rather than preordained poetic topics and roles. And it is this mystery that makes this broader definition of the poet spiritual and therefore the foundation of changes in history, at least as a symbol. That mystery seems also to be analogous to those undefined but affirmed values exemplified by the chain in "Figure." Finally, many of Hayden's poems link this process of transformation to spiritual self-awareness, implying that the "angle of ascent" is process more than product or pursuit. There is no explicit quest and certainly no single goal, only internal changes that get expressed in art or activism or art as activism.

Hayden associates the artist's self-discovery with the second lyric of "Two Egyptian Portrait Masks," called "Akhenaten," linking the artist's imagination to the transformation of the saint and the movement of history. Seeing just one creator in opposition to the polytheism of his Egyptian society, Akhenaten literally embodies the progressive revelation that leads to Baha'i spirituality, historical change, and Hayden's own artistic achievement.

> The royal prophet reeled
> under the dazzling weight

of vision,
exalted—maddened?—the spirit moving
in his heart: Aten Jahveh Allah God.

(lines 11–15)

Akhenaten had a vision of a single God just as Baha'is do, a vision that encompassed for Hayden the progressive spiritual revelations of human history from the Egyptian deity Aten through Christianity and Islam to God in one man's spiritual conversion. Such is the relationship among individual spirituality, individual self-knowledge, creativity, and human history. The idea that the ancient Egyptians were worshiping the same God as the Baha'is is doctrinal and it is also anti-assimilationist, since this shared spirituality is enhanced in our understanding by historical specificity. Rather, historical moments overlap in the broad retrospective of this historical poem, giving the poet the capacity to suggest dimensions of the same spirituality without didacticism or the erasure of the "merely ethnic." In this way, Hayden's art functions similarly to Akhenaten's conversion, an association that answers the mystery of the achieved flight in "For a Young Artist." Perception of the spirit is what makes for the personal transformation necessary for art and prophecy and for art *as* prophecy.

This symbolic process of personal spiritual introspection as a parallel to historical prophecy was brought to full fruition in *Word in the Mourning Time* (1970) and *The Night-Blooming Cereus* (1973). The two volumes constitute Hayden's conception of Baha'i spirituality in history—including the "mourning time" before prophecy in Baha'i doctrine—and the symbolism needed to illuminate it, a combination that led Hatcher aptly to consider the two the descent of the volume's narrative. Hayden himself claimed that *The Night-Blooming Cereus* constituted significant gains in his artistry. And when included in *Angle of Ascent,* these poems heighten the symbolic implications of the rest of the volume, consolidating these ideas of transformation as imagination and history. Exemplifying the innovative syllabic and accentual verse structure by which Hayden makes introspective process into a model of historical and spiritual process, "Richard Hunt's 'Arachne,'" from *The Night-Blooming Cereus,* is worth quoting in its entirety.

Richard Hunt's "Arachne"

Human face becoming locked insect face
    mouth of agony shaping a cry it cannot utter

eyes bulging brimming with the horrors
of her becoming

Dazed crazed
by godly vivisection husking her
gutting her
cutting hubris its fat and bones away

In goggling terror fleeing yet powerless to flee
Arachne not yet arachnid and no longer woman
in the moment's centrifuge of dying
becoming

Embodying the dynamics of change in staggered accentual lines with no concluding punctuation, the poem, by repeating "becoming" three times, emphasizes potentiality, suggesting that, though Arachne's horrific transformation is not explicitly heroic, it is governed by a sense of promise. As Hatcher
observes, "Like Arachne, mankind, from Baha'i perspective, is not aware of its
destiny, what it is becoming; therefore the 'godly vivisection' is all the more
awesome" (183). The poem suggests that transformation is divine and traumatic, since Arachne's is mandated by the gods and, as Hatcher says, such
painful transformation reveals the difficult proof of spirituality. Potential and
pain coincide with only the hope and expectation that the emerging self
may be better than the previous self, despite the fact that Arachne's (and humankind's?) transformation is mandated as punishment. "Richard Hunt's
'Arachne'" links art, history, and ethnic identity, because it is Hayden's poetic
reflection upon African American sculptor Richard Hunt's sculpture of
Arachne's transformation into a spider. The poem is therefore as much about
how art (beauty) captures change and *is* change as it is about mythology.
Moreover, it is about artistic heritage and continuity, about how the hybrid
black artistic self participates in the powerful legacy of Western artistic trans-
formations from Ovid to Hayden.

The way the poet speaks for the race, then, is by speaking for the ultimately
spiritual meaning of human introspection and transformation and of the historical change associated with it. This ideal attributes to the explicitly symbolic poems of these two middle volumes the implication that the meaning-
making power of the mind is Hayden's ultimate social ideal. Hayden never put
it that way, but these two volumes are rife with artist figures such as Richard

Hunt, clarifying how the beauty of change is also the meaning and motivation of history. In "The Peacock Room," Hayden wonders:

Ars Longa   Which is crueller?
Vita Brevis   life or art?
                              (lines 1–2)

The titular Peacock Room in the Smithsonian is a "Triste metaphor" for these questions:

Thus history scorns
    the vision chambered in gold
and Spanish leather, lyric space;
rebukes, yet cannot give the lie
    to what is havened here.
                              (lines 12, 14–18)

Arguing against the escapism of which he was accused by critics such as Angela Jackson, who called such symbolism "coreless," and who declared that Hayden's poetry is "never at the enter of Black/activity in the world [the slash is Jackson's]" (69). Hayden asserts that history rebukes the claims of the artist for pure lyricism, first in the social irrelevance of any such purity, if achieved, and, secondly, in its actual impossibility, since that "lyric space" cannot actually escape its dialectical juxtaposition with the outside world. After all, the "horrible malice" of the peacocks on the wallpaper of the room, the speaker asserts, actually recalls the horrible competition between artists who vied for the commission to create the Peacock Room, as Whistler also used that malice to criticize the vanity of those who commissioned it. Moreover, those peacocks, "Whistler's satiric art," allegedly drove his rival mad with that very social commentary, what the rival perceived to be a compromise of artistry. Finally, the mortality of the speaker's friend and fellow artist, who once celebrated a birthday in the room, reminds him of art's cruelty in being immortal; it outlives the horrors and pains of the world as it recalls them. Art is therefore never entirely transcendent in the first place. It always evokes the pain associated with human impermanence and mortality and the social world that rebukes it.

This idea leaves Hayden with a problem: how can an art that is always invested in reality be a transcendent indication of the spiritual ideal? The analogies between Hayden's art and the divine may be the wishful thinking of a foolish idealist and failed artist who cannot reconcile symbolic ideals to historical fact, while "too much" reality may lead the black artist especially to limited political ideals. We can recognize Hayden's solution best if we look not for political ideology but for the construction of the poetic self, in which Hayden unites these two opposed possibilities in the process of meaning making of which the poem is a trace and in the process of tension in the structure of the poetic form. Art *does* endure, and it endures in part as an embodiment of the enduring human pursuit of meaning that constitutes both the enduring humane values and the process of intellection by which poetic meaning reveals those values. Each of these components of the poem's ideal potentially enacts the divine. "The Peacock Room" concludes:

> What is art?
> What is life?
> What the Peacock Room?
> Rose-leaves and ashes drift
> its portals, gently spinning toward
> a bronze Bodhisattva's ancient smile.
>   (lines 49–54)

Life is no more true or real, transcendent or degrading, on its surface than art is, so that it is not any direct correspondence between specific terms, images, or ideology in art and specific social actions or practices that matters. Rather, it is the process of perceiving meaning through the dubious surface of phenomenal experience that forces the viewer or reader to look beyond appearances, artifacts, and social forms to the eternal human quest for meaning. Can the proximity of the Peacock Room to this spiritual sculpture be anything more than coincidence? If it is more than coincidence, then the artist serves as the Bodhisattva guiding souls into heaven though the artist, like Moses, may not see that promised land. In this guidance, beauty is the end point of artistic pursuits of meaning and thus the aesthetic absolute that embodies the absolute of the divine. And all of this gets its ultimate proof in the process of mind that either perceives or makes that meaning. So the artist clearly gets into heaven by getting his mind into the art. And that heaven is of transformation, the beauty of change that makes evolving selfhood into evolving spirituality and changing history.

Thus, the poems from *Words in the Mourning Time* function as Hayden's declaration of his theory of history derived from the spiritual vision of *The Night-Blooming Cereus*, a theory of history that associated spiritual perception with fighting for freedom and beauty with social activism. Like the confused poet or the tortured Aten, Malcolm X in "El-Hajj Malik El-Shabazz" was prey to various illusions and, like that speaker, Malcolm X had to "'Strike through the mask!'" in order to come to a true sense of himself, a private process of spiritual transformation with obvious and exemplary social, political, and spiritual implications because of Malcolm X's status as a Civil Rights leader. Following the trajectory of *The Autobiography of Malcolm X*, Hayden's poems treat Malcolm X's spiritual insights as an emerging and truer sense of himself that led to his defiance. But that transformation and defiance was also cut off by the social world unprepared for this vision of African American wholeness and antiracist social unity:

> He fell upon his face before
> Allah the raceless in whose blazing Oneness all
> were one. He rose renewed renamed, became
> much more than there was time for him to be.
>   (lines 52–55)

Spiritually, Malcolm X "became" transformed in the "full moon" of Allah's "blazing Oneness" and, in becoming, became much more than the world could acknowledge or accept, as his assassination and Baha'i teachings suggest (Hatcher 132). That Malcolm X was a preacher in the African American tradition makes this transformation a symbol of how the role of spirituality in African American liberation is evidence (always potentially) of the movement of Baha'i spirituality. The traumas of African American history are part of both the mourning time and revelation. In other words, as he moved closer to Allah, Malcolm X presumably moved close to the Baha'i faith. Like Akhenaten and Hayden himself, Malcolm X is simultaneously a religious "prophet" and an artist figure of a particular artistic and cultural tradition. And as a wordsmith, Malcolm X's analogy to both Akhenaten and the artist figure in "For a Young Artist" validates the overlap of political, aesthetic, and spiritual meaning in individual transformation.

Thus, Hayden's analogous personal transformation parallels that of this freedom fighter in "Words in the Mourning Time," a poem that follows "El-Hajj Malik El-Shabazz" and confirms in the poet's personal experience what Malcolm X's death means. The poem's first section sets the tone:

For King, for Robert Kennedy,
destroyed by those they could not save,
for King for Kennedy I mourn.
And for America, self-destructive, self betrayed.
I grieve.

(lines 1–5)

But the speaker finds solace "through power of / The Blessed Exile's / trans-illuminating word" (lines 6–8). He comes to recognize that "the agonies of our deathbed childbed age / are process," by which "oh dreadfully, our humanness must be achieved" (lines 10–12). This process is the central paradox of the original poem, as in section 2: "Killing people to save, to free them? / With napalm lighting routes to the future?" (lines 13–14). In the fifth section, also, the speaker wonders "*what a world we make, oppressor and oppressed*": "We hate kill destroy / in the name of human good / our killing and our hate destroy" (lines 34–35, 39–41).

In *Angle of Ascent*, the middle sections of this poem are deleted, making it all the more personal. For this persona, this poem is a version of the Baha'i faith's Obligatory Prayer, which is spoken "as a reminder of God's ultimate ascendancy, whatever else ensues" (Hatcher 173). As such, the poet's declaration links his artistic purpose to his spiritual purpose.

I bear Him witness now—
mystery Whose major clues are the heart of man,
the mystery of God:

Baha'u'llah:
Logos, poet, cosmic hero, surgeon, architect
of our hope of peace,

wronged, exiled One,
chosen to endure what agonies of knowledge, what
auroral dark

bestowals of truth
vision power anguish for our future's sake.
"I was but a man

"like others, asleep upon
My couch, when, lo, the breezes of the All-Glorious
were wafted over Me . . ."

Called, as in dead of night
a dreamer is roused to help the helpless flee
   a burning house.

I bear Him witness now:
towards Him our history in its disastrous quest
   for meaning is impelled.

(lines 35–55)

Using enjambed, juxtaposed, and truncated syntax and accentual rhythm similar to that in "Richard Hunt's 'Arachne,'" this poem clarifies how, by seeking to perceive spiritual meaning in this devastating history, the poet is testifying to how the pursuit of meaning reveals spirituality and how spirituality motivates a pursuit of meaning. This "becoming" is more ordered than Arachne's and is parallel to "For a Young Artist." Poetic structure is thus a symbol. The poem purposefully elides the question of which comes first in order to identify the paradoxical process by which the horrors of life lead to the promise of divinity. By offering his own words as the culmination of that seeking, the poetic speaker, an ordinary man (like Baha'u'llah, "but a man"), is bearing witness to the truth of Baha'i spiritual process, individual and historical, and to the spiritual meaning of poetry. Bearing witness is central to Christianity in general and to African American Christianity in particular. And it is his symbolic poetry that is his means of bearing witness. The poet becomes a prophet, echoing Baha'u'llah's declaration that he was but an ordinary man before he was called by God.

In this context, as well as on its own terms, "A Ballad of Remembrance," one of Hayden's most important poems, transforms the autobiographical moment into a parallel of personal growth and poetic growth. It is, in other words, a persuasive rewriting of the commitment to human unity that tempers the potential naïveté of suggesting that whites and blacks are unified equally in their suffering. In the case of "A Ballad of Remembrance," first published in *The Lion and the Archer* and then revised for *A Ballad of Remembrance* (1962), Hayden offers one of his most impressive conceptions of the bardic self as an ethnic self and the ethnic self as an ideal of history, the union of beauty and social reality that enacts populist ideals through a model of self-affirming ethnic self-definition. It is also Hayden's version of Baker's conception of the black artist as blues translator. New Orleans at Mardi Gras thus becomes symbolic of both historical and psychological conflicts and transforms the externally directed call to accountability in "Figure" into a personal one which is meant to be a model for all introspection. Says Hayden, "The central motifs [in the poem] of the mask, of disguise, illusion, were suggested by the Mardi Gras, including the Zulu parade, a parade by Negroes which used to be a feature of Mardi Gras and perhaps still is, if the civil rights movement hasn't caused it to be eliminated" since the "Zulus" "made such a raunchy spectacle of themselves as stereotypes, outlandish caricatures of black people" (*Collected Prose* 153). These caricatures motivate the speaker to look within himself to see if any of these masks of stereotypes fit in order to discover the truest notion of the self available and necessary for social unity.

In essence, the poem depicts the process of an African American mind moving from an engagement with the circumscribing effects of racism to the self-affirmation of existential self-definition predicated on shared humane ideals. The poem opens:

> Quadroon mermaids, Afro angels, black saints
> balanced upon the switchblades of that air
> and sang. Tight streets unfolding to the eye
> like fans of corrosion and elegiac lace
> crackled with their singing: Shadow of time. Shadow of blood.
>
> Shadow, echoed the Zulu king, dangling
> from a cluster of balloons. Blood
> whined the gun-metal priestess, floating
> over the courtyard where dead men diced.
>
> (lines 1–9)

The speaker encounters "contrived illuminations" that challenge his sense of security and urge him to consider bad options.

> Accommodate, muttered the Zulu king,
> toad on a throne of glaucous poison jewels.
> Love, chimed the saints and the angels and the mermaids.
> Hate, shrieked the gun-metal priestess
> from her spiked bellcollar curved like a fleur-de-lis:
>
> As well have a talon as a finger, muzzle as a mouth,
> as well have a hollow as a heart. And she pinwheeled
> away in coruscations of laughter, scattering
> those others before her like foil stars.
>
> (lines 20–28)

The speaker in the poem wrestles with various socially and historically oppressive conceptions of African American identity that are full of anger and danger and that are symbolized before him both in actual people and in the masks they wear. Their masks are both symbolic and real, as are the aspects of the African American self they represent.

Like the lynching, the ugly beauty of a self-deprecating and racist New Orleans embodies how, as the poem suggests, self-definition for anyone, but especially for blacks, must be derived from resistance to the limiting options created by race politics. The oppositions are between masquerade and actual psychology, stereotypes and genuine mental and emotional states. Rather than directly addressing a community, the speaker in the poem is addressing himself, listening to opposed personal impulses that are embodied in the external reality he observes. In essence, this poem can be read as the African American bardic poet's becoming. Here is the emergence of the "indigenous creativity" that Baker suggests is derived in part from racist material conditions.

It seems to me no coincidence that it was the 1962 volume that garnered Hayden his initial international fame, since that volume most fully articulates the relationship between African American poetic and cultural selfhood and the act of introspection as a defining pursuit of social unity. It also most fully articulates how an artist connects individual selfhood to communal affirmation. Though the poet's becoming is, in Hayden's actual terms, based on a spiritual essence, his poem represents that becoming as a complex process of social construction in which racial differences are real but can be refuted through genuine mutual understanding. Thus, the connection with poet Mark Van Doren is not based on some specific political ideal such as integration or interracial love but on the recognition of another's humanity beneath the masks that the dancing of the poet's fears and frustrations with self embody. In other words, the speaker sees the meaning of another and thus the meaning of himself:

> Then you [poet Mark Van Doren] arrived, meditative, ironic,
> richly human; and your presence was shore where I rested
> released from the hoodoo of that dance, where I spoke
> with my true voice again.
>
> (lines 34–37)

Contrary to the reservations of many Black Nationalists who felt that the saving presence of a white poet compromised the black speaker's identity, making the poem simply an affirmation of the ideology of assimilation, the truth is that, as Hatcher observes, Van Doren actually "is a poignant example for the speaker of human possibilities" because he "demonstrates his individual ability to transcend such matter." As a result, says Hatcher, the speaker "realizes profoundly that individual spiritual ascent can overcome 'the minotaurs of edict' [Hayden's name for such dogmatic people as Black Nationalist literati], and the poet can speak with his 'human voice again', not as a Negro or as the advocate of a cause, but simply as one artist to another" (111). Hatcher is largely right, except that it is not Van Doren's knowledge or ability to transcend that matters; rather it is Hayden's *friendship* with Van Doren—one that literally transcends race—that embodies the "richly human" commonalities masked by the Mardi Gras. The speaker always speaks as a "Negro" but his blackness is now tied not to the mandates of political action or the self-fulfilling stereotypes of black Mardi Gras in particular and black southern life in general, but to the humane values that allow humans to interact healthfully in spite of race. African American identity is about an experience of the world anchored in genuine human connection, not in blacks becoming white or in blacks rejecting whites. Both stances accept the masks as truth. In fact, Van Doren's irony about the speaker's anxiety implies his lack of sensitivity to the struggles of the speaker, since that irony seems to come from sarcastic responses to the masking of New Orleans. His irony masks as much as it reveals. Differences in experience remain, the poem declares, but the artist can recognize that those differences are not absolute and that memory, combined with introspection, produces the richly human verse that, as much as Van Doren's friendship, constitutes the speaker's endurance of the horrors of his experience. The ballad hero here is the poet in particular and the African American mind in general, as both reconcile the tensions between mask and reality, self and world, black and white, in the modes of expression they offer. In this way, the African American artist produces, by the identifying conventions of such art as the ballad, a mark of individuality that is also, as Baker puts it, "an invitation to energizing intersubjectivity" (*Blues, Ideology* 5).

Thus, by the end of *Angle of Ascent,* the reader is guided to Hayden's well-known history poems as expressions and confirmations of the ways in which historical specificity and cultural difference are the primary substance of spiritual incarnation and transcendence. In these poems, the traditional terms of ethnic affirmation too simply prized in African American literary study is offered as both foreground and backdrop to the spiritual process that makes such ethnic affirmation possible. In "Middle Passage," the most important and exemplary poem of the series, Hayden posits his largest vision of how spiritual transformation, poetic symbolism, historical heroism, and political ideology require one another in order for the world to have meaning. In the poem, Hayden juxtaposes revised quotations from official historical documents, primarily those of the slave traders, with each other in order to articulate the third term of humane values that most critics ignore or treat only as cultural assimilation. For example, Vera Kutzinski asserts:

> Resituated in a new context, the [historical] texts Hayden purports to quote lose not their appearance of authenticity [with his revisions] but their historical authority. Broken into textual fragments, they are no longer capable of offering a coherent, unified historical narrative. They become voices among many other, competing voices, or better perhaps, images of language, of the discourse of slavery without claims to representational authority and historical truth. (172)

Though Kutzinski's analysis is apt, breaking down claims to representational authority and historical truth was not Hayden's only aim. He also breaks down the unification of history and religion that the slave traders had constructed for themselves in order to articulate a new unity of history and religion in the quest for meaning impelled toward Baha'i spiritual revelation. Nor was he interested only in challenging the conservative elitism of the allusive techniques of *The Waste Land*, as Brian Conniff argues (489). What Hayden was primarily suggesting through the dialectics of his poetic structure was a synthesis that could potentially suggest that the middle passage could be part of progressive revelation. How are African American identity and history the substance of a spiritual ideal? The answer to this question is more comprehensive, more fundamental, and more epistemological—in short, more substantive—than a progressive poet's answer to a conservative predecessor.

Meant "to change the very texture of history," as Kutzinski put it, then (174), the poem uses Hayden's characteristic dialectical symbolist techniques and syllabic poetics to embody what Charles Davis aptly calls "the mystical emergence of freedom from circumstances that appall and degrade, and the making of a man, a Black man in America" (125). That emergence must account both for commonality and difference, spirit and social activism, the horrors of slavery and the emerging and sustained resistance. In fact, the poem is structured in the microcosm and macrocosm of its two refrains to portray both history and the writing of this poem as both personal and communal spiritual transformation. This is the first of the two refrains:

Middle Passage;
    Voyage through death
        to life upon these shores.
                (lines 5–7)

As with the previous poems of transformation, the form here is an analogy for the angle of ascent, a structure that is repeated three poems later in "Runagate Runagate," where runaway slaves themselves ("runagate" is a vernacular transliteration of renegade) become that poem's analogous refrain:

Runagate
    Runagate
        Runagate
(lines 8–10)

Though clearly about "the making of a black man in America," what becomes even clearer in "Middle Passage" especially, but in all of the history poems in this sequence, is that such freedom is tied directly to the Christianity of African American freedom fighters. Through various symbolic indications of progressive revelation, the series articulates the new texture of history based on Baha'i beliefs, expressed through black Christian ones making these individual black heroes into secular prophets of historical change.

These unnamed and usually unacknowledged black prophets are construed as such by the poet simply because they lived at all. On the opposite pole of Hayden's dialectical method, then, and equally responsible for implying the unstated third term of spiritual truth and social action, is a second set of refrains that embody the trauma or transformation out of which the ideal, the new identity, emerges.

Deep in the festering hold thy father lies,
of his bones New England pews are made,
those are altar lights that were his eyes.

Jesus   Saviour   Pilot   Me
Over   Life's   Tempestuous   Sea

We pray that Thou wilt grant, O Lord,
safe passage to our vessels bringing
heathen souls unto Thy chastening.

Jesus   Saviour

(lines 17–25)

In Hayden's words, the revision of Shakespeare's famous "sea-change" passage from *The Tempest,* where a dead body is transformed into an immortality of riches beneath the sea, emphasizes "the change from human beings into things—objects, suffered by the enslaved African—the idea that slavery was a kind of death" (Wilburn Williams, "Covenant of Timelessness" 80). Moreover, Hayden forces the reader to recognize the idea that the slaver's journals and the speaker of this poem both suggest the same thing: that the middle passage improved the spirituality of Africans. The Christianity that will be the manifestation of the African American will to freedom is also the terms of their oppression. Since he questions its validity, Hayden is clearly not accepting the racist narrative that such Christianity justifies slavery. Rather, he is showing the inadequacy of the African American assimilation of that culture. The poem suggests ways to look beyond the cultural specificity of a racist Christianity to the ideal spirituality that motivates the truer aspects of African American culture.

The second version of the sea-change refrain reveals that the traders' vision emphasizes death while Hayden transforms the "living" Africans into the nameless agents of a historical change. He also reveals how the transformation of the Africans is predicated on their interior lives, their resistance to being absorbed into a racist culture, a mysterious motivation analogous to the "angle of ascent" of the artist figure and the transformation of Akhenaten.

> *Deep in the festering hold thy father lies,*
> *the corpse of mercy rots with him,*
> *rats eat love's rotten gelid eyes.*
>
> *But, oh, the living look at you*
> *with human eyes whose suffering accuses you,*
> *whose hatred reaches deep through the swill of dark*
> *to strike you like a leper's claw*
>
> *You cannot stare that hatred down*
> *or chain the fear that stalks the watches*

and breathes on you its fetid scorching breath;
cannot kill the deep immortal human wish,
the timeless will

(lines 108–19)

Just as Malcolm X "became" his people's anger, these surviving Africans become their people's will to freedom and the promised resurrection of mercy and love by resisting the way they are portrayed in the racist culture. This refrain thus reiterates the trajectory of the first refrain, adding here the specific human agency by which the transformation is made possible. That resurrection of mercy and love is in the bodies of the Africans, who could not be assimilated into the racist narratives of Christianity except as slaves, even though they almost literally embodied the ideals of the faith. The Africans' will to freedom is their alternative to this oppressive culture.

The "living" Africans survived the middle passage and, led by divinely inspired heroes such as Cinquez, initiated a cycle of repetition and change in history that was the very essence of freedom and should become a model both for how the reader understands herself and for subsequent action. Despite the white deponent in the *Amistad* case who declares the imminent death of Cinquez, the poem belies his certainty:

The deep immortal human wish,
the timeless will:

Cinquez its deathless primaveral image,
life that transfigures many lives.

(lines 172–75)

Like Cinquez, then, each successive African American hero on this shore, like each religious prophet in progressive revelation, gives the same will to freedom a new name to which Hayden dedicates a poem: Cinquez, Nat Turner, Harriet Tubman, Frederick Douglass. Consequently, in this third version of the first refrain, "Voyage through death / to life upon these shores," the poem is no longer contained by the middle passage—the middle passage, poem and journey, is over. And what is resurrected is an American history improved and spiritually enhanced by the ironically liberating middle passage and the new and representative subjectivity of Africans in America. And the reader is thus constructed as recognizing the futility of assimilating humanity into racist narratives. That humanity—ultimately spiritual in nature—will always resist.

And of course the poem's own beauty is at the heart of its claims on the reader's imagination. It is artistic perception, finally, that allows us to comprehend these spiritual principles of an otherwise horrific historical transformation, a perception that Hayden affirms as his poem's role in progressive revelation. Without the poem, these living but still unnamed Africans would perhaps remain unrecognized, their spiritual humanity unacknowledged despite its powerful reality in the living heritage of African Americans today. Since the prophecy of freedom is not yet fulfilled, Hayden and his reader must rely in part on art to embody the principles of that prophecy and then rely on their own actions of meaning-making pursuits and quests for unity to fulfill that prophecy. In a voice independent of revised historical documents (and therefore "free" of the racist narrative of those documents), Hayden articulates the third component of symbolism.

> Shuttles in the rocking loom of history,
> the dark ships move, the dark ships move,
> their bright ironical names
> like jests of kindness on a murderer's mouth;
> plough through thrashing glister toward
> fata morgana's lucent melting shore,
> weave toward New World littorals that are
> mirage and myth and actual shore.
>
> Voyage through death,
>   voyage whose chartings are unlove.
>   (lines 94–102)

The American coast, "fata morgana's lucent melting shore," a mirage brought about by the meeting of sky and sea, appears to be a false shore, but within the refrain, "voyage through death / voyage whose chartings are unlove," and the "shuttles in the rocking loom of history," are images of creation that make the shore a true shore indeed. With the loom imagery as a metaphor both for historical change and for poetic creation, Hayden suggests that, just as from the weaving of historical documents comes a poem that illuminates the spiritual motivations of black history, and from a continuing practice of poetic weaving comes his own career—the aesthetic and spiritual proof of *Angle of Ascent* itself—so from the "weaving" together of Africans and Europeans, Africans and Americans, slaves and free, in lived history, comes a reconstitution of humanity, the earliest weaves of a new human garment. Significantly, these images of artistic and human unity—reflective of each other—come at the point in the poem where its "plot" of the middle passage is at its worst, affirming both the human and the aesthetic potential that will bring unity from the tensions of evil and trauma.

What matters for Hayden in the end is the capacity of the individual to perceive spiritual value in human life and act on it, a process and practice that made those individuals themselves into symbols of that spiritual meaning. As he put it in "Frederick Douglass," that famous freedom fighter will be remembered when we quite literally "flesh" his ideas of freedom, allowing them to become, as Hayden suggests, "diastole, systole," the very functioning of our bodies. And that fleshing had its start in the fundamentally human and irrepressible spirit of Frederick Douglass himself as it motivated his resistance to slavery in his escape, his *Narrative,* and his many abolitionist activities. In this way, freedom will be more than the "gaudy mumbo jumbo of politicians" and Douglass will be remembered more substantively than "with statues' rhetoric" or "with legends and poems and wreaths of bronze alone" (lines 6, 11–12). In other words, living Douglass's dream of freedom will be more substantive than the artistic representation of it. But the irony of the poem is, of course, it is quite successfully fleshing that spirit, claiming to be a "living" rather than a static monument. Hayden makes that claim in this poem by evoking the sonnet form, that monument to Western artistic achievement, and revising it through the same accentual metrics that characterize poems of transformation such as "Richard Hunt's 'Arachne.'" In addition to using its fourteen lines to associate his poem with the sonnet form, Hayden also claims to offer only five accented syllables per line, even though each line exceeds ten syllables. If mastery of the sonnet is a monument to poetic gift, then exceeding its conventions can be read as a visual and structural emblem of how the active memory of Douglass and the enactment of his will to freedom both exceed proscribed limitations, even in a poem as memorial. The distinction is that it is not primarily calling for Douglass to be remembered. It is primarily calling for Douglass to be alive in the minds and acts of Hayden's readers. Like the "living" who enacted the revolt in "Middle Passage," the living will bring the dead Douglass to life in the process of history that makes his dream manifest. Thus, at the very least, we have art to illuminate this process for us.

In this way, Hayden's art is a political self-assertion in the broadest possible terms, his affirmation of the spiritual value and meaning of African American social pursuits and his assertion that African American history is a centerpiece for understanding that pursuit. Accepting his ethnic heritage meant simultaneously asserting its ideal meaning, which was constituted by the humane values that were ultimately distinct from the social codes of racial ideology. And to do Hayden's verse justice, we must take this possibility seriously. For what Hayden has in mind is an agency predicated on a spiritual motivation, a humble commitment to make one's life mean its truest meaning, the freedom of spiritual unity. His 1975 *Angle of Ascent* verifies that he took up that pursuit and joined a long-standing African American poetic tradition that celebrated the African American mind as a social and cultural ideal. As such, Hayden's anti-ideological poetic ideal becomes a defining model of a bardic poetic activism. Both reader and poet share in the capacity of poetic self-definition to exemplify—indeed, to *live*—the ideal meaning of the social world. Readers of Hayden's verse must thus be as resolute as he in linking spirituality to history, common humanity to ethnic difference in order to recognize the *meaning* of their lives and souls. This is clearly not a traditional notion of the political in poetry but it is an appropriate way for understanding how Hayden's commitment to the transcendent was never either about cultural assimilation or being entirely apolitical. It was rather about making poetry that could make ideal values and transcendent meaning real in poetry in order to see it as real in history and to live as real in the individual life. Hayden's poetic persona in *Angle of Ascent* exemplified his articulation of his soul's strict meaning throughout Hayden's career. The result: the complex symbolism of process as the framing of personal spiritual history that makes Hayden's poetic artistry a powerful affirmation of African American ethnicity and a unique idealist and symbolist version of the African American bardic self.

6 A Port Worth the Cruise
Melvin B. Tolson's Epic Imagination

Black Boy, O Black Boy,
is the port worth the cruise?

—Melvin B. Tolson, *Harlem Gallery*

In his magnum opus *Harlem Gallery, Book 1: The Curator* (1965), his first book of a proposed five-book epic of African American history, neglected poet Melvin B. Tolson culminates his career and the African American bardic tradition by characterizing both the intellectual qualities and the artistic ideals that make African American poetic genius a prophetic enactment of principles of social unity that would, as a result of this genius, come to be realized in history. Expanding to epic proportions the ethnic spiritual history that distinguished Robert Hayden's poetry, as I argued in the last chapter, and conceptualizing the broadest social possibilities of artistic distinction for the African American poet, Tolson's last poem characterizes bardic genius as the dialectical and unifying function of African culture and history in the African American person's adaptation of Western culture to African American art and life. Tolson's simultaneous construction of poetic genius and ethnic selfhood in epic narrative conventions paradoxically rejects the limited notions of national unity so central to the tradition of the epic, to the binary logic of white supremacy, to the framing logic of ethnic identity that both fetters and liberates the bardic tradition, and to the ideals of ethnic authenticity central to African American literary culture. Instead, he develops an ideal of a transnational historical consciousness constituted in its internal and historical dynamics by the westward spread of African peoples and cultures. In this vision, representing the African American self becomes a mode of postcolonial critique of Western notions of race and self that fetter the (African) American imagination. An *ars poetica*, *Harlem Gallery* portrays the ideal of the American epic journey of individual spiritual self-discovery initiated so beautifully by Walt Whitman as the cultural and historical self-discovery of marginalized peoples. Through this process, Tolson implies, marginalized people originated the Western tradition from which they were excluded. Perhaps no African American poet so tenaciously pursued one ideal of African American historical and cultural selfhood as Tolson, and none offers so full an achievement of the ethnic self-definition possible in Western poetics. Theorizing and enacting the social value of African American cultural self-worth, Tolson's epic imagination was well worth the neglect it brought.

In this chapter, therefore, I seek to resurrect Tolson's reputation by recovering how fully his ideal of a synthesizing diasporic self, as enabled almost paradoxically by his adaptation of modernist artistry, rejected exclusion of Africans and African Americans from equal social opportunity by asserting African American artists and African diasporic culture into the pantheon of the West. In its innovation, Tolson's modernist artistry anticipates critiques by contemporary theorists such as Paul Gilroy of the flawed construction of racial identity as static and coextensive with equally static and limiting notions of nation. In his art, Tolson eventually envisioned a "black Atlantic" (Gilroy 2) of the African American mind whose journey from Africa through ancient and modern Europe to the United States was fulfilled when it transformed the cultural limitations imposed upon it by Western society into what Henry Louis Gates called "a full and sufficient self" (*Signifying Monkey* 169). Instead of being compromised by conventions of modernist poetics, Tolson's representation of that ethnic self was enhanced by his revision of the principles of modernist formalism and European cultural references. While fully invested in the elitism of modernist poetics, this hybrid art claimed that such elitist culture could serve egalitarian social ends by attributing all of its cultural capital to the African diasporic consciousness that, paradoxically enough, exemplified the imagination that was the source of that "white" culture.

By articulating its internal and historical complexity in the complex artistic representation of its journey of self-discovery, the African American diasporic mind became its own greatest potential resistance to the legacy of imperial power. That mind itself rewrote (or could rewrite) the patterns of thought that emerge from the racist binary logic of Western society and that are essential in the production and internalization of the principles and practices of social hierarchy. Rather than either accepting the opposition of African American identity and American culture as Ronald Cansler suggests or simply "deterritorializing" modernism by rewriting the "master's" narrative, both of which are reminiscent of the logic his verse rewrites, Tolson claims that a nondualistic cultural narrative was always already written in the African mind and was warped by the Western culture that African mind founded. Modernist poetics was not a master narrative to claim for black people but an innovative literary culture that had its roots in African culture and that needed to be reclaimed for the egalitarian principles of thought it could convey. Rather than imperial metaphors, then, scholars should turn to the metaphors of transformation associated with postcolonial theories of the hybrid nature of the culture. Metaphors of hybridity help to reveal how, for Tolson, culture was not constituted by competing territories but by aspects of mind that exist always in contention and combination. Following in a long line of epic poets in the American tradition, Tolson's opus traces the individual journey as a historical, democratic one that, while constructed by history, could reconstruct it.

What most readers of Tolson have missed, then, is the fact that this ideal of a self-defining African American mind and its complex, modernist artistry is also the foundation of an alternative ideal of mutually supportive social relations across racial lines. It is not the simple cultural assimilation or the double consciousness that some critics have seen it to be. Tolson rightly saw no inherent or unchanging opposition between ethnic affirmation and modernist formalism, because such oppositions were based on the binary, dualistic logic that was the defining social and cultural fetter that an oppressive capitalist or tyrannical society imposes upon humanity. Just as fellow bardic modernist Gwendolyn Brooks saw the mind of ordinary African American people as the battleground for resisting such fetters, as I suggested in chapter 4, Tolson saw every mind as a locus of the unifying hybridity of culture as that hybridity was exemplified by African Americans. And just as fellow bardic modernist Robert Hayden posited the mind as a symbolic parallel to history, Tolson made that mind the prime mover in social life, with the added ideal that there was but one human cultural mind of which the poet was exemplary, not a possible spiritual manifestation that needed to be proven. As Tolson put it in one of his *Washington Tribune* "Caviar and Cabbage" columns called "How Can You Tell an Intelligent Mind?": "An intelligent mind is a mind that thinks in terms of sunshine and shadow. It sees things in terms of antithesis—contrasts," "places opposite ideas in juxtaposition," and, most important, "sees the underlying unity in contrasts" (*Caviar and Cabbage* 186–88). Unlike the minds of white supremacists and fascists, according to Tolson, and unlike the argumentative trends in African American literary culture, this intelligent mind rejects the binaries of race politics because "the black Zulu and the blond Anglo-Saxon have a oneness, an identity of I-ness," especially since "biological evolution is nothing more than the theory of the underlying unity of animals" (188). Not a plea for integration or assimilation, Tolson's definition of this "underlying unity" is a declaration of an ideal of the human self that Tolson called "tridimensionality: biology, psychology, sociology."[1] This tripartite construction of the self is what unifies, making this constant process of selfhood the ideal universal for the artist, not a set of literary themes.

As such, Tolson's conception of all human selfhood refutes the liberal humanist ideal of a coherent and consistent abstracted self that is central to Western rationalism and racism and the associated bourgeois capitalist individualism. This conception of selfhood as inherent and singular rather than dimensional has been central to the idea that African American writers must transcend blackness to be human, as Harvey Curtis Webster implied. In refuting this idea, Tolson's work also rejects the conception of blackness as a preexisting ethnic cultural monolith that an African American artist must articulate in the forms of that authentic culture. Instead, Tolson offers a vision of social construction through which he can perceive and represent the underlying human unity that allowed him to transform the binary logic of the West into the dialectical, synthesizing logic of the culture of diaspora. And the poetic self consisted of the ways in which black consciousness enacted that alternative synthesizing logic.

Reading the poetry of Tolson's career calls for a method of analysis that operates through this dialectical process of the African American mind represented in his poetry. Instead of measuring Tolson's eclectic virtuosity against an unquestioned notion of a preexisting black self, readers must acknowledge how Tolson proposes to contain within the mind of the poetic genius all aspects of the African and Western cultures and to synthesize the two to create the social values by which that poetic mind could reject hierarchy. By construing African American poetic genius as a version of this intelligent mind and its simultaneous journey to itself and its place in history, Tolson made the black self and the poetics by which he defines it into a broad locus of the conflict, contradiction, and reconstruction of the historical discourses by which whiteness, blackness, Americanness, and literary value were constructed as oppositions to one another. In other words, this "intelligent mind" provisionally resolves the African's Janus-like problem of double consciousness, of "facing two cultural directions at once," as Paul Gilroy put it, that characterizes the diasporic self and that models the most genuine universal human condition more fully than presumptions of a stable distinct self. By doing so, Tolson's art forces readers to "the theorisation of creolisation, metissage, mestizaje, and hybridity" rather than the "ethnic absolutism" that is usual in discussions of race and culture (Gilroy 2). In this vision, African and African American traditions, because they have at times been predicated on resisting exclusion from nations, contain within their dislocation from the nation a truer model for understanding all socially constructed human identity. These excluded black selves—these African intelligent minds—also therefore contained the shared and fundamental humane values necessary to resolve that dislocation and to provide to the West the greatest fulfillment of its ideals. This black self constitutes what Brent Hayes Edwards called "the black diasporic *décalage* [an untranslatable French word for *gap, interval, loss*]" (13). Social unity requires recognizing the historical dislocation caused by the fixing of identity, and embracing the gaps in those allegedly unified selves in order to adapt the self to the unachievable end of self-definition. As such, reading Tolson's verse requires recognizing that the means by which we fill those individual gaps can reinforce the construction of oppressive social institutions by being an extension of the logics that support them, or they can enact the values that will lead to alternative thinking and to alternative institutions.

In other words, Tolson's poetics models social unity because it models the introspective self-knowledge and historical self-awareness by which this ideal dialectical mind was, to borrow Edwards's terms, "a changing core of difference" with "'differences within unity'" that allows for more persuasive, enduring, and egalitarian conceptions of selfhood, community, and nation (14). Readers of Tolson must therefore discern these complex linkages of commonality and difference, affirming ethnic cultural discourses and oppressive Eurocentric ones, that underlie and complicate Tolson's assimilation of modernist poetics into an African diasporic poetic genius. After all, the misreading of Tolson hinges upon critics' failure to grasp well enough this antibinary construction of his genius as modeled by dialectical poetic texture. On one hand, conservative critic Allen Tate was only partly right in his preface to Tolson's 1953 *Libretto for the Republic of Liberia*, commissioned by that nation, when he claimed that Tolson had assimilated the poetic language of his day and had become "more intensely Negro" for it (3). Tate's condescending language and Tolson's apocryphal claim to change his art to accommodate Tate's taste notwithstanding, Tolson did indeed "assimilate" mainstream poetic language in order, paradoxically, to intensify the terms of his ethnic self-definition, a paradox that is exactly the gap Edwards had in mind in his definition of diaspora. Tate was more right than he could have known, since the paradox he identifies is part of a radical political revision of poetic meaning that would have challenged some of the principles by which he identified that paradox. On the other hand, leftist critic Karl Shapiro also correctly suggested in his preface to the first-edition *Harlem Gallery* that Tolson writes "in Negro, which is to say a possible American language" (13) as a consequence of his modernist mastery. But Tolson goes further than acknowledging black language as a possible American language, as studies of Black Vernacular English have since revealed. In addition for Tolson, speaking "in Negro" was in fact speaking in a foundational Western language. The insight and confusion in these critical assessments reveal how fully Tolson's artistry conveyed its dialectical self to its readers. The problem of understanding is in the logic of the criticism, not the structure and priorities of the poem. Tolson's conception of genius rejected the false "to be or not to be a Negro" dilemma that these critics and such scholars as Ronald Cansler too often emphasize as Tolson's concern. Instead, Tolson's art makes his complex formalism simultaneously an extension of an unacknowledged African past, a revision of the known Western past, and a prophecy of a quasi-socialist revolution, a unification of presumed opposites that produces the biggest, baddest African American self in African American poetry.

Finally, then, Tolson's opus must be read in light of epic conventions and ambitions in order to accept the full complexity of Tolson's modernism. While I am certainly proposing a teleological development in Tolson's career that can be overstated, I am nonetheless convinced that Tolson's goal as a poet remained fairly consistent throughout his career, justifying at least the modest teleology I am offering here. When seen as this big bad selfhood capable of filling gaps in diasporic culture and in the fulfillment of Western egalitarian cultural ideals, Tolson's bardic self-fashioning expands the African American bardic imagination from lyric to epic self-assertion, expressed in increasingly complex poetic structures. Believing that "wise men judge a race by its geniuses," that "no race is civilized until it produces a literature," and that "the literary epic is the supreme achievement of a civilization" (*Caviar and Cabbage* 67), Tolson sought to write such an epic in each of his four major works—*A Gallery of Harlem Portraits* (completed in 1935 but never published in his lifetime), *Rendezvous with America* (1944), *Libretto for the Republic of Liberia* (1953), and *Harlem Gallery*. In each, Tolson tried to meld artistic innovation to the recovery and preservation of an ethnic cultural heritage as a literary embodiment of this African American cultural self. In this pursuit, he moved from a social realism modeled on Edgar Lee Masters and Carl Sandburg to a democratic romanticism inspired by Walt Whitman to the modernist allusiveness of T. S. Eliot and Ezra Pound, each of which reflected Tolson's evolving sense of the breadth of the African American self, its capacity to assert through the complexity of its distinctive cultural memory the defining commonality of human life. As he put it in manuscript notes, "Four Stages of M.B.'s poetry: / / I. concern with myself / / II. concern with my race / / III. concern with my country / / IV. concern with man."[2]

Thus, though Tolson's diasporic ideal does not emerge explicitly until the 1950s, what remains consistent is the sense that the journey from self to humanity was the defining trajectory of the epic poet and the ideal mind-set of a reader, both of which would trace the possibility of social justice from the practice and process of African American cultural self-definition. By the end of his career, Tolson's art had fertilized the aridity of the modern colonial and postcolonial wasteland with visions of a rich, culturally fertile Western African self that embodied the best possibilities of our world. That it has fallen through the cracks testifies to subtle limitations in Tolson's artistic choices that have alienated readers, to be sure. But, more important, this neglect testifies to substantive flaws in the ways in which Tolson was read. Though Tolson's social agency was ultimately limited, his verse nonetheless is largely successful in fulfilling the broadest possible manifestation of bardic genius as I have defined it in this book.

The story of Tolson's career is thus his epic journey from a fairly conventional individualist protest and "a concern with self" in his juvenilia written in his boyhood in the nation's heartland to an epic modernism and "a concern with man" that was fulfilled by the African diasporic mind. First of all, though his juvenilia are not available, it is still quite clear that Tolson began his career imagining a bardic role, even though its earliest manifestation was apolitical. Embellishing the story of his young conformist art to prove this point in "The Odyssey of a Manuscript," a posthumously published essay about the development and fate of his first collection, *A Gallery of Harlem Portraits*, Tolson wrote that as "iambic and trochaic feet pattered across my boyhood on the level uplands of Iowa," "the sinking of the *Titanic* rocketed me into a Parnassian frenzy, and I composed a ballad of twenty-five quatrains." In it, he lauded "a missionary on his way to Darkest Africa," and "taking a cue from William Cullen Bryant, I closed with a climactic apostrophe to the Deity. I was now ready for the Hall of Fame, if not for Westminster Abbey" (6–7). Scoffing at this individualism, Tolson declared, "I scorned the prosaic Jewish and Italian and Polish boys, wore a Windsor tie, and affected the mannerisms of the poets we studied" (6). In short, as Tolson said of his English teacher, "No swarthy organ grinder was ever prouder of a trick-performing monkey." This was Tolson's approach well into his adult years: "In 1932, I was a Negro poet writing Anglo-Saxon sonnets as a graduate student in an Eastern University. I moved in a world of twilight haunted by the ghosts of a dead classicism" (8). Even if Tolson is overstating the case to validate his later artistry, that dramatization would prove the point. Tolson retrospectively declares this single-minded investment in the mainstream of Western poetics to be both artistically and politically moribund, an empty bardic role predicated on a minstrel-like performance of a tradition he failed to make his own.

What gave Tolson's bardic ideal its initial substance was the idea of an epic rooted more in the realities of African American people than in the traditions and conventions of Britain—the beginnings, in other words, of this diasporic consciousness and its epic journey. Again, even the exaggerated claims Tolson makes in "The Odyssey of a Manuscript" are telling. In the essay, he recalls that he showed a sonnet called "Harlem" to a German friend who read it and said, "'It's good, damned good, but—'": "The brutal words knifed into my consciousness: 'You're like the professors. You think the only good poet is a *dead* one. Why don't you read Sandburg, Masters, Frost, Robinson? Harlem is too big, too lusty for a sonnet. Say, we've never had a Negro epic in America. Damn it, you ought to stop piddling!'" (8–9). Apparently, after this traumatic aesthetic experience, Tolson read the authors listed, in addition to all of the major Harlem Renaissance writers about whom he wrote his master's thesis at Columbia University ("Harlem Group" 121). Taking his cue from these realists, Tolson turned his attention to common language, everyday themes, and ordinary people to fulfill his emergent social consciousness. He also adapted to his own art the commitment of the Harlem Renaissance writers to a defiant romantic imagination rooted in racial experience and African American cultural heritage. Rejecting the niceties of social decorum and genteel aesthetic representation that he associated with his early art and with that of some Harlem Renaissance writers, Tolson declared, "I hear Negroes grumbling because Negro writers portray the vulgar side of Negro life. They make me think of the woman who sweeps the dirt under the bed and says 'There ain't no dirt!'" Genteel black writers need "to put some chitterlings in [their] mouth[s] and write like Dostoevsky and Dos Passos and Dreiser" (*Caviar and Cabbage* 70). Essentially, Tolson shifted his attention from the role of affecting

the aloof persona and idealist poetics of a romantic poet to the ideal of linking artistic achievement and spokesmanship to the distinctive experiences,
reality, and culture of African American people. This shift was rooted in the
social consciousness characteristic of 1930s American literature of all ethnic
traditions. This new ideal also led Tolson to the representation of all facets of
African American existence, finding in that complete complexity, rather than
in bourgeois polish and narrowness, the affirming selfhood most capable of
defying racism.

Out of this shift in consciousness come Tolson's first "Negro epic," *A Gallery
of Harlem Portraits,* in which Tolson adapted the model of Edgar Lee Masters's
Spoon River Anthology to represent, through one-poem sketches of individual
Harlem people, the cultural, social, and personal diversity and vitality of
Harlem as a representation of the race as a whole. That realism and vitality
substituted here for the ego of the poet, though it was a substitution that was
ultimately uncomfortable for Tolson and unsuccessful in the volume. In this
practice of bardship, Tolson did not combine the epic imagination with the
process of the people's cultural self-definition the way, paradoxically enough,
he would with the elitism of high modernist poetics. "Stillicho Spikes," one of
Tolson's most accomplished portraits in the volume, hints of the dialectal balance that would characterize Tolson's mature art.

> Stripped to the waist,
> His muscles gnarled like ebony cord,
> Stillicho swung his mighty pick
> As the ballad of this dusky Ulysses
> Climbed the perpendicular tenements:
>
> *John Henry said if you give me a drink*
> *I'll finish dis job befo' a cat kin wink,*
> *When Gawd made me, He made a man*
> *Who's de best steel-driver in all de lan'.*
>
> The sweat rolled down Stillicho's body,
> And the sweat rolled down his face,
> And the blurs of objects wavered before his eyes.
>
> He wiped his face with a soggy rag.
> The rise and fall of the curving pick
> matched the rhythm of his song:

John Henry worked in all kinds ov weather . . .
'Cause a workin' man cain't do no better.[3]

The poem continues on like this, with the folk song encompassing both the triumphs and the deprivations of Spikes's condition, and articulating the representative strength he has that is analogous to that of John Henry. That strength is both a celebration of African American strength and an indictment of the society that prevents a "workin' man" from doing any better. Nonetheless, Spikes also uses the tale of John Henry to keep himself mindful of the fruits of his labor: a new suit for his son's graduation, the evening time with his wife, and even the pride of the work itself. In Tolson's poem, this character becomes a realistic folk hero in his own right, a unification of John Henry and Ulysses, an African American hero and a classical giant, a good neighbor and a budding proletarian revolutionary. The voice of the speaker balances with the omniscient voice of the poet, just as the folk culture is fruitfully if simply balanced with Greek myth. Here the journey to self-awareness is ordinary but substantive, Tolson's version of Gwendolyn Brooks's existential imagination in which individual characters make the most out of the culture that justified their isolation in poverty.

No longer the cheap tricks of an organ-grinder's monkey, the aesthetic of *A Gallery of Harlem Portraits* addresses all of the social and cultural dynamics that made Harlem a mecca and a legend, serving well Tolson's purpose of demonstrating the "genius" of the race, its presiding spirit. In this volume, Tolson is closest to the vision of vernacular cultural affirmation that dominates conceptions of the African American poetic tradition even today, as the conception of poetic genius is directly rooted in the folk culture of African American people. All of the Harlem portraits follow a pattern similar to that of "Stillicho Spikes," presenting simultaneously individualized and representative portraits that tie the diversity of the characters to the diversity of African American culture, refuting the ways in which white supremacy reduces African Americans to a monolithic mass. For example, Tolson interpolates the blues into the poem "Big Bessie" and other aspects of vernacular language in poems such as "Deacon Phineas Bloom" and "Grandma Lonigan," both of which articulate folk wisdom. Tolson also portrays characters who are based on historical figures, such as Grand Chancellor Knapp Sackville (a nationalist reminiscent of Marcus Garvey), Napoleon Hannibal Speare (comparable to W. E. B. Du Bois), and Madame Alpha Devine (similar to Madame C. J.

Walker), as well as poems that deal with passing, with violence, with poverty, and even with artist figures. Decentering the poet and rejecting romanticized or stereotypical portrayals of African Americans, Tolson posits the community realistically as its own epic narrative.

But this strict emphasis on the vernacular as somehow opposed to traditional literary achievement is a contradiction that prevents Tolson's volume from distinguishing itself enough from its proletarian models, preventing it from being published at the time. Rather than making formalist poetics an extension of the ethnic self by making the poet one with the people the way Brooks did, in other words, Tolson imposes an artistic structure on the material that is not justified by the conception either of the people or of the poetic self and that speaks to an odd, contradictory alienation of the poet from the people. It is a tension in the use of the vernacular for the construction of poetic genius that is not always acknowledged in African American literary study in general and certainly not in studies of Tolson, which tend to gloss over this volume. On one hand, Tolson's approach is predicated upon depicting the thoughts, words, and deeds of the individual characters in each poem, muting the poet's presence except as the omniscient conveyor of the characters' minds and lives, a practice that is Brooks's great artistic and political triumph in her early verse. To the extent that poems in the volume follow this model, it is successful. Yet, on the other hand, not only does Tolson call the collection a gallery of portraits, suggesting his presence as painter, but he also makes mention, in the introduction, of a Curator who collects them (Pinson 43). Moreover, the section labels—"Chiaroscuro," "Silhouettes," "Etchings," and "Pastels"—call attention to an aesthetic, not a social, structuring of a work that is ostensibly predicated on minimizing any aesthetic structure. However, the groupings of portraits in the collection offer little demonstrable or consistent variation to justify the titles of the sections. This lack of aesthetic structure and narrative development undermines Tolson's pronouncement of the "advance" of the downtrodden in a poem near the end of the book called "The Underdog," a poem that uses racial and ethnic slurs to chronicle the divisions among workers created by the privileged. The poem concludes:

Then a kike said: *Workers of the world, unite!*
And a dago said: *Let us live!*
And a cracker said: *Ours for us!*
And a nigger said: *Walk together, children!*

WE ARE THE UNDERDOGS
ON A HOT TRAIL!
                (lines 41–46)

This advance was supposed to be the ultimate result of an appreciation of the culture and unity of the common folk of Harlem, but the character sketches and gestures of aesthetic structure are parts that do not add up completely to the larger epic whole that Tolson wished to achieve. In other words, it is not enough to be close to the people, as most vernacular theories of the tradition assume, and as critics of Tolson have proffered as reasons to dismiss him. The folk cultural realism does not always provide the best models for broad visions of African American life. For Tolson that vernacular and social realism failed to provide a space large enough to unite traditional aesthetic ambition with ethnic affirmation. In effect, Tolson's construction of himself in that volume did not conform to his definition of an intelligent mind, an ideal of artistic self-constitution between the poet and his public that could not happen until Tolson adapted and transformed modernist literary techniques.

In these terms, it makes sense that Tolson offers his first version of the diasporic consciousness not by his attention to race but by his attention to "nation," a turn that led him to adapt the model of Walt Whitman's bardic voice to Tolson's own conception of American democracy in World War II and the place of African Americans in that democracy. In this way, his decision to locate African American culture in a national context allowed him greater space to unite what even he seemed to have opposed in the previous volume. In *Rendezvous with America,* Tolson's second volume and the first instance of his successful construction of this diasporic self, he used the occasion of World War II to revive aspects of Whitman's claim to assume what all others assume—the democratic meaning of the individual romantic imagination— and to adapt it to the leftist political mandates and communalist vision he claimed for himself in the early 1930s. His poetic adaptation of the democratic ideals of the nation and of the Allies to his poetic self-concept unified race and art more fully than a proletarian poetics could by locating in them a shared mode of mind, a shared set of values that were manifest in different social forms at different times but that were historically consistent with the poet's pursuit of individual distinction. With explicit allusion to Whitman in his volume's title and in a poem called "A Song to Myself," Tolson conceived of a similar representative selfhood in which the "the physical, emotional, moral, intellectual, and aesthetic Personality" of the poet could "tally" the nature of the nation (Whitman 313). For Tolson, as for Whitman, that self was simultaneously social and symbolic, imbued with the historical principles of democracy that allowed the individual poet's perceptive visions of present and future society to render that individual personality representative. In this way, as in Whitman's case, Tolson could commit himself to the poet's ego and to traditional literary achievement without being a performing minstrel and without the hints of alienation from the masses that marred *A Gallery of Harlem Portraits*. In essence, he was a black version of the Good Gray Bard, producing the terms by which Tolson and his audience could construct a mutually informing and affirming identity that made the poet both a leader of the people and one with them. And Tolson achieved this unity not with African American vernacular poetics but with his innovative versions of various traditional formalist techniques.

In the context of the World War II publication of *Rendezvous with America*, then, the construction of a collective poetic persona in "Dark Symphony," which won an award at the 1935 Negro Exposition, unites an interracial community as a nation through the racialized individuality of the poet's bardic self. In the third section of the poem, Tolson makes this bardic persona clear.

Andante Sostenuto

They tell us to forget
The Golgotha we tread . . .
We who are scourged with hate,
A price upon our head.
They who have shackled us
Require of us a song,
They who have wasted us
Bid us condone the wrong.

They tell us to forget
Democracy is spurned.
They tell us to forget
The Bill of Rights is burned.
Three hundred years we slaved,
We slave and suffer yet:
Though flesh and bone rebel,
They tell us to forget!

Oh, how can we forget
Our human rights denied?
Oh, how can we forget
Our manhood crucified?
When Justice is profaned
And plea with curse is met,
When Freedom's gates are barred,
Oh, how can we forget?[4]

Here is no Stillicho Spikes with whom the reader can identify and through whom aspects of a culture speak in some presumed objectivity or realism. Instead the poet takes on the voice of the people, shifting from the third-person omniscient voice to a first-person plural omniscience both spoken for and addressed to a collectivity of which the speaker is a part. Along with the capitalization of "Democracy," "Justice," and "Freedom," the terms of the speaker's address—the "we" and "they"—create archetypes that allow for the layering of historical eras that become the substance of the poet's method and authority. The poet can represent a people from different times and different locales in the nation by identifying the principles that can and should unite them.

In the process, the Bill of Rights becomes an emblem more meaningful than the first ten amendments of the United States Constitution alone, just as democracy becomes more than one nation's form of government. Both are abstracted into the principles or ideals of justice as they inhabit the mind and perhaps even have objective existence in the world independent of those documents. The United States is both real and potential justice here, a microcosm of the possible realization of these values in human society in general. Also, the rhetorical grandeur and the repetitiveness echo Whitman's voice and vision, including the paratactic structure of his well-known catalogs that substitutes grammatical and metaphorical parallels for rhyme and narrative. Here Tolson adopts that parallelism to traditional rhyme schemes, distinguishing himself from Whitman in order, paradoxically, to claim Whitman's voice. And this oratorical stance is enhanced by the reference to music, suggesting that this one voice encapsulates the harmony, melody, counterpoint, and other unifying structures of symphonic music. The one voice is the many, national, racial, and human, and it is, in its structure, an egalitarian prophecy. Thus, "the fundamental rhetorical strategy of 'Dark Symphony' is to project the history of black American experience as a prophecy of the fate of a nation, and, ultimately, the world" (Wilburn Williams, *Desolate Servitude of Language* 104). And Tolson does so by embracing his predecessor's inclusive attitude, optimism, and moral authority.

In "The Bard of Addis Ababa," from the same volume, Tolson makes explicit the principles by which he can link this oratorical, symphonic voice of American bardic poetry to the multicultural self of an African poet. The poem transforms Tolson's association of himself with the Ethiopian bard into a fuller definition of this diasporic self, his vision of the linkages of difference that actually hold African and Western culture on equal footing in the African and African American mind. For Tolson, the ideal bard was not Shakespeare or even Whitman but a semihistorical Ethiopian who criticized the Fascist invasion of that country in the Second World War. As I suggested in the introduction, the bard here evokes a parallel between African freedom fighting and the principles of the Allies in that war (Thomas 125). I also argued that the bard combined calls to action with personal celebrity in order to offer an inspirational prophecy analogous to the kind of poet usually celebrated in the study of African American literary culture. But what makes the poem particularly telling for Tolson's epic imagination is its conclusion in the parallel celebrations of African heroes and the bard that makes the poet as much an African as a Western cultural hero. In other words, the American poet enacts part of his rendezvous with America through the valor and validation of the African bard. On one hand, in the first stanza of its last section, the poem represents the returning soldiers.

> Along the Imperial Highway
> The heroes of Takkaze ride;
> The silver-gilt shields and knife blades
> Vie with the patriot's pride;
> And the crows in Addis Ababa
> Swirl like a surfy tide.
>
> (lines 75–80)

These heroes return triumphant to welcoming communities shining with the "patriot's pride." On the other hand, in their return, they either encounter the bard leaving Addis Ababa or see him leading their way into the city. Either way, they include the bard in their community and yield their heroism to him.

> The Imperial Highway discovers
> A great dog and a graybeard ahead.

"O Bard of Addis Ababa!"
Cry the heroes to wake up the dead.
And the Bard's face shines with a glory
No crown, no lumot can shed.

(lines 105–10)

The shine of the bard derives from both the inner vision and power of the imagination and the warm reception of the heroes. The bard's self is a weapon for justice just like the shields and blades. The bard's self is also rooted in an African tradition as much as an American one. The bard must be embraced by Ethiopia to have his shine validated. The "oratory" here is not explicitly musical, but the ballad stanza of the poet's call in the second section of the poem aligns his voice with that of the speaker in "Dark Symphony." In these terms, Tolson's enacts two call-and-response traditions, an African and an African American one, to motivate implied listeners to substantive political action.

The bard of Addis Ababa thus models Tolson's ideal for his own African American bardic personality, its unity of visually opposed cultural traditions in one song and consciousness. Rather than compromising Tolson's ideals, then, the references to Whitman substantiate his affirmative poetic identity and his own balance of East and West, his capacity to inhabit simultaneously the roles and aesthetics of the white American democratic poet and the black Ethiopian revolutionary poet. As such, Tolson's accomplishment in this work is facilitated by his traditionalism, his almost complete reliance on formal literary language, sonnet, ballad and epic conventions, and the affirmation of national rather than ethnic cultural ideals. The fact that none of the poems in the volume makes use of African American vernacular language testifies to Tolson's almost entire rejection of the method of *A Gallery of Harlem Portraits*. He writes animal fables of the African American folk in sonnets to "elevate" them, an ambivalent gesture reminiscent of the Harlem Renaissance. He turns to Pompeii instead of Harlem and to Whitman rather than his mother's stories. For what Tolson wanted to do in this volume, it worked very well. Not only did it remake Whitman for Tolson's purposes, it also allowed Tolson to remake the boundaries on poetic genius imposed by race loyalty. Though Tolson's investment in resisting race undermined to an extent the full validation of ethnic selfhood that is occasionally implicit in the volume, the result was nonetheless a flawed but substantive poetics of democracy.

Thus, not only does this conception of the bardic genius of diaspora illuminate the ambition and accomplishment of Tolson's neglected *Rendezvous with America,* it also clarifies how this turn to Anglo-American poetic models facilitated Tolson's most substantive revision both of the fetters of national identity and of the binary logic of racial authenticity that characterize the achievements of his most important work, *The Libretto for the Republic of Liberia* and *Harlem Gallery.* Tolson's ambition of ethnic bardship was not compromised by this turn to modernism, then, but was fulfilled by it, as Tolson adapted those techniques designed to reconstruct fragments of a shattered Western heritage to the unearthing and reconstructing of an ignored and repressed (and therefore shattered) African heritage. In the process, Tolson asserted that the reconfigured fragments of the African past constituted the answer to the lost sense of meaning of the Western one for all Western people, not just those of African descent. It is telling, then, that, once Tolson was made poet laureate of Liberia and was commissioned to write a poem on the occasion of that African nation's fiftieth anniversary, he transformed this Whitman-like bardic selfhood into the fullest reaches of his diasporic identity in his most complete and imitative assimilation of modernist poetic techniques. Having been granted an official bardic role, Tolson successfully navigated the potentially compromising impact of his two cultural "patrons"— Liberia and the literary canon so beholden to modernism—by using the modernist techniques to temper the celebration of Liberia and African culture and history with images of its compromised history to provide the substance of the modernist techniques. In this position, Tolson found himself to be quite analogous to the Celtic bards after British colonization, poets who were treated as inadequate and imitative poets by that imperial culture to whom they owed their livelihood and, in their own communities, treated as politically compromised lackeys. Like them, Tolson found himself co-opted by the imperial culture that disparaged them, in Tolson's case in the person and review of Allen Tate, even as he expressed aspects of his vernacular cultures. And it is this position on the margins—this liminal space of "both/and" rather than "either/or"—that constitutes the agency of Tolson's renovation of his Whitman-like bardic ideal. The result was the first full instance of Tolson's innovative and neglected diasporic consciousness and his richest public challenge of the binary logic of race that Tolson yearned to dismantle. In the process, instead of reaching back into the past to reconstruct lost culture, Tolson articulates the creation of new versions of the old certainties in the emerging African cultures exemplified by Liberia.

Tolson's first and most comprehensive adaptation of high modernist poetics, *The Libretto for the Republic of Liberia* chronicles the history of the cyclical move of Africans to the United States and back to Africa as Liberians, tracing that history as the social and historical manifestation of the diasporic consciousness that made it possible. By structuring itself as a song, a public ode organized as a single octave with eight sections from "do" to "do," the poem effectively articulates what Homi K. Bhabba theorized as the "location" of culture. It identifies the union of minds and practices that constitute the possibility and reality of this diasporic culture:

> It is in the emergence of the interstices—the overlap and displacement of domains of difference—the intersubjective and collective experiences of *nationness,* community interest, or cultural value are negotiated. How are subjects formed "in-between," or in excess of, the sum of the "parts" of difference (usually intoned as race/class/gender, etc.)? How do strategies of representation or empowerment come to be formulated in the competing claims of communities where, despite shared histories of deprivation and discrimination, the exchange of values, meanings and priorities may not always be collaborative and dialogical, but may be profoundly antagonistic, conflictual and even incommensurable? (2)

For Tolson, the Liberian mind and nation together constitute just such a locus, an enactment of such interstices, a matrix of sorts whose inner workings emulate and even motivate the course of history that made Liberia a possible resolution of antagonistic and incommensurable meaning. It is a multivoiced and egalitarian hybridity inherent in the poem's highly allusive form that fills the diasporic gaps in identity that both separate and connect Africans and African Americans in the construction of Liberia. Calling this the "deterritorialization of modernism," Aldon Nielsen compares Tolson's revision of Eliot to how Frederick Douglass learned to read and write out of his master's copy book, a gesture of imitation that is a gesture of resistance, a reclaiming by rewriting (241–42). More important, Tolson represents the cultural collaboration that produced the "strategies of representation and empowerment," which could indeed reconcile meanings that "may be profoundly antagonistic, conflictual and even incommensurable."

> My work [in the *Libretto*] is certainly difficult in metaphors, symbols and juxtaposed ideas. There the similarity between me and Eliot separated. That is only technique, and any artist must use the technique of his time.

Otherwise we would have the death of Art. However, when you look at my ideas and Eliot's, we're as far apart as hell and heaven.[5]

Using the operatic form and the elitist allusive method he derived from the models of Eliot and Pound to complicate the traditional public function of the ode, Tolson creates an African diasporic song form that articulates the centrality of the African self to African American culture in particular and Anglo-American culture in general. It also suggests the interstices of that self-constitution through the abstract meaning-making function of musical form. The result is a persuasive vision of democratic or egalitarian cultural meaning that justifies the historical prophecy with which the poem concludes. The heaven of the dialectical intelligent mind replaces the hell of an attempt to reconstruct a singular and dualistic European mind. The poet has become a world-historical bardic singer (almost literally, though the *Libretto* could hardly be sung) and the African American self has become the defining "location" of a culture of justice.

In essence, using the poetic texture as emblem of the psychological trauma of the cultural and historical antagonisms that create nations, Tolson also uses it as an emblem of the unifying social values across time and national borders that may lead Liberia to be a revision of these faulty notions of nation. The song form is crucial, because the poem is an ode of eight sections labeled by the notes of the musical scale, the first six of which detail and celebrate Liberian history and make it symbolic of all quests for freedom, while the last two articulate the dynamics of past and contemporary history in order to offer prophecies of justice in Africa and in the world. This structure calls attention to the bardic voice that sings it, attributing to that voice the knowledge and even an embodiment of the history and prophecy of which it sings. Initiating the historical cycles of the rise and fall of empires that are made to be broken by egalitarian ideals, the first section, "Do," defines Liberia as both product and rejection of this history. The section concludes:

> *Liberia?*
>
> No wasteland yet, nor yet a destooled elite,
> No merry-andrew, an Ed-dehebi at heart,
> With St. Paul's root and Breughel's cheat:
> You are
> The iron nerve of the lame and halt and blind.

Liberia and not-Liberia,
A moment of the conscience of mankind!
(lines 49–56)

Also called "*Mehr licht* for the Africa-to-be," Liberia is not the evidence of a decaying culture (Eliot's wasteland) but is an inspiration for all dispossessed people, an indication of what has been wrong with the world and what can be right. That is why it is "Liberia and not Liberia"; it is real and potential liberty, just as America was real and potential democracy in *Rendezvous with America*.

The allusions enrich the implications of this dialectic. For example, the leaders of Liberia are not yet a "destooled elite," a reference to how, on the Gold Coast, the stool is a mark of royalty and to take it away is to take away power. The reference to the iron nerve, Tolson notes, is from Tennyson's "Ode on the Death of the Duke of Wellington," a poem in part about the defeat of tyranny. Liberia will grant the marginalized and the dispossessed the nerve to act, as it will act for them. The claiming of an African aristocracy (or at least the memory of one) is juxtaposed with European pursuits of liberation, then, implying that the two are part of the same pursuit of freedom, with the paradox that an African aristocracy is necessary for an egalitarian society. Finally, the concluding line of the section about a moment of conscience, a reference to Anatole France's address at the bier of Emile Zola, thus culminates the analogy between the broader historical meaning of Liberia and the value of an artist who can spur the conscience of humankind to the ideals that Liberia allegedly represents. All of these allusions juxtapose a real Liberia with an ideal one, African leaders with European liberators, the representative African American poet with European arts, all to clarify the world-historical meaning of Liberia as an awakening of the best humane values of the Western tradition and the bardic poet as a purveyor of these values in song. This is where the octave cycle starts, with Liberia already accomplished and with its meaning established in all art, but especially the poetic consciousness of this poem.

Placing Liberia so squarely in the center of "the conscience of mankind" is the poem's first explicit rejection of the binary logic of race, its first assertion that this African and African American *décalage*—this untranslatable but nonetheless highly expressive self—constitutes the central ideal of the history of humankind. The second rejection of the West's binary logic is in the poem's assertion of how this mind reclaims the history of Africa as an original and originating history of civilization, suggesting that the just values Africans embody did not come only from resistance to colonization. In the second section, "Re," the speaker implies that the Songhai Empire preceded not only Liberia but European civilization as well, reminding readers of what they have been led to forget in their imperial or postcolonial amnesia: "The Good Gray Bard in Timbuktu chanted: / *"brow tron lo—eta ne a ne won oh gike"* (which Tolson translates as "The world is too large—that's why we do not hear everything"). The Good Gray Bard here is an amalgam of an African, Tennyson (whom Tolson mentions in his notes), Whitman, and Tolson himself.

This multicultural bard juxtaposes the various social and literary histories of our too-large world in order to validate this poet-speaker's historical memory:

> *Lia! Lia!* The river Wagadu, the river Bagana,
> Became dusty metaphors where white ants ate canoes,
> And the locust Portuguese raped the maiden crops,
> And the sirocco Spaniard razed the city-states,
> And the leopard Saracen bolted his scimitar into
> The jugular vein of Timbuktu. *Dieu seul est grand!*
>
> And now the hyenas whine among the barren bones
> Of the seventeen sun sultans of Songhai,
> And hooded cobras, hoodless mambas, hiss
> In the gold caverns of Galeme and Bambuk,
> And puff adders, hook scorpions, whisper
> In the weedy corridors of Sankore. *Lia! Lia!*
>
> The Good Gray Bard chants no longer in Timbuktu:
> "The maggots fat on the yeas and nays of nut empires."
> (lines 87–100)

The rivers of the first quoted stanza are metaphors for both the geographical locales and the passages of time in which colonialism happened. The destruction of the African empire is an emblem for all such violent rises and falls of empires, especially when partly motivated by racism. Moreover, the racist destruction of African empires had led, later in the section, to the greater crime of the historical erasure in which Africa is simply an animal safari, not a continent of many nations, and only animals "sing" of the glorious past. These voiceless animals seem to be alone in the knowledge that only God, not the works of humanity, is grand. Empires can rise and fall by all manner of plagues, including racism, greed, and colonialism, while the goodness of God (or of what God represents) is eternal. Only dedication to what is good and just and holy (a dedication Liberians possess) is the answer to this course of history. Thus, "Sol" is a long section about Elijah Johnson, the "founder" of Liberia, as he imbibes folk wisdom from African *griots* in the manner of religious litany. The section is composed almost entirely of West African proverbs. Johnson becomes the biblical type to Jehudi Ashmun, then president of Liberia, whom Tolson lionizes in "La." The poem therefore illuminates the recurring abuses of power that have made Liberia necessary and that Liberia may possibly end through this African wisdom, made manifest in the lived experiences of these descendants of both Africa and America. And the poet's multifaceted, multiethnic mind is as important for the rejection of these tyrannies as it is for the acts of the political leaders of Liberia. After all, it is the bard, not the politicians, who makes readers aware of the historical patterns of empires rising and declining, of oppression and resistance, and of the possible liberating breaks in these cycles of history represented by Liberia.

Thus, it is in the bardic poet's analysis of the compromises of the present and the prophecy for the future that Tolson validates his own epic imagination as a component of these nonbinary, Pan-African values of heroism and freedom and as an even more central and enduring enactment of these just social values. In "Ti," the first of the two deeply allusive and difficult concluding sections that end the poem, Tolson characterizes how the multicultural reality of the world is ignored to preserve the power of the few and casts his poetic persona in the role of the American Jeremiah, a prophet called to identify how citizens of the United States are not living up to their ideals. In the third stanza, for example, he makes explicit the power dynamics involved in cultural production as they affect the workings of the human mind.

All cultures
walk hard
fall,
flout
under class under
Lout,
enmesh in ethos, in *masoreth,* the poet's flesh,
intone the Mass of the class as the requiem of the mass,
serve *adola mentis* til the crack of will,

castle divorcee Art in a blue-blood moat,
read the flesh of grass
into the bulls and bears,
let Brahmin pens kill
Everyman the Goat,
write Culture's epitaph in *Notes* upstairs.

(lines 303–17)

Centered on the page, these balanced and parallel syllabic lines suggest a symbolic center and symmetry in aesthetic meaning that will embody the center of the social and historical meaning Tolson hopes to convey. They also imply a descent, especially in the first part of this stanza in which lines are constituted by one word. While each line has self-contained organization of repetition, assonance, and consonance in addition to the largely syllabic structure, they combine to contribute to the visual image of the stanza pouring its substance from the top of the page to the bottom.

The ordered disorder of the form is thus a contrast to the way "Culture" can be entirely reduced, distorted, and disordered in order to support the established and fully disorganized hierarchy of racial binaries and religious institutions. For example, the Catholic Mass maintains the authority of the few over the mass, whether by justifying colonialism or by advocating political passivity for the dispossessed as an alleged but false version of heavenly patience. The rhyme of "mass" and "class" and the repetition of "Mass" in the lowercase "mass" reveal the aesthetic balance that contrasts with the historical imbalance this stanza envisions. This enduring pattern of institutional hierarchy is what Liberia and the poet's artistry will resist. As such, Liberia becomes more and more an abstract ideal rather than an actual nation, a poetic device through which the bardic poet articulates the proper mind-set, which Liberia represents. This mind-set, not the celebration of this specific nation, is the ultimate ideal of the poem.

Moreover, the poem clarifies how its difficult form is more allied with those ideals that Liberia represents than other aspects of so-called high culture, including its own elitist origins in high modernism, a distinction that, while compromised, does ultimately ring true. Tolson's modernism is not an oppressive institution such as the Church nor is it entirely his surrender to that oppressive cultural institution, the Western canon. In fact, this section of the poem reveals how the Good Gray Bard is fettered and potentially compromised by the forms of culture by which those ideal values are expressed but ultimately triumphs in his/its embodiment of an alternative history and set of values. In a moment of self-critique, Tolson points out that writing culture into "*Notes* upstairs" destroys it. During the writing of the *Libretto,* Tolson even published "The Man of Halicarnassus," a poem that examines Herodotus's laureate role for Athens, like Tolson's laureate role for Liberia, and his potential compromise of his art in order to fulfill that responsibility. Like so much else in history, even the poet can be used to reinforce negative political power, and may even wittingly do so to make a living. The passage concludes: "*O Cordon Sanitaire,* / thy brain's tapeworm, extract, thy eyeball's mote! / *Selah!*" (lines 318–20). Perhaps culture is not such an ideal alternative to tyranny after all, and certainly the Jeremiah must recognize the mote in his own eye before he can critique others' angle of vision. Aware of the pitfalls of his own investment in linkages of difference, in other words, Tolson recognizes that his vision of diaspora is potentially as hierarchical and oppressive as the modernism he is trying to revise, especially in this difficult modernist form. And it is my contention that this self-critique is more effective than scholars recognize. As with the rest of the bardic tradition, then, the poet's investment in this culture provides the paradoxical power for this Jeremiah to extricate himself from the worst of the culture in which he is otherwise enmeshed.

In essence, the poem does suggest how art can change history. It does so through the represented mind of the poet, because the complexity of that mind, revealed even in its compromises, provides an alternative of cultural heritage to the reductive binary logic by which ethnic traditions are separated and hierarchies of culture are created. As such, the difficulty of the poem is not, in Tolson's mind, opposed to the folk, because, first of all, he believes that everyone can learn to read it and, secondly, the poem's complexity should reflect the complexity of the African American mind, including the diasporic mind of the folk. "Away with the simple Negro!" as Tolson put it. Thus, at the end of "Ti," after outlining the horrors of human history attributable to cyclical abuses of power, including the hierarchies reinforced by "Culture," Tolson's complex "Negro" bard suggests, in part, that

> the ferris wheel
> of race, of caste, of class
> dumped and alped cadavers till the ground
> fogged the Pleiades with Gila rot.
>
> (lines 472–75)

At the same time, he argues that

> the Beast with a Maginot Line in its Brain,
> the staircase Avengers of base alloy,
> the *vile canaille*—*Gorii!*—the *Bastard-rasse*

and its nine other allusive and ironically disparaging names

> ride the merry-go-round!
> *Selah*!
> (lines 476–78, 485–86)

The divisions of race, caste, and class ("idols of the tribe," as Tolson calls them, following Bacon) have led to piles of dead bodies whose rot has blocked the view of the stars. Tyranny kills beauty as it kills people.

Nonetheless, according to this Jeremiah, the many-named and universally despised masses are described as being more egalitarian and are ordered to get on the merry-go-round of history. As Tolson put in a "Caviar and Cabbage" column of October 19, 1940, called "The Merry-Go-Round and the Ferris Wheel of History": "Have you ever looked philosophically at a Ferris wheel? The car-riders go up—and come down. No particular car stays at the top. Why? because the giant power-driven wheel is always turning. Now, follow me. The Ferris Wheel of History turns on the axis of Time. Rome was at the top 2,000 years ago; today Germany occupies the top seat in Europe. Tomorrow—another conqueror, of course" (*Caviar and Cabbage* 90). Though this lesson of history is obvious according to Tolson, "a ruling class never learns anything from the downfall of other ruling classes," including the fact that "racial superiority and class superiority produced the hellish contraption called the Ferris Wheel of History. Democracy will produce the Merry-Go-Round of History" (92). In order to get to this merry-go-round, the masses must defy invading cultural forces who are seeking a way around the Maginot Line in the brain, that part of their minds given over to hierarchy through the social construction of their individual and collective subjectivity.

And the difficulty of this poem does just that by challenging that complacency. It forces the effort of reading that pushes beyond those internalized and automatic responses. By defending their own minds against elite culture through the version of elite culture the poem claims is of the masses, the mass can reject the many insulting names that the elite have bequeathed to them and resist such power as the Mass has and thereby become democratic in theory and practice.

In other words, Tolson is an artistic elitist, who paradoxically accepted a cultural hierarchy based on presumed universal values of art in order to link high artistic achievement by black people to the erasure of social hierarchy. While this paradox cannot work entirely in the social world, it works quite effectively in the aesthetic structuring of the poem, which is, after all, where the social agency of any poem would be. Thus, the musical scale is again the central source of this empowering conception of the bard and this attempt to associate this complex modernism with the minds of the masses of dispossessed people. The musical scale can be seen either as a progression upward and downward like the Ferris wheel, with each "Do" bringing a new hierarchy, or it can be a level cycle, an equalizing merry-go-round, since "Do" and "Do" are the same note. This tension in the meaning of the musical scales provides a means to question other modes of institutionalized meaning and to side with the complexity and mutability of music and poetry over the falsely stable meanings that nations institutionalize.

Ultimately, Tolson validates the meaning of his poem as an alternative to the problems it raises by validating the antinationalist implications of its relationship to music. In the sixth stanza of "Do," the "she-fox today" says,

> naïfs pray for a guido's scale of good and evil to match
> worldmusic's sol-fa syllables (*o do de do de do de*)
>> worldmathematics' arabic and roman figures
>> worldscience's greek and latin symbols
>>> the letter killeth five hundred global tongues
>>> before esperanto garrotes voläpuk *vanis vanitatum.*
>>>> (lines 517–22)

The craftiness of the status quo can baffle and confuse. About the pursuit of a scientific basis for morality that Tolson, like his modernist and New Critical peers, despised, this passage questions notions of universal ordering principles, from math to science to a common language. Western logocentrism and literacy destroy thousands of nonliterate languages—those of non-Western oral cultures especially, as those cultures were colonized—and science serves as a poor morality, since it implies no fellow feeling and fails to acknowledge the simultaneous historicity and universality of human experience. What is the value of the musical scale as an ordering principle, then, especially as it is mirrored in Lear's lunatic "*do de do*"? Perhaps "worldmusic" does have the universal ordering of the musical scale, an ordering that is not scientific and for which there is no match in scientific morality. Or is it another powerless, wandering king, a hierarchy that masks the social construction of its meaning?

By comparing this music to the sections of his poem, Tolson implies that the music of the world, like the old music of the spheres, sings of harmonious interactions more true and just than those allegedly explained by science or any other socially constructed form of meaning. Perhaps it is not mere lunacy to believe so. In these terms, the poem claims, Tolson's vision of history, because it is modeled on music, is more substantive than any of these other attempts at order because it is a harmony of many voices rather than the privileging of one. As in the choric strophe, antistrophe, and epode of the Pindaric ode, the opera, with its many singing parts, works for Tolson as a communal celebration. As such, the musical scale should lead to a harmony of voices of the ages rather than the dictatorship of a soloist, as Tolson suggests in a note to this passage. Music—and all that it represents: the will to expression, beauty, complementarity, poetry—is the ideal model of historical meaning. In this ways, the song of this Jeremiah moves through the culture in which it is fettered to derive from that culture the terms to articulate its possible alternative.

Thus, in "Do," the hinge between the potential despair of the she-fox's observations and Tolson's more optimistic prophecy of African unity is a brief section of questions the answers to which only the bardic consciousness seems to know. The possibility of the merry-go-round rather than the Ferris wheel of history is based upon the literary illumination that can motivate the proper use of human agency.

> Tomorrow . . . O . . . Tomorrow,
> Where is the glory of the *mestizo* Pharaoh?
> The Mahdi's tomb of the foul deed?
> Black Clitus of the fatal verse and Hamlet's arras?
> The cesspool of the reef of gold?
> *Der Schwarze Teufel*, Napoleon's savior?
> The Black Virgin of Creation's Hell Hole?
> Tomorrow . . . O . . . Tomorrow,
> Where is Jugurtha the dark Iago?
> The witches Sabbath of sleeping sickness?
> The *Nye ke mi* eyeless in the river of Blood?
> The Tagus that imitates the Congo?

The *Mein Kampf of kitab al suden wa'lbidan?*
The black albatross about the white man's neck?
O Tomorrow,
Where is the graven image *pehleh* of *Nash Barin?*
Their white age of their finest hour?
The forged minute book of ebony Hirsch?
The chattel whose Rock vies with the Rime of the upstart Crow?
Ppt. knows.

(lines 553–72)

Essentially wondering if the future holds more of the same as the past of "Ti"
and the present of the she-fox, the stanza provides for the reader an opportunity to change the course of history, if the reader is perceptive enough to know
that, for instance, a "*mestizo* Pharaoh," a mixed-race tyrant, is no better than
a "racially pure" tyrant. The stanza conveys a distinct fear that history will repeat itself much in the manner of the Ferris wheel, even once the masses take
control. Trying to peer into the future, the voice realizes that perhaps only
William Blake knows, since the refrain of "Tomorrow" is a reference to Blake's
"The Bard," as Tolson tells us in the note, and to Goethe's *Faust* ("Enough, the
poet is not bound by time"). With a reference to a Shakespeare line about the
immortality of poetry, Tolson's speaker claims for itself a bardic, prophetic
authority similar to "The Bard of Addis Ababa," as if it knows the answers to
these questions, and offers those answers in the rest of "Do." In other words,
we must turn to artists, especially this African American diasporic consciousness, rather than historians or scientists for answers to historical order and to
our future. The poem goes on boldly to prophesy the merry-go-round of history in the "Futurafrique" and the "Parliament of African People," and to
posit the visionary who sees this as an authoritative bard, whose voice(s), if
heard, can make this prophecy a reality. It will be manifest in the poem's "Parliament of African Peoples," which Tolson derived from his expectation that
African nations would gain independence from colonial powers soon and
lead the world's people of color in throwing off colonial rule and installing a
true worldwide democracy. Though he seems to have been wrong so far about
African nations leading democratic movements, Tolson was not wrong to
imagine that the answer to the horrors of the past is the perceptive, prophetic
music of the Pan-African historical and poetic consciousness.

Harlem Gallery is Tolson's most important poem because it most fully the-
orizes and enacts his celebration of the artistic self as the ideal political leader

and the artistic construction of meaning as the agency of resignification (the rewriting of meaning) through which African nations would redefine nationhood in the "black Atlantic mind." Even more than *Libretto*, this poem claims to be an epic and self-reflexively defines the terms of its own ideal art while practicing those principles. Though a bit out of step with the modernists, many of whom had died by the time it was published, and African American literary culture, which had become nationalist at the time, the poem traces the personal intellectual journey of the Curator of the title gallery in order to demonstrate how usually elitist ideals of art, represented by the Curator, can effectively be married to the folk heritage and social purpose of African American literary culture. In this way, Michael Berube is correct: the neglect of Tolson's poem has less to do with the poem itself than with interpretations of its historical position. In the process of theorizing these terms, Tolson has the Curator come to conclusions close to his own about the inevitability and antiracist power of modernist art in order to invite readers to transform their perception of African American art from marginal culture to the canonical center of Western culture, and African peoples from marginalized savages to mainstream cultural esquires. More than the simple assimilation it seems to be, the poem seeks to identify the unifying principles of all art in order to identify the value of producing and collecting art by African American people as a means of social inclusion. Also, though its neglect contradicts my claim about the poem's actual agency, I still insist that the terms of its neglect constitute its ongoing challenge to our literary culture. Its claim that universal values of art are what make African American art a seed of social revolution and the neglect of that claim testify more to the entrenched nature of the ideological hegemony of white supremacy than to the aesthetic coherence and effectiveness of Tolson's poem.

Transforming racial alienation into ethnic self-affirmation, the poem reveals how an idealistic, universalist modernist art—Tolson's own—is not only one of the most powerful components of the antiracist struggle for freedom, it is also paradoxically the most powerful means of constructing an affirming ethnic self. *Harlem Gallery* therefore brings to full fruition the diasporic self and prophecy of cultural and political unity of Tolson's career. Read in light of such playful African American cultural practices as hip hop, Tolson's poem becomes an example of the full possibilities of the postmodern performance of racist social codes in order to undermine them that scholars like Kimberly Benston celebrate. As Benston suggests about a performance of comedian Dick Gregory, Tolson's poem uses its "hyperbolic and parodic adherence to institutional order" in order to suggest that "the wit and irony of performance could supplant the classifying norms of sanctioned writing" (2). Because of the seriousness of Black Nationalism and the backlash of the legacy of New Criticism against that nationalism, scholars have not fully recognized Tolson's wit nor how he supplants the "classifying norms" of mainstream literary culture by imagining an artistic ideal embodied in an ethnic mind. The recourse to the historical narrative by which Tolson was neglected shows how fully this supplanting performance does indeed enact the contradictions of the literary culture it embraces (Berube 193). Analyzing the poem contradicts that historical narrative and, though I cannot do full justice to this epic in these pages, I can demonstrate its central narrative of individual intellectual transformation, the constitution of the "intelligent mind" that makes *Harlem Gallery* a port well worth the cruise.

The poem opens with several sections of the title Curator meditating on his ideal of art, a process through which Tolson establishes the problems in the Curator's mind about the political value of those universal ideals that the poem will seek to solve. Alluding to canonical aesthetic philosophies and ideal artists, the Curator tells himself that such great art is separate from social concerns, is created by geniuses, and therefore may not exist at all in the race-conscious art of Harlem, making his job as Curator of the Harlem Gallery potentially a waste of time. But he also suggests that such self-sufficient independent art would paradoxically initiate the "people's dusk of dawn" in Harlem. Such apolitical art would be just what Harlem needs. One source of his discomfort is clear:

> Like ironstone in its bed
> or a fixed idea in the head
> spin of a Ph. D.,
> I am pegged as an ex-professor of Art

so that

> *Ex* sets me in my status: *formerly*
> *but not now;*
> and quoth the Raven, "Nevermore!"
> ("Beta," lines 82–85, 93–95)

Fired presumably for some incompatibility with his bosses about what art to display and resolved to remain independent of such social concerns, the Curator turns to the Harlem Gallery because he need only choose the art he believes to be truly artistic. He believes therefore that "not even a godling ism of Art rises up to bow to, / nor a horseshoe bias perches above the door" ("Beta," lines 97–98). But Tolson is implicitly acknowledging that this idealism is in itself political and traces the Curator's gradual realization of the social meaning of his ideals of art, especially when manifest in African American society. The Curator thus comes to realize that the social value of artistic self-definition makes for enduring art. Thus, in the end, he comes to exemplify the ambivalent, self-contradictory diasporic consciousness defined so much more explicitly in *Libretto*.

The Curator's ideals of art are socially meaningful, the poem implies, because they are historically consistent manifestations of the best acts and values that humans have to offer. Those enduring ideals resist inimical social ideologies, the "godling isms" that have excluded African American artists and the Curator himself from the artistic and cultural mainstream. The Curator thus models himself after the artists themselves, who do not succumb to outside pressure, even in the fight for social justice:

> As serpents, sly,
> The Lost, The Bright, The Angry, The Beat
> (tongues that tanged bees in the head around the clock)
> did not stoop the neck to die
> like a dunghill cock.
> ("Beta," lines 126–30)

These generations of artists, each rooted in its own time, shared the desire for expression and a rejection of the limited ideas of their society. By getting closest to the heart and soul of truth, the artist reveals the limits of social convention and the socially and historically unifying power of the imagination.

> Who knows, *without no,*
> the archimedean pit and pith of man?
> (Ask the Throttler at Giza!)
> But if one seeks the nth verisimilar,
> go to Ars by the way of Pisgah:
> as the telescope of Galileo

deserted the clod to read the engirdling idioms of the star,
>> to the ape of God,
>>> go!

>>>> ("Beta," lines 7–15)

Tolson's Curator suggests that art provides a greater sense of humanity and truth than any other cultural form, as truth-seekers must go "to the ape of God," the human creator whose visions are substantial if lesser mimics of the divine creation of the world. Art illuminates the human heart in much the same way science clarifies the laws of the physical world. Believing that artists produce portraits of transcendent truth, the Curator suspects, like so many critics, that an art about the "pit and pith of man" cannot be about racial identity. As a result, he fears that a Harlem art may be a contradiction in terms.

These tensions between art, artists, and curators on one hand and the social world, race politics, and viewers on the other hand actually lead the Curator to become a man at odds with himself, and it is the reconciliation of the Curator's double consciousness that testifies to the power of art to unify. It also exemplifies the ideal epic imagination that Tolson has sought to articulate and to embody from the beginning of his career. The Curator's first impulse, stated in the very opening stanza of the poem, is to hope that "The Harlem Gallery, an Afric pepper bird, / awakes me at a people's dusk of dawn" and that "In Africa, in Asia, on the day / of Barricades, alarm birds bedevil the Great White World, / a Buridan's ass—not Balaam's—between no oats and hay" ("Beta," lines 1–2, 13–15). Perhaps there is great art in Harlem that is a wake-up call to artistic innovation and to racial self-definition, and an end to the colonialism of the "Great White World," an artistic popular uprising like the day of the Barricades, which removed a French king.

But, unfortunately, the Curator is not sure that there is such an art or that it can have such an effect: "Black Boy, O Black Boy, / is the port worth the cruise?" The opening section, "Alpha," concludes,

Although the gaffing *"To ti?"* of the Gadfly girds
>> the I-ness of my humanness and Negroness,
>>> the clockbird's
>>> jackass laughter
>>> in sun, in rain,
>>> at dusk of dawn,

> mixes with the pepper bird's reveille in my brain,
> where the plain is twilled and the twilled is plain.
>
>   ("Alpha," lines 43–51)

Though Socratic dialectics actually "gird" his sense of an African American and a human self in a synthesis of presumed opposites, the Curator is not sure that the dialectics of "Negroness" and humanness can produce a truly artistic "I," despite the evocative shape of this stanza. In other words, though the Curator is worried that dialectics do not synthesize but merely confuse the oppositions, making twill plain and the pepper bird into a clockbird, Tolson's poem suggests through its centered structure and the shape of this stanza that these very dialects are what make the "I" what it is. The "I" is the process and product of the questioning of itself. So though the alarm birds at the beginning of the poem may actually be the laughing clockbird that sings at both dusk and dawn, confusing reveille with dirge and mocking the pretensions of an artistic renaissance, what seems more likely is that the pursuit of a resolution to this question produces an affirming "I."

This self-doubt is this epic's heroic flaw, a faulty idealist individualism that leads potentially to a lack of will, a passive acceptance of the logic of race. That idealism spurs the Curator to his epic journey. And because of his illuminating experiences, the Curator overcomes this flaw, rejecting the tragic possibilities the poem evokes. Quoting "the Amharic eunuch's voice," the Curator first disparages his own abilities by quoting an aphorism that, he believes, he fails to achieve:

> "Great minds require of us a reading glass;
>   great souls a hearing aid."
>   But I,
>   in the shuttlebox world,
>   again and again,
>   have both mislaid.
>
>   ("Beta," lines 46–51)

After making an excuse for his perceived incompetence, the Curator then minimizes his role to justify both his taste for a certain kind of art and his potential inaction:

> In the drama *Art,*
> with eye and tongue,

> I play a minor vocative part
>
> . . . .
>
> So none shall censure me

because "I lost my sight and voice to the vanity of the Uppermost" ("Beta,"
lines 52–54, 61). With the classic pun on vanity, Tolson's Curator defends his
commitment to his ideals of a transcendent art and his resistance to social activism, suggesting that such a commitment excuses any lack of action, and
may in fact even necessitate that inaction. In other words, though his search
for the "Uppermost" may be futile, he must remain true to his calling, which
Tolson implies to be an abdication of the social responsibility paradoxically
tied to the pursuit of the "uppermost." But since curators have much smaller
roles than artists and since art is not social anyway, the Curator can justify his
withdrawal from activism. In this way, Tolson frames the logic of his own imitative beginnings and the defining potential problem of the African American bardic poet as I have been defining it in this book.

The rest of the poem traces the Curator's development of the awareness of
the dialectical mind that he already has in order to rethink the binary logic by
which he defined the social meaning of art in the beginning of the poem. It
also reveals how the texture of Tolson's poem validates this evolution and attributes to Tolson himself the ideal to which the Curator turns at the end of
the poem. With the Curator's journey, Tolson provides a model for the
reader's pursuit of a similar dialectical thought as both reader and character
encounter various dialectically opposed artist figures through which Tolson
creates the synthesis that both sustains and justifies *Harlem Gallery*. In the
process, Tolson validates the political idealism of his modernist artistry and
his ambivalent Curator by rejecting the creation of a monolithic black self that
would oppose itself to this model of poetic creation. He creates instead a hybrid self that incorporates the best of both Western and African American cultural traditions, including important references to African culture.

From his first encounter in the poem, a visit to painter John Laugart in
"Zeta," then, the Curator learns that even an artist committed to independence from the social world can create an independent, self-sufficient work of
art that offers a trenchant social commentary.

> My thoughts tilted at the corners like long Nepalese eyes,
> I entered, under the Bear, a catacomb Harlem flat
> (grotesquely vivisected like microscoped maggots)

> where the caricature of a rat
> weathercocked in squeals
> to be or not to be
> and a snaggle-toothed toilet
> grumbled its obscenity.
> The half-blind painter,
> spoon-shaped like an aged parrot-fish,
> hauled up out of the ruin of his bed
> and growled a proverb in Yiddish.
> ("Zeta," lines 1–12)

First of all, since Laugart's isolation leads to extreme poverty, the Curator's "to be or not to be" becomes a life-or-death situation rather than merely the naïve, abstracted dilemma about the relationship between race and art with which the Curator starts the poem. As Houston Baker observed in *Modernism and the Harlem Renaissance,* his definition of the ethnically distinctive "modernist" practices, African American artists do not have the luxury of worrying about the lost "old certainties": "Without food for thought, all modernist bets are off" (10). While Tolson does not believe that modernist bets are off, he does recognize that different social circumstances produce different investments in the modernist literary problems and ideals. A flat vivisected into too-small units by a slum lord; an unhealthy rat merely a caricature of a rat; a ruin of a bed: these are the social conditions attendant upon the isolated African American artist and are therefore more pressing issues than the false concern of whether or not to be an artist concerned with race.

However, even in these impoverished circumstances, Laugart creates a work of art that represents the ideal that quality art "transcends" its circumstances not by being outside the social world but by being a self-contained, coherent entity. It nonetheless challenges social codes and conventions. Laugart asserts,

> A work of art
> is an everlasting flower
> in kind or unkind hands;
> dried out,
> it does not lose its form and color
> in native or in alien lands

and says that "'I shall never sell / mohair for alpaca / to ring the bell'" ("Zeta," lines 59–64, 137–39). Though his drinking may demonstrate the wasteland of culture and the lack of will that sap his art ("perhaps this bootleg liquor eclipses my will / as dram steps on the heels of dram" [lines 135–36]), Laugart remains dedicated to his intellectual independence and to an ideal art independent of the marketplace. Thus, his isolation and independence come at a cost to the person, allowing Tolson to criticize the stereotype of the romantic artist isolated from the world in a garret. And he also criticizes the idea that African American artists have to be so concerned with race politics that they cannot deal with the "modernist bets" of the fundamental constitution of Western culture and the place of the culture in social organization. In effect, Tolson constructs the Curator to be a figure for his reader and attributes to the Curator the racial stereotypes and conceptions of art that Tolson considers to be inimical to the social health and expressive tradition of African American people.

As a result, Laugart's painting functions in the poem as a contradiction to the Curator's apolitical notion of the role of independent artistry in society. It is not predicated on anything romantic about isolation, nor is it ignorant about the social cost of artistic independence. In looking over Laugart's "Black Bourgeoisie," the Curator muses that

> Perhaps the isle of Patmos
> was like this
> *here emerges the imago*
> *from the impotence of the chrysalis*
> *in the dusk of a people's dawn.*

He goes on:

> *this,* somehow, a synthesis
> (savage—sanative)
> of Daumier and Gropper and Picasso.
> As a Californian, I thought *Eureka;*
> but as Ulfilas to the Philistines I said,
> "Oh!"
> ("Zeta," lines 33–37, 44–49)

The painting *Black Bourgeoisie* was the black butterfly emerging from the chrysalis like the dawning of the Harlem Gallery itself, as Laugart, a lone prophet in his Patmos slum, provides a challenge to the Philistines that is not merely an aesthetic one:

> Although
> the regents of the Harlem Gallery are as eye-
> less as knitting needles, *Black Bourgeoisie*
> retching foulness like Goya's etching
> *She Says Yes to Anyone*
> will wring from their babbitted souls a Jeremian cry!
> ("Zeta," lines 50–55)

Prophetic, Laurgert makes his most powerful commentary against the black bourgeoisie by incorporating Western artists who have been commodified as status symbols for that bourgeoisie, and by using them to reject that commodification of art. The artists themselves would never "say yes to everyone" for the sake of financial gain, a point of hypocrisy in the bourgeoisie that the painting seems to point out to its viewer. Like his life, Laugart's painting reveals the cost to selfhood caused by a failure to validate both the distinctive experiences in heritage and the common Western values of the African American self, especially in the face of the compromising commodification of culture in capitalism. The prostitution of capitalism is made evident by art that rejects such compromise. Here is the first lesson in the social value of art that declares its independence.

As such, the painting prepares the way for Dr. Obi Nkomo's more social view of art in the next section, "Eta," an alternative to the Curator's pessimistic elitism that more neatly ties together the paradox that the social independence of art constitutes a central component of its agency of social commentary. An African freed from the particular anxieties of African American double consciousness and a former participant in African freedom struggles, Dr. Nkomo declares, "'The lie of the artist is the only lie / for which a mortal or a god should die'" ("Eta," lines 24–25). Nkomo asks,

> "Curator of the Harlem Ghetto, what is a masterpiece?
> A virgin or a jade,
> the *vis viva* of an ape of God,
> to awaken one,
> to pleasure one—
> a way-of-life's aubade."
> ("Eta," lines 93–97)

Whether virginal, pure, and independent of society as the Curator hopes, or a jade sullied somehow by grosser concerns as Laugart's painting is, a masterpiece is the dawning of a new way of life through aesthetic sensibility, and it announces that the dusk of dawn is actually the beginning of the day and not the end. It is the living face—*vis viva*—of the "ape of God," and thus the living visage of all humankind. Its social function is to awaken people to social commonality, the cultural union through antiestablishment imagery. Laugart's painting is a version of Tolson's own masterpiece, then, and it initiates the Curator's education by confirming Nkomo's perspective.

In essence, with Nkomo as the "alter ego" to the Curator, the poem posits these two figures as components of the balanced African American "intelligent" mind that is Tolson's ideal and that he claims to be his own mind. The presence and thinking of Nkomo thus provides the social scientist's antithesis to the Curator's extreme aesthetic individualism. For example, unlike the Curator, who at first despairs of the possibility of art emerging from artists living in poverty, Nkomo believes in positive social and cultural potential in all people everywhere. For him, the universals of artistic beauty and truth and the cultural aspects of identity are interrelated due to a biological and sociological relativity. According to Nkomo,

> "since virtue has no Kelvin scale,
> since a mother breeds
> no twins alike,
> since no man is an escape running wild from
> self-sown seeds—
> then, no man,
> judged by his biosocial identity
> in toto
> can be,
> a Kiefekil or a Tartuffe,
> an Iscariot or an Iago."
>
> ("Eta," lines 72–82)

Arguing against a scientific scale for human behavior and human essence as Tolson did in the *Libretto,* Nkomo identifies the social construction of racial identity that challenges the very possibility of a pure artistic individualism, a conception that is a poetic version of Tolson's ideal of "tridimensionality." Since virtue has no science, since no person can truly be self-made, given the influence of social forces, and since even twins are not completely alike, Nkomo rejects the idea of social or cultural purity of the sort that leads to white supremacy, cultural nationalism, or the quasi-modernist withdrawal from society into "pure" art that the Curator seems to advocate. Nkomo believes that the best of culture, experience and expression can be everywhere because it is always created in the crucible of social forces. Nkomo declares that "Hubris is an evil the Greeks / boned and fleshed to wear the mask" and that "Pride is the lust- / sinewed wench the churchman speaks / of first in the table of Deadly Sins." Given these egalitarian principles, "Doctor Nkomo's *All hail to Man* / was a vane on the wing / to winnow the grain / in person, place and thing" ("Eta," lines 44–45, 47–49, 50–53). Rather than hubris or pride, Nkomo preferred to pursue commonality—the "grain in person, place and thing." That equality of possibility therefore argues against a pure hierarchy of talent and suggests that the value of art is almost entirely social. The most valuable art for Nkomo is that which provides terms for a way to live.

Thus, both the Curator and Nkomo are after the "uppermost" in art, which, for both of them, is the defining commonality of humankind, with each filling the diasporic "gap" in the other's thinking. But because his vision of this commonality is rooted in analysis of the dynamics of the social, Nkomo can understand how art in Harlem can be a dawning of a new age, declaring what seems to be Tolson's own ideal, at least in part, of the social value of art.

> "Life and Art," said Doctor Nkomo, "beget incestuously
>   (like Osiris and Isis)
>   the talented of brush and pen.
>   Artistic instinct draws
>   on a rock in the Kalahari Desert,
>   a crocodile for Bush-born men.
>   Without Velasquez and Cranach,
>   what would Picasso be?
>   or Leger without Poussin?
> Or Amedeo Modigliani without Sandro Botticelli?"
>   ("Omicron," lines 1–10)

Not only does life motivate and indulge "artistic instinct" ("When a caveman painted a rubric / figure of his mate with a gritstone, / Eros conquered Thanatos"), but each artist provides a precursor for the next artist, in both a living and an artistic example. No artist is self-made, in other words, and each genius has a social explanation that levels his or her distinction with that of others produced by the same cultural history.

This social emphasis, a hint of Tolson's interest in socialist thought, provides a meaningful contrast to the Curator's fear that, even if art could offer social commentary and be great art, such art could not actually create conditions for social change. But, according to Nkomo, if one artist can motivate another in life and art, then this dynamic must also account for the effect such art can have on the rest of its audience. In "Kappa," Tolson describes Harlem Gallery regent Guy Delaporte's encounter with Laugart's painting:

> before the *bete noire* of John Laugart's
> *Black Bourgeoisie*
> Mr. Guy Delaporte III takes his stand,
> a wounded cape buffalo defying every thing and Everyman.
> ("Kappa," lines 42–45)

The Curator laments, "On its shakedown cruise, / the *Black Bourgeoisie* runs aground / on the bars of the Harlem blues," as if the painting did not have its proper effect on Delaporte (lines 74–76). In response,

> Dr. Nkomo quicks the quid of an analogy:
> "This work of art is the dry compound
> fruit of the sandbox tree,
> which bursts with a loud report
> *but* scatters its seeds quietly."
> ("Kappa," lines 77–81)

In this formulation, art affects its audience beyond a mere private interaction, and beyond the initial responses. The implication is that Delaporte's rage demonstrates that the social seeds of Laugart's painting have been planted. The poem thus characterizes the challenge the poem offers to the Delaporte-like sensibility of most readers of the poem, most of whom seek to have art by African Americans fit preconceived notions either of rejecting racial difference or being about that difference exclusively. Thus, Nkomo can argue that artist and critics must be active, pointing out to the Curator that, among other things and in essence, "The bane of the hinterland, / as well as the outland, / is the mirage of the Status Quo" ("Kappa," lines 57–59). Since change is inevitable, including change in the meaning of art, the critic must help the viewer to cultivate the antihierarchical seeds of artistic meaning that have been planted so quietly. Given the interaction between the social world with the world of art, art can affect the world as much as the world affects art. Curators and critics have to be legitimate intercessors. There is no excuse for the Curator's self-justifying inaction. For Tolson, this combination of American idealism and African communal and militant politics justifies the idea of art in general and his epic poem in particular, especially the elitist poetics. These categories are a bit reductive, but they operate for Tolson as opposed components of one unified artistic ideal.

Having established these dialectical terms of the value of art and the ideal artistic consciousness in the Curator's and Nkomo's philosophy, Tolson offers a long narrative section that synthesizes these poles into a rejection of nationalism and an affirmation of the avant garde as the expression of the African American diasporic mind. If the Curator, in his rage to be blameless, abdicates his social role, then, in his rage to end all hierarchy, Nkomo—the African—rejects the idea of genius, for Tolson a flaw in his otherwise admirable worldview. Tolson offers a third foil, the "people's poet" Hideho Heights, who enters the poem, bringing with him the specifics of race politics, the fallibility of critics, and the consequences of social relativity that Nkomo's ideals raise and that the Curator's seeks to downplay. Heights announces himself: "From the mouth of the Harlem Gallery / came a voice like a / ferry horn in a river of fog":

> "Hey man, when you gonna close this dump?
> Fetch highbrow stuff for the middlebrows who
> don't give a damn and the lowbrows who ain't hip!
> Think you're a little high-yellow Jesus?"
>   ("Lambda," lines 1–7)

This assertion articulates the class distinction between the Curator and Heights that underlies their approaches to art. But though class distinctions are central to Tolson's critique of the apolitical elitism of his own modernist poetics, this section of the poem ultimately suggests that the avant garde that will emerge from the lower-class African American culture looks a lot like his own. Heights is the crystallization of the false dilemma of "to be or not to be a Negro," as Tolson implies that such class and race politics are the worst limitation to a substantive political art for African American people.

As Heights takes the Curator to the Zulu Club, the low-brow artistic milieu reminiscent of the salons and cabarets of Harlem during the 1920s, the Zulu Club becomes a second crucible for the Curator's belief in artistic isolation and the acid test of Nkomo's social context theory of art. These scenes can be

considered the Curator's epic descent into the underworld and his confronta-
tion with the shades of his own thinking, of which Heights is the concrete
manifestation, making the bulk of *Harlem Gallery* the Curator's dark night of
the soul. Emerging from that dark night, the Curator can testify to the social
and aesthetic value of art, synthesizing his personal dialectic with Dr. Nkomo
into a new vision of art. And he is able to do so because the people's poet, in
his public acceptance of the opposition that the Curator and Nkomo represent as a tandem, reveals how destructive the binary logic of race is to art, to
the artist, and to the antiracist possibilities of both. For Tolson, such a perspective reinforces racism more than his poetry does and, to an extent, he is
largely correct.

In the next ten sections—from "Lambda" through "Upsilon"—Tolson
mounts a persuasive argument against what he sees to be the too simplistic de-
pendence on the political role of the folk poet and the vernacular in African
American literary culture for conceptions of the liberating power of African
American poetics and the African American intelligent mind. It is a critique
that, while subject to the objection raised by Michael Berube that Tolson takes
the evolution of literary culture to high modernism too much for granted,
does illuminate how the discourses of ethnic authenticity often limit conceptions of African American literary culture and its social relevance. This limitation will be the lesson of the fate of Hideho Heights. On one hand, then,
Heights's artistry is one possible ideal of communal interaction and ethnic
affirmation as a substantive alternative to Laugart's elitism and isolation and
to the Curator's and Nkomo's abstraction.

For example, in the "Zulu Club," the "lowbrow" alternative artistic venue
to the Harlem Gallery, as Frog-Legs Lux's band plays,

> The creative impulse in the Zulu Club
> leaps from Hideho's lips to Frog-Legs' fingers
> like the electric fire from the clouds
> that blued the gap between
> Franklin's key and his Leyden jar.
> ("Xi," lines 111–15)

Here is a distinctive vernacular tradition in action, as two African American
folk artists respond to and enliven each other in a black milieu rather than in
a European tradition or a polite context of a gallery. Instead of being memo-
rialized, in other words, culture is being immediately created. It is a dynamic

that is clearly positive for Tolson and for the characters in the poem. After all, Heights is greeted by the emcee of the venue with the words

> "the Zulu Club has a distinguished guest tonight
> who has never let us down
> . . . .
> Let Harlem give a great big hand, therefore and *henceforth,*
> to a great big poet and a great big man."
>
> ("Nu," lines 10–11, 20–21)

Moreover, readers have tended to concur with Hansell that Heights is Tolson's response to Gertrude Stein's assertion that "the Negro suffers from nothingness" (125). After all, Heights alludes to the claim himself, and since African American literary culture privileges the vernacular too simply even now, Heights's comment seems to justify the fact that verses from this section of the poem are often the only excerpts by which Tolson is represented in anthologies. Such selections and assessments assume that Heights embodies the ideal audience-artist relationship and aesthetic ideals in the poem, a notion that is seemingly confirmed by Heights's being repeatedly called the "People's Poet," and by what Hansell points out as the "messianic" power of Heights's presence in the Zulu Club (125). But these readers fail to believe that black art and great modern art can be the same thing. They even miss how his role as the people's poet represents his lack of faith in black people, a lack of faith that Tolson would gleefully and sardonically attribute to those critics who think of African American culture only in the terms of the vernacular. Heights is cast as the proof that, without synthesizing the Curator's and Nkomo's ideals, the African American self will be trapped in limiting conceptions derived from the hierarchies of white supremacy.

In other words, and paradoxically, Heights reveals for Tolson one of the worst consequences of racial logic and white supremacy for the African American artist and the African American self. In "Chi," the Curator discovers the manifestations of Heights's dilemma when he discovers "the bifacial nature of his poetry: / the racial ballad in the public domain / and the private poem in the modern vein" (lines 12–14). Heights writes two kinds of poetry and keeps them separate, rejecting the unification of the two that has been Tolson's ideal. Worse, Heights yearns for modernist achievement but accepts the racial logic and status quo of his black audience, becoming a people's poet more because he is "supposed to" than because he wants to. Thus, though a people's poet, he separates art from life and Negroness from what he calls "Negro not-ness" even more firmly and pessimistically than does the Curator, remaining in the end unable to reconcile his sense of black self and audience with his understanding of great art. As a result, Heights is twice compared to Ozymandias: "the scorn in the eyes that raked the gallery / was the scorn of an Ozymandias" and, according to the MC Rufino Laughlin,

> "in a thousand years,
> when the Hall of Fame
> lies in ruin on genesis ground,
> the poems and the name
> of Hideho Heights,
> the poet laureate of Lenox Avenue,
> will still be kicking around."
> ("Chi," lines 12–18)

Heights, like Ozymandias, Percy Bysshe Shelley's poem of that title, is presiding over bygone ruins of a black wasteland of an outmoded aesthetic, a vernacular poetics that Tolson and Heights himself eventually oppose unfavorably to high modernism. If his name is still "kicking around," it will only be in reference to ruin. Therefore, in the Curator's words, the leadership he provides as the people's poet is a false one.

> In spite of the Mocker's Mask,
> I saw Hideho
> as a charcoal Piute Messiah
> at a ghetto
> ghost dance.
>
> Does a Yeats or a beast or a Wovoka
> see and hear
> when our own faculties fail?
> ("Zi," lines 17–21, 22–24)

The poem suggests that a Heights does not "see and hear when our own faculties fail." If Heights is a messiah, he is leading his people to their doom like Wovoka, who claimed to his tribe that a ghost dance would make them immune to bullets.

Unlike Tolson and, ultimately, the Curator, Heights actually separates his racial milieu from his aspirations for great art, becoming a false prophet in large part because he fails to challenge his community in the way that modernist art was supposed to. While that elitist challenge for poets such as Eliot was meant to distinguish the initiated from the uninitiated, Tolson's ideal elitism was meant to bring everyone up to the level of the poet by leading them to recognize the full complexity of their social and cultural worth. Heights motivates his audience but fails to push them to new dialectical ways of thinking, an ideal that would have been his true contribution. This lack of synthesis is revealed in Heights's version of Tolson's "E. & O.E.," a poem in which the speaker, like the Curator at the beginning of *Harlem Gallery*, confesses his compromise of himself. In a footnote, Tolson avers, "In an attempt to establish his *I-ness* as a Negro—a concept that is itself a unity of opposites—the [poetic speaker] combines the Cartesian definition with a variant of the Law of Synthetic Identity. This is the key to the allusions in the poem." In the original version, published in *Poetry* magazine in 1951, the speaker of "E. & O.E." spends the first seven of the poem's twelve sections trying to devise a conception of identity and then, in the last five sections, comes to understand how his failure to do so affects his art. For example, in section 2, where the speaker asserts that "[therefore] I think [therefore]"

> I am what I am not:
> if Nazarene
> by lot,
> if no Hellene
> in the Old Gadfly's sense,
> I am, perhaps, a Roman and no Roman, save
> among the dense.
>
> (lines 30–37)

Tolson's footnote, where he describes the "key to the allusions" in the poem, refers to this passage, in which the African American speaker tries to base his sense of selfhood on his capacity to think and yet, by calling himself "no Hellene," the speaker remains trapped in binaries rather than dialectics. Thinking is equated with being civilized while being black is equated with being uncivilized.

This tension creates a split that makes "I think therefore I am" no solution for the deluded character. He tries to erase this second binary (civilized versus uncivilized) by unifying opposites, calling himself "a Roman and no Roman" and calling culture "Madame de Civilis," "a zombi slut who came to preen." If culture is so devalued, then the opposition between civilization and barbarism should not matter either, yet even here he cannot rest comfortably with both "Negroness" and "Negro not-ness," in part because, as a would-be artist, he values culture. Consequently, in section 6, facing a mortality with no spirituality, the speaker must try to reject the implications of his own thinking:

Death?
It's a jot less
than iota.
Dying
is the ogress
lying
in penumbra
wrying
identity to the dregs
with tentacles of
the seven plagues.
      (lines 183–93)

If to be is life and death is "not to be" then where is the dilemma? "To be or not to be" should, as Hamlet knew, really only be about life and death, rather than about identity, meaning that a self is not determined by being or not being some social identity, but by both. The process of dying (or living) is the issue, making identity a matter of philosophical antithesis and synthesis and social interaction rather than being or not being. But until the speaker of this poem grasps that sense of process, he will continually oppose aspects of himself and expectations with his reality, dividing himself and being of no use to anyone as an artist.

By becoming philosophical and Socratic, the speaker should be able to turn the binary into a dialectic, into a process of thought that leads to a synthesis, but the speaker in "E. & O.E." falls prey to the self-indulgent advice of the Tartuffean shill, the double-dealing gambler, who suggests that if identity has no meaning then there can be no higher purpose to art. Says the shill in the poem,

"Why place
an empty pail

before a well
of dry bones?
Why go to Nineveh to tell
the ailing that they ail?
Why lose the Golden Fleece
to gain the Holy grail?"
                (lines 137–43)

If the speaker cannot conceive of himself properly and thus comes to feel, as Heights seems to, that his culture is a well of dry bones, why should he sacrifice himself for the sake of that culture? Why should he commit himself to a port in art that is not worth the cruise? Thus, the speaker, like Jonah, does not go to Nineveh to tell the ailing that they ail. Unlike the Jeremiah speaker of *Libretto,* then, the speaker in "E. & E.O." fails in his bardic role. Like Jonah, had he warned others of mortality—that great equalizer—and of the spiritual cost of their "sin" of social division and stagnation, perhaps he could have found a new way to understand himself. Lacking Jonah's new piety after his rebirth, and left with Ishmael's uncertainty about identity and knowledge throughout Herman Melville's *Moby Dick* but without Ishmael's equanimity at the end of that novel, the speaker in "E. & O.E." is

a Jonah—
a jonah shrunk
by a paraclete
Malebolgean,
in funk
Tartarean
and heat
Gehennan,
from his scalp to the balls of his feet!
                (lines 349–57)

Like Milton's Satan, the speaker of "E. & O.E." himself is hell.

In *Harlem Gallery,* the public warning of "E. & O.E." becomes a private struggle for the people's poet. Heights's "E. & O.E." cites divisions in himself that have an explicit manifestation in his self-destructive popular poetic leadership and his pessimistic private modernism. Thus, instead of facing someone else's tempting offer of material wealth and abdication of social and aesthetic responsibility, Heights is his own Tartuffean shill, actually resigning himself to his ineffectual art. And he fails to conduct this introspection, unlike the original speaker in the poem published in *Poetry*.

Centered in *Harlem Gallery*, the conclusion to "E. & O.E." reads

> "Beneath
> the albatross,
> the skull-and-bones,
> the Skull and Cross,
> the Seven Sins Dialectical,
> I do not shake
> the Wailing Wall
> of Earth—
> nor quake
> the gethsemane
> of Sea—
> nor tear
> the Big Top
> of Sky
> with Lear's prayer,
> or Barabas' curse,
> or Job's cry!"
> ("Chi," lines 184–200)

In Tolson's original version, the speaker is frustrated at his own confusions and impotence, with a sense that a stronger will could make his art more effective. For Heights these words are utter despair, as if the philosophical considerations of the speaker in "E. & O.E." have become merely emotional despair for Heights. Entering the poem with what the Curator calls "a death rattle," Heights writes a kind of poetry that has become useless and will die out. The vernacular art, oddly enough, is the African American wasteland. And as for Heights himself, at the end of "Xi," "slumped in a shoal of a stupor," he "slobbers and sobs, / 'My *people*, / *my* people— / they know not what they do" (lines 278–83). Heights, in accepting and despairing of his split identity that confirms his people's errors, does not even offer to lead them aright, does not go to the Zulu Club to tell the ailing that they ail. Heights is a false prophet indeed.

But what makes Heights false is not his commitment to vernacular culture alone but his resistance to innovation within and against that vernacular culture. Most readers of the poem have missed this point. Berube, for example, suggests that Tolson would have disparaged hip-hop music, when the truth is that Tolson would have loved the underground music for its political consciousness and, most important, for its creativity, its commitment to originality and making it new. Thus, the Curator discovers Heights's fatal flaw. This passage implies two crucial components of Tolson's critique of vernacular poetics. First, by marrying the black poet to those forms and that single audience, critics and poets alike ignore what Tolson saw to be the inevitability of what he called "modern poetics" and what is now called "modernist poetics." While it is odd and a little misguided for Tolson to choose *The Waste Land* and *The Cantos* as models of this inevitable modernism, since neither Eliot nor Pound was continuing in that style, the commitment to innovation is still valuable and valid. Tolson did seem to underestimate the possibilities of innovative artistry in folk poetics but not as much as critics and scholars underestimate the ways in which Tolson could in fact "deterritorialize" modernism, as Nielsen puts it. The other component of that critique is more important, and that is the hypocrisy of the black artist who avoids innovation publicly because he conforms to audience expectations. If the African American poet continues to critique white society for its "reception" of black people, why should that poet then turn around and fail to resist the simplistic ways in which the black community receives the black poet? What kind of political leadership is involved if the poet says nothing new about black culture or the political situation of black people? In other words, Heights falls prey to the problem that critics usually attribute to Tolson: accepting too wholeheartedly the established values of an audience. Just because the audience is black does not mean that it inherently has the ideals appropriate to the black artist.

With those dialectics in mind, it becomes clear that Nkomo and the Curator together provide Tolson's ideal of what I am calling the diasporic consciousness necessary to sustain the epic imagination. The Curator's status as bardic genius clarifies the misreading that has led so many scholars to think that Tolson is worrying about "to be or not to be Negro." This is a false problem actually attributed to Heights, not one Tolson was claiming for himself. After reading Heights's modernist poetry, the Curator muses,

Poor Boy Blue
the Great White World

> and the Black Bourgeoisie
> have shoved the Negro artist into
> the white and not-white dichotomy,
> the Afroamerican dilemma in the Arts—
> the dialectic of to be or not to be
> a Negro.
>
> (lines 29–37)

Blaming the black writer's problems on the Great White World and the Black Bourgeoisie instead of on Omniscience, the Curator has become aware of the falseness of the black writer's (and critic's) dilemma and the very real effects social forces have on artistic production. Heights's dilemma not only argues for the independence of the artist that the Curator values in Laugart but also articulates the need for black writers (and Curators) to accept the full complexity of black identity in order to be an artist. Finally, it means that such an acceptance will lead the artist to reject the limited and limiting binary logic of black people that, Tolson rightly points out, is the black mirror image of the binary logic of white supremacy.

In fact, for Tolson, being for the African American artist was not an ontological or epistemological dilemma; rather, it was a matter of social purpose. In his notes he writes "V. No American Dilemma. In a dilemma a man faces the two horns, of a psychological or moral Scylla and Charybdis. It's To be or not to be." For Tolson, the African American artist has a particular version of this dilemma: "It's the Negro who faces the dilemma; to fight or not to fight. J. Saunders Redding pictures this in 'On Being Negro in America'. Langston Hughes pictures it in 'The Big Sea.' Dunbar faces it: to write jingles or an epic? To create a stereotype or a hero?"[6] "To be or not to be" is the choice of whether or not to engage in the fight against racism and how to engage in that fight. If the black writer succumbs to the false dichotomy, he or she will not go to Nineveh to tell the ailing that they ail, instead lamenting the personal difficulties caused by that dichotomy. Or he or she will reinforce stereotypes or existing conceptions, as Heights does. Thus, the passive practice of Heights in giving the audience what it wants is analogous to creating a stereotype whereas Tolson suggests that, had Heights made his modernism public, he would have become the hero that the Curator turns out to be by the end of the poem. But that heroism does not derive from the artist's regurgitating African American folk culture. It is the transforming of that folk culture into the alternative complexity of the diasporic self that makes the Curator and Tolson himself the ideal of his poem. If Tolson's anthologizers continue to use Heights's celebration of Louis Armstrong as their sole selection from Tolson's art, as was often the practice until recently, then they not only misrepresent his aesthetic, they misunderstand Tolson's vision of this multiethnic diasporic self.[7]

Doing away with the binaries of "to be or not to be" in the last two sections of the poem, the Curator devises a sense of the social, psychological, and biological amalgam of African American identity from which genius actually can emerge and challenge both white supremacy and the complacencies of the African American folk cultural community. He starts "Psi" by examining the contingency of identity and forms of culture that will produce African American poetic genius:

> Black Boy,
> in this race, at this time, in this place,
> to be a Negro artist is to be
> a flower of the gods, whose growth
> is dwarfed at an early stage.
> ("Psi," lines 27–31)

The writer recognizes, as before, that

> you ["Black Boy"]
> have not
> dined and wined
> (*ignoti nulla cupido*)
> in the El Dorado of aeried Art,
> for unreasoned reasons.
> ("Psi," lines 37–42)

But he also acknowledges that this mischance is no reason to believe the black artist never will develop beyond the growth that has been allowed to this point. Just as the Curator earlier realized that formal aspects of art are

> of *this* race,
> of *that* time,
> of *this* place,
> of *that* psyche,

he now realizes that aspects of identity and cultural achievement are likewise situated in time, positing a relationship between time and artistry that makes the universals of that art a hybrid of social and transcendent ideals ("Psi," lines 29–32). Leaving the external trappings of art and identity to the specialists, the Curator commits himself to "the pit and pith of man," to which race and racial identity are not opposed, the most fundamental and common truth of human life.

Instead of worrying about the particular trappings in a particular time that constitute the manifestation of this common emotional pursuit of self-knowledge, the Curator will validate how those trappings convey that ideal "pith" of the person. The Curator even asks "Black Boy" to "summon Boas and Dephino, / Blumenbach and Koelreuter," thinkers who have studied the culture of the African past and the contingency of racial identity, in order that "we may ask them: / 'What is a Negro?'" ("Psi," lines 68–69, 80–81). The Curator uses himself as a model for accepting the theories of social contingency and cultural evolution by which scholars such as Boas refute the fiction of absolute biological difference and inferiority: "my skin is as white / as a Roman's toga," and "since my mongrelization is invisible / and my negroness a state of mind conjured up / by Stereotypus, I am a chameleon" ("Psi," 259–60, 253–55). For the Curator, since he is of "mixed" race and has white skin, blue eyes, and blond hair, "Negroness" is a state of mind, the development of an internal psychological and cultural life in response to stereotypes that exceed its origins in stereotypes. By tracing the complex manifestations of this claim to "Negroness," the African American artist will produce great art and the Curator will collect it.

From these considerations, the Curator derives a new commitment, one commensurate with Tolson's own, in which blackness is the elaboration on the claim to community and heritage in a given time. That claim will lead to art engaged in its time and capable of articulating the pith of the person within and against the social categories of race and cultural forms of that heritage. As such, that great art, even in its elitism, will be proof ultimately of egalitarian social ideals. Not just seeking to avoid professional limitations as he was in the beginning of the poem, the Curator is now seeking to motivate social justice through artistic collection.

> Those in the upper drawer give a child
> the open sesame to the unknown

> What and How and Why;
> that's *that* which curators, as Pelagians, try
> to
> do in exhibitions,
> when a genius gets through
> with a nonpareil of art whose exegesis
> exacts patience.
> ("Omega," lines 19–27)

By illuminating this genius, the Curator can recognize, as a Pelagian, that there is no original sin, not even black identity, and that human genius needs cultivation. Given the complexity of that genius, it produces an art "whose exegesis / exacts patience." The Curator can use his position and knowledge to spread the know-how necessary for that exacting exegesis, including the idea that race and inheritance do not determine genius. The Curator warns "Black Boy" to

> beware of wine labels,
> for the Republic does not guarantee
> what the phrase "Chateau Bottled" means—
> the estate, the proprietor, the quality.
> ("Psi," lines 209–12)

Neither the democratic republic nor the republic of letters can guarantee the meaning of tradition or substantiate claims to lineage, and so the black citizen and the black writer need to be aware of possibilities of exclusion on utter pretense rather than on talent or quality. In the end, "we know *without no* / every people, by and by, produces its 'Chateau Bottled'" ("Psi," lines 238–39), and it does so by claiming the complexity of its own heritage, allowing its social situation and individual tri-dimensionality to be filtered through innovative artistic forms. Harlem will have its genius, and that genius will emerge from and with a genuine cultural and aesthetic lineage operating in defiance of the racist aspects of the Western cultural tradition, even as it attempts to define the pit and pith of man in part within the Western tradition. And when the Curator cultivates that art, he will be participating in the pursuit of social justice.

Because scholars have been so concerned with Tolson's rejection of traditional definitions of African American ethnicity, they have missed how substantively *Harlem Gallery* functions as an *ars poetica*. They also therefore miss how fully this *ars poetica* validates an alternative, more comprehensive, and more affirming conception of African American ethnicity than these critics have. For example, Berube too simplistically affirms the preference of the vernacular and, despite his desire to reject binary logic, Nielsen chooses terms that reinforce them. With these meditations, Tolson—through his Curator—validates his own "intelligent mind" and his mode of artistry as an ideal ethnic self to be celebrated. The entire poem, by balancing vernacular language with formal literary language, African cultural heritage with European, liberal humanism with African communalism, defines "The Negro" by its contradictions and synthesizes those contradictions into an ideal of self that incorporates the vast cultural traditions and knowledge that constitute Tolson's copious research. As in the *Libretto*, Tolson in *Harlem Gallery* has placed the African American artist at the heart of what it means to have an artistic masterpiece derived from the full complexity of African diaspora. It creates the "Negro language" that is a possible American language by assimilating modernist poetics and transforming it with biblical history, literary history, and African and African American folk culture. Like the poets of the entire bardic tradition, Tolson is largely right. Tolson demonstrates how a people's dusk of dawn emerges from a poetic complexity that mirrors the complexity of black identity and history.

As a writer of such poems, Tolson becomes a bard, as the Curator's mind becomes exemplary of African American literary history and solves the problems of African American (and, therefore, human) identity. Both minds synthesize the common antithesis between aspects of race and aspects of writing. *Harlem Gallery* not only announces the epic of a people, then, but also announces itself as the culmination of its own aesthetic musings, its resolution of "the black diasporic *décalage*" by recognizing those gaps as an inevitable part of the process by which African Americans pursue and achieve the self-knowledge that redefine the postcolonial mind (Edwards 13). This synthesizing art, like the mind that creates it, becomes in its difficulty the "interstices" in which national selfhoods are dissolved by the negotiations that create them and that therefore constitute the truest location of culture. It is not in one tradition and certainly not the Anglo-American tradition or the African American folk tradition alone.

Though Tolson and the Curator are not one and the same, they sing in unison at the end of "Omega": both declare,

> In the black ghetto
> the white heather and white almond grow,
> but the hyacinth
> and asphodel blow
> in the white metropolis!
> (lines 238–42)

Thus, when the poem concludes, the Curator has indeed seen the light of Tolson's vision and voices it as Tolson would.

> Our public may possess in Art
> a Mantegna's arctic rigidity;
> yet—I hazard—yet,
> this allegro of the Harlem Gallery
> is not a chippy fire,
> for her, in focus, are paintings that chronicle
> a people's New World odyssey
> from Chattel to Esquire!
> ("Omega," lines 248–55)

The white flowers of life grow in the black ghetto, while the blackness of death hovers in the white metropolis. The people's poet, like the people's Curator, will demonstrate the heights of African American cultural achievement, in Tolson's case in high modernism, making the art of a people's dusk of dawn the next great modern art. By articulating a national history through the representative mind of the Curator; by displaying the representative virtuosity and cultural knowledge of Tolson himself; and by offering these aspects of the poem as an argument for the new art that the poem itself embodies, *Harlem Gallery* is the new American epic.

What makes Tolson's port worth the cruise, in the end, is the reconciliation of social ideals with aesthetic ones and a redefinition of how African American art garners its aesthetic effect through a complex, hybrid ethnic imagination predicated on the culture of the African diaspora and the ambition and conventions of the Western epic tradition. In the process, Tolson affirms the versions of cultural mastery formalized in the Harlem Renaissance and broadens them with the proletarian modes of meaning and the modernist construction of consciousness. Though Tolson does not fully address the problems that modernist elitism creates for his own work, his belief in the representative capacities of high art, which is a cornerstone of his epic imagination (and of African American formal poetics), suggests that he takes such elitism as a necessary aspect of his poetry's social effect. So Tolson manages to affirm openly the individual pursuit of genius characteristic of practically every artist, while articulating how that individual genius in itself, and its expression in certain cultural forms, serves the social concerns of African American poets very well. No other African American poet so fully and explicitly combines these poles, making Tolson's *Harlem Gallery* a fulfillment of the various terms and practices of that tradition. Thanks to the Black Arts Movement, black poets do not feel as strong a need for cultural mastery today, but Tolson's example still rings true as an articulation of a sense of self much larger than that of nationalism. And since it is this sense of self that counts in African American poetic expression, Tolson's epic imagination, in its dialectics, in its self-consciousness, in its idealism, and in its epic African American selfhood, constitutes the logical and beautiful end of the African American formalist poet's attempt to represent the race.

Conclusion

"Because everything belongs to me."

—Ruth Simmons, President, Brown University

The president of Brown University and the first African American woman president of an Ivy League university, Ruth Simmons captured well what I consider to be the most important implication of my conception of the fettered genius of the African American formalist poet. A PhD in French, Simmons was asked in a *60 Minutes* interview, "But why does a kid, a tenant farmer's kid from the wrong side of the tracks in this country decide to study French literature?" Her response: "Because everything belongs to me. There is nothing—there is nothing that is withheld from me simply because I'm poor." I find this claim persuasive and even inspiring not only for an individual's education but also for a poet's relationship to form and tradition, a literary scholar's relationship to critical heritage, and an entire history of African American people relating to the history and culture of the West. From the first moment that Africans encountered Europeans and were forced in various ways to adopt aspects of European culture, this claim that it all belongs to black people, while problematic, has been sustaining. While we must acknowledge the oppressive nature of the simultaneous inclusion in and exclusion from Western culture and society that African Americans have faced, we must also see that the study of African American literature in general—but especially the study of African American formalist poetry—needs to be conducted with an awareness of how one mode of resistance to that exclusion was actually to claim and thereby almost inherently to revise Western culture. And we should pursue this study with all of the means at our disposal. While there are elements of cultural self-sacrifice in this formalist poet's claiming, and while the history of this attempt to adapt an imperialist culture to the African American self is certainly as much a consequence of imperialism as an expression of self-affirmation, this cultural assimilation did in fact facilitate modes of resistance and attributes a subversive character to all aspects of the African American expressive tradition. The approach has not been the main strategy of resistance for all African American artists, nor is it necessarily the most effective one, but it has been a productive one in which the construction of traditional genius and the claim to social and cultural belonging affirm African American identity and culture in much same way as the more fully valorized vernacular tradition. Bardic genius is a powerful act of ethnic self-definition.

So my suggestion throughout this book that the year 1967 was the beginning of the end of the African American bardic tradition is meant as a validation of the ways in which the artistic modes of claiming of African American formalist poets anticipate the powerful claiming of folk traditions, ethnic community, militant activism, and institution building enacted in the Black Arts Movement of the late 1960s and in African American literary culture ever since. Not only did a new, more directly affirming movement begin but it superseded a movement that had substantively reached its full potential. By 1967, Gwendolyn Brooks, Robert Hayden, and Melvin B. Tolson had, together, powerfully achieved just about all that was possible in the artistic and cultural logic of what I have been calling bardic genius. Just as the mainstream of the Civil Rights Movement, the political analogue to this cultural tradition, faced the disaffection of young activists who saw the very real limitations to social integration and cultural assimilation, namely in the potential erosion of racial self-worth, these formalist poets quite literally confronted the literary pronouncements of these militants. In that year, the year of Melvin Tolson's death, young militant writers had organized and put on the First Annual Fisk University Writers' Conference, one of the first collective announcements of the nationalist aesthetic theories of the Black Arts Movement. In this and other venues, militant writers rejected the pursuit of traditional mastery as a faulty acceptance of white power and redefined the African American poet's "genius" as exclusively racial or ethnic in nature, a position that led Robert Hayden, a professor at Fisk at the time, to the brilliant anti-ideological ethnic affirmation of *Angle of Ascent*. But because both Black Power and the Black Arts Movement were necessary responses to the slow, painful progress of Civil Rights and the wicked retrenchment of segregation in some quarters, Gwendolyn Brooks was persuaded by the new ethos and ideals and joined in this shift from accommodation and integration to nationalist resistance, offering her own versions of a more explicit priority on racial self-worth and a firmer sense that African American self-definition need not meet with mainstream approval.

But this transformation was not simply an improvement on the failed politics of the preceding formalism. Only studies of African American literary culture too deeply rooted in its nationalist heritage could come to such a conclusion. African American formalist poetics was not a complete abdication of self-worth nor was it devoid of the kind of claiming of self rightly privileged in African American literary culture since the Black Arts Movement. That movement was in fact the crest of the wave that had developed from the continuous and burgeoning groundswell of African American social, cultural, and political self-assertion since Emancipation. The bardic tradition was part of this historical upsurge, since its continuous construction of this complex self was the foundation of both formalist and nationalist poetics. And the defining components of that historical trajectory are best understood as the dynamics of postcolonial cultural life—in which culture is located, as Homi Bhabba suggested, in the interstices between a valid vernacular culture and the imposition of and resistance to an imperial culture, a space in-between where subjectivity is constructed and imagination resides. Within that interaction, mastery is subversive, especially since African American poetic mastery has always been tied to the validation of the distinctive perspective and, later, of that distinctive cultural heritage. Bardic formalists were not wrong in their faith in traditional artistry to convey black identity even if readers objected to the terms of social integration by which they operated. In fact, that is the point: the concept of bardic genius should demonstrate that the politics of artistry is more complex than the direct assertion of a single ideology. It is rather the politics of representation, the mediation of cultural forms, and the complex revelation of the inextricable relationship between self and world, imagination and social discourses, that made this claiming of traditional poetics a valid and persuasive aesthetic *and* political precursor to nationalism. Bardic genius is a set of contradictions and, in claiming them, we claim a tradition.

Therefore, by turning to the models of hybridity and mutation central to postcolonial studies instead of to the logic of cultural purity central both to white supremacy and to Black Nationalism and its legacies, readers of this formalist tradition can recognize three important components of antiracist cultural meaning in the bardic genius's fettered claims of self that, as Simmons avers, have remained central to African American culture since the Black Arts

Movement. First of all, the artistic and political coherence of African American formalist poetics was constituted not by the relationship between poetic artistry and some preexisting ethnic self or by some stated political ideology but rather by the manipulation of bardic self-definition in evolving formal innovation. The friction in its own making revealed the validity of African American ethnic selfhood and also refuted even as it claimed a culture of authenticity. Because they helped construct rather than failed to represent an ethnic self, these poets do not fit conveniently in the faulty but far-too-common traditional categories of African American literary criticism of protester or sellout, self-affirming masker or self-hating capitulator. While self-hatred and certainly self-doubt are components of this tradition, they are minor compared to the self-affirmation and the self-assertion that ranged from the moderate whisperings of Phillis Wheatley's claim to citizenship to Melvin B. Tolson's brash historical revisionism. The complex unities of this tradition constitute blackness in the making, revealing the boundaries that fetter and the imagination that resists.

Therefore, the complex coherence of this tradition validates my second conclusion, namely, the importance of cultural hybridity for conceiving of the aesthetic and the political meaning of African American poetic expression of all sorts. By attending to the dialectical and provisionally synthesizing nature of African American traditional formalism, I have shown that traditional poetics balances the opposing terms of our conceptions of race. In that balance, it reveals that the complex, dialectical, and interactive relationship between racial ideology and aesthetic meaning creates in individual poems, in collections of poems, and in bodies of works a set of disparate strategies and conflicting ideas about how racial identity relates to art. Not only has literary scholarship neglected the combinations of black and white color imagery, themes of identity, community and democracy, sonnet forms, ballad forms, odes, and epics in this formalist tradition, it also has neglected how fully formalism is a defining component of poetic meaning, whether traditional as in this tradition or vernacular as in the Black Arts Movement. While hybridity need not be the only watchword for the aesthetic legacy of this bardic tradition, formalism should be, in other words, since it is the construction of poetic form commensurate to the poet's conception of ethnic identity that makes for a large measure of the formal innovation and achievement of African American poets from Wheatley to the present. Scholars of this bardic tradition and of all African American poetry must be much more careful in the analysis of the complex hybridity of poetic form, following scholars such as Aldon Nielsen and Meta Jones in recognizing that discussing the shift in politics in poetry is inadequate without exploring the forms through which that politics is conveyed. By treating all poetics as modes of various competing formalisms, it becomes much clearer how fully engaged African American formalist poets were in the cultural subversion of racism that is almost always at least a backdrop to African American expressive culture.

Finally, then, in the idea of the complex construction of an ethnic self through the formalist construction of poetic achievement across time, we have a dynamic conception capable of dealing with how the social, cultural, and artistic struggles of the poets of the bardic tradition continue in African American cultural production today even as their particular strategies of response have long since been superseded. Though I will go into this conflict and continuity in more detail in the second volume of this history of African American poetic formalism, it is worth noting here that the problems of potential cultural strangulation and the dynamics of aesthetic effect in relationship to race politics are very much the same, even though most poets since the Black Arts Movement have fully embraced various modes of formal innovation that more directly subvert the manifestation of postcolonial cultural power. Nonetheless, a major strain of late-twentieth- and early-twenty-first-century African American poetry similarly constructs poetic genius as an ideal ethnic self, even though these poets function more fully in the mold of the popular conception of the bard. At the heart of it all is this point: African American cultural self-definition remains a primary and sometimes underestimated antiracist agency, and it remains tied intimately—in certain important, public cases—to conventional mainstream terms of achievement. Moreover, African American identity continues to be an amalgamation of disparate and sometimes competing and contradictory elements that validates African American self-worth and at times provides a model for just social relations. Trey Ellis was on to something when he defined the postmodern "cultural mulatto," and though he overstates the uniqueness of the cultural identities of bourgeois black people of his generation, he is ultimately right in stating that "we no longer need to deny or suppress any part of our complicated and sometimes contradictory cultural baggage to please either white people or black" (235).

As such, we should not judge cultural production for the radicalism of its politics or the uniformity of its representation of black folk culture alone. Not only will we simplify the African American expressive tradition, we will do a disservice to a part of the spectrum of being black that is as true to the lives of African American people as it is to the ways of the masses. This insight is what makes Ellis's articles so compelling. While I am not as invested in defending the middle class as he is, I am likewise trying to remind readers that cultural production not only sometimes reflects aspects of the culture of which it is a part, as most critics read it, but also is more significantly a mediating factor for constructing and disseminating that culture. And its complexities always push the boundaries even of its definitions of the blackness it represents.

With these conclusions, I do not mean simply to make apologies for the conservatism of artists such as Wheatley or Paul Laurence Dunbar, or to deflect attention too simply away from institutional practices of racism, nor do I mean to imply that cultural assimilation is a wise political strategy. In fact, I concede that African American poetry in particular and literary culture in general since the 1960s has had antiracist effects more powerful and more concrete than the preceding bardic ideal. Those effects include a broader range of poetic innovation, more direct affirmation of African American culture, a more direct refutation of oppression, and greater numbers of publishing venues and other such institutions, including the institution of Black and African American Studies that, in its current incarnations in colleges and universities, has provided the social and scholarly infrastructure that allows me to develop the contrary perspective offered in this book. But I do mean to validate how the bardic commitment to cultural crossover was nonetheless a significant precursor to Black Power, cultural nationalism, and multiculturalism, because it demonstrated the complexity of the African American self by making African American experience and culture the defining components of formalist poetic achievement and literary genius for African American poets. I also mean to suggest that the construction of black community in cultural and social practice has always included assimilationism, the adaptation of formal literary culture and the bourgeois norms associated with both. These positions have always been subject to criticism for perhaps giving too much away to racism, but that criticism should not obscure the awkward fact that these components of black community building have also contributed important components of cultural practice and social unity to African American heritage, especially in the world of the arts. Such practices have sometimes usefully separated ideals of artistic achievement from the white mainstream norms that defined those ideals, allowing for genuinely black versions of these ideals. In short, I claim it all, from Dunbar's parodies in dialect to Brown's complex affirmations; from Wheatley's claim to cultivation to Tolson's redefinition of cultivation; from the moralism of Bill Cosby to the complex didacticism of Spike Lee. The analogies are here if we would just see them.

Finally, this book is my answer to that nagging question about how to discuss the relationship between ethnic selfhood and the so-called universals of literary culture. The most defining universal—at least as practiced and represented in bardic genius—is the construction of selfhood from disparate sources within and against socially imposed and sometimes oppressive boundaries of convention and discourse. Thus, to offer my own instance of the bardic imagination, I am suggesting in paraphrasing Walt Whitman that the African American cultural self contains multitudes, and we should embrace this fact. In the particular case of the bardic tradition, the poets were conservative and liberal, Christian, Baha'i, and agnostic. There were neoclassical poetics and the blues, a racist dialect and an innovative African American vernacular language, African proverbs and allusions to Shakespeare. All formed components of a distinctive ethnic experience and each, read through both the poet's and the reader's lens of racial ideology, contributed to a distinctive use of traditional poetics to rewrite the sometimes racist norms associated with those poetics. In the end, then, as Simmons implies, what matters in an understanding of culture is what is shared, both within groups and across all social boundaries, especially if we seek to understand, as these poets did, how culture can refute social hierarchy and motivate just social relations. And that sharing, that human commonality, must be understood and appreciated through the distinctive cultural forms in which it is expressed, and this is the beautiful paradox of African American formalist literary culture. Recognizing this paradox will keep us from thinking of cultural difference as absolute, or as somehow inevitably tied to greater than or lesser than. We can also see how African American identity is ethnic, not racial, and always in the process of being made and therefore constantly remaking its boundaries. Though I remain haunted by Harvey Curtis Webster's review of Gwendolyn Brooks, I am comforted by the idea that the trend in literary study is to acknowledge this multifaceted nature of the human self and the multiple literary means by which that self is represented.

In the end, then, the creation of African American ethnicity in public culture of the past two hundred plus years has expanded the boundaries of blackness set by racism. Oppression, self-hatred, and cultural violence are not to be denied and are in fact the continuing expressions and consequences of an American society founded on injustice and dedicated, in its own often genteel, idealistic ways, to maintaining the practices that oppress and do the violence. In this context, white Americans especially but also all people who are not African American need to stop treating blackness as an absolutely different commodity that can be put on or discarded like clothes or that is somehow opposed to what we as humans share. African Americans need not—indeed cannot—transcend blackness, so we all must accept it as an inextricable and even fundamental thread of American culture. African American people need to stop embracing the same notion of absolute difference or we will continue thinking of ourselves as victims and outsiders, which is only partly true. Worse, we will victimize ourselves by internalizing the racist logic that white society created to disparage us and reduce ourselves to a monolithic opposition to whiteness that maintains whiteness as norm and center and that comes from old-fashioned boundaries of social segregation. Thus, for me, the chief lesson of the bardic tradition is that, whatever social limitations that were and still are imposed upon black people, our cultural selfhood knows no such bounds. By embracing the expansion, we can find new strategies to change the terms and social practices of race, to rewrite the logic of white supremacy, to make racial authenticity unnecessary, and to pursue genuine equal opportunity. That is my bold faith. But at the very least, with this approach to poetic expression, we can appreciate more fully the marvelous artistry and agency of the African American bardic poet.

Notes

Introduction

1. Tolson, "The Bard of Addis Ababa," lines 43–49, in *Harlem Gallery and Other Poems*. All subsequent references to Tolson's poetry are from this edition and are cited in the text.

1. "Bid the Gifted Negro Soar"

1. Horton, "A Poet's Feeble Petition," line 16, in Sherman, *Black Bard of North Carolina*. All subsequent references to Horton's poetry are from this edition and are cited in the text.

2. Wheatley, *Poems of Phillis Wheatley*, 48. All subsequent references to Wheatley's poetry and prose are from this volume and are cited in the text.

3. Harper, "Bury Me in a Free Land," lines 29–32, in *Complete Poems*. All subsequent references to Harper's poetry are from this edition and are cited in the text.

2. "Writ on Glory's Scroll"

1. Daniel Webster Davis, "The Biggis Piece ub Pie," lines 57–64, in *Idle Moments*. All subsequent references to Davis's poetry are from this edition and are cited in the text.

2. Dunbar, "The Party," lines 6–9, in *Lyrics of Lowly Life*. All subsequent references to Dunbar's poetry are from this edition and are cited in the text.

3. *Encyclopædia Britannica Online*, s.v. "trochee," http://www.search.eb.com/eb/article?tocId=9073458 (accessed December 11, 2004).

3. "To Make a Poet Black"

1. Cullen, "Yet Do I Marvel," lines 3–8, in James Weldon Johnson, *Book of American Negro Poetry*. All subsequent references to Cullen's poetry are from this anthology and are cited in the text.

2. Georgia Douglass Johnson, "The Heart of a Woman," lines 1–8, in *Selected Works*. All subsequent references to Johnson's poetry are from this edition and are cited in the text.

3. *Encyclopædia Britannica Online*, s.v. "anapest," http://www.search.eb.com/eb/article?tocId=9007363 (accessed December 11, 2004).

4. McKay, "If We Must Die," lines 1–5, in James Weldon Johnson, *Book of American Negro Poetry*. All subsequent references to McKay's poetry are from this anthology and are cited in the text.

5. Hughes, "The Weary Blues," lines 9–30, in *Collected Poems of Langston Hughes*. All subsequent references to Hughes's poetry are from this edition and are cited in the text.

6. Brown, "Southern Road," lines 3–6, 25–36, in *Collected Poems of Sterling A. Brown*. All subsequent references to Brown's poetry are from this edition and are cited in the text.

4. "Weaponed Woman"

1. Tate, "Gwendolyn Brooks," 40. As she put it in a 1983 interview, "Our people have been looked at as curios . . . something other than ordinarily human," though she has "fought that idea, a little less . . . than formerly because I used to feel it was my DUTY to change everybody's idea about Blacks! . . . [But] it is my duty to express what I feel, to say certain things to Blacks that others are not going to say to them . . . . But I don't sit down now and write, hoping I can change the hearts of white people."

2. Brooks, "Weaponed Woman," lines 1–4, in *Blacks*. All subsequent references to Brooks's poetry are from this edition and are cited in the text.

5. "Our Souls' Strict Meaning"

1. Hayden, "'We Have Not Forgotten,'" lines 6–8, in *Heart-Shape in the Dust*. References to subsequent poems from this edition are cited in the text.

2. Hayden, "The Lion," lines 19–30, in *The Lion and the Archer*. References to subsequent poems from this edition are cited in the text.

3. Hayden, "For a Young Artist," lines 33–47, in *Angle of Ascent*. References to subsequent poems from this edition are cited in the text.

6. A Port Worth the Cruise

1. Tolson Papers, box 10.

2. Tolson Papers, box 8.

3. Tolson, "Stillicho Spikes," lines 7–23, in *Gallery of Harlem Portraits*. Subsequent references to poems from this volume are cited in the text.

4. Tolson, "Dark Symphony," lines 34–57, in *Harlem Gallery and Other Poems*. Subsequent references to poems from this volume are cited in the text.

5. Tolson Papers, box 12.

6. From Tolson's notes. I have corrected parts of it for spelling and the conventions of capitalization.

7. See, for example, Henderson, *Understanding the New Black Poetry,* 148–50.

Bibliography

Andersson, Theodore. "The Displacement of the Heroic Ideal in the Family Sagas." *Speculum* 45, no. 4 (October 1970): 577.

Baker, Houston. "The Achievement of Gwendolyn Brooks." In Mootry and Smith, *A Life Distilled*, 21–29.

———. *Blues, Ideology and Afro-American Literature: A Vernacular Theory*. Chicago: University of Chicago Press, 1987.

———. *Modernism and the Harlem Renaissance*. Chicago: University of Chicago Press, 1987.

Bassard, Katherine Clay. *Spiritual Interrogations: Culture, Gender and Community in Early African American Women's Writing*. Princeton, NJ: Princeton University Press, 1999.

Benston, Kimberly. *Performing Blackness: Enactments of African American Modernism*. New York: Routledge, 2000.

Bergin, Osborne. *Irish Bardic Poetry: Texts and Translations*. Dublin: Dublin Institute for Advanced Studies, 1970.

Berube, Michael. "Avant-Gardes and De-Authorizations: *Harlem Gallery* and the Cultural Contradictions of Modernism." *Callaloo* 12, no. 1 (1989): 192–215.

———. *Marginal Forces/Cultural Centers: Tolson, Pynchon and the Politics of the Canon*. Ithaca, NY: Cornell University Press, 1992.

———. "Masks, Margins, and African American Modernism: Melvin Tolson's *Harlem Gallery*." *PMLA* 105, no. 1 (1990): 57–69.

Bhabba, Homi K. *The Location of Culture*. New York: Routledge, 1994.

Boone, Joseph Allen. *Libidinal Current: Sexuality and the Shaping of Modernism*. Chicago: University of Chicago Press, 1997.

Bowra, C. W. *Heroic Verse*. London: Macmillan, 1952.

Boyd, Melba Joyce. *Discarded Legacy: Politics and Poetics in the Life of Frances E. W. Harper, 1825–1911*. Detroit: Wayne State University Press, 1994.

Brooks, Gwendolyn. *Blacks*. Chicago: Third World Press, 1991.

————. *Report from Part One*. Detroit: Broadside Press, 1972.

Brown, Fahamisha Patricia. *Performing the Word: African American Poetry as Vernacular Culture*. New Brunswick, NJ: Rutgers University Press, 1999.

Brown, Sterling. *The Collected Poems of Sterling A. Brown*. Evanston, IL: Triquarterly Books, 1980.

Burgett, Bruce. *Sentimental Bodies: Sex, Gender and Citizenship in the Early Republic*. Princeton, NJ: Princeton University Press, 1998.

Burstein, Andrew. *Sentimental Democracy: The Evolution of America's Romantic Self-Image*. New York: Hill and Wang, 1999.

Butler, Judith. *Gender Trouble: Feminism and the Subversion of Identity*. New York: Routledge, 1990.

Campbell, James Edwin. *Echoes from the Cabin*. Chicago, 1895.

Carby, Hazel. *Reconstructing Womanhood: The Emergence of the Afro-American Woman Novelist*. New York: Oxford University Press, 1987.

Chrisman, Robert. "Robert Hayden: The Transition Years, 1946–1948." In *Robert Hayden: Essays on the Poetry*, ed. Laurence Goldstein and Robert Chrisman, 129–54. Ann Arbor: University of Michigan Press, 2001.

Cobbs, John L. "George Moses Horton's *Hope of Liberty:* Thematic Unity in Early Black American Poetry." *CLA Journal* 24, no. 4 (June 1981): 441–50.

Collins, Terence. "Phillis Wheatley: The Dark Side of the Poetry." In Robinson, *Critical Essays on Phillis Wheatley*, 140–49.

Conniff, Brian. "Answering 'The Waste Land': Robert Hayden and the Rise of the African American Poetic Sequence." *African American Review* 33, no. 3 (1999): 487–506.

Davis, Arthur P. "Gwendolyn Brooks: Poet of the Unheroic." *College Language Association Journal* 7 (1973): 114–25.

Davis, Charles. "Robert Hayden's Use of History." In *Modern Black Poets: A Collection of Critical Essays*, ed. Donald Gibson, 96–111. Englewood Cliffs, NJ: Prentice Hall, 1973.

Davis, Daniel Webster. *Idle Moments, Containing Emancipation and Other Poems*. Baltimore, 1895.

Dickson, D. Bruce, Jr. "On Dunbar's 'Jingles in a Broken Tongue': Dunbar's Dialect Poetry and the Afro-American Folk Tradition." In *A Singer in the Dawn: Reinterpretations of Paul Laurence Dunbar*, ed. Jay Martin, 94–113. New York: Dodd, Mead and Company, 1975.

Du Bois, W. E. B. *The Souls of Black Folk*. New York: W. W. Norton and Company, 1999.

Dunbar, Paul Laurence. *Lyrics of Lowly Life*. New York: Citadel Press, 1984.

————. *The Paul Laurence Dunbar Reader*, ed. Jay Martin and Gossie H. Hudson. New York: Dodd, Mead and Company, 1975.

Edwards, Brent Hayes. *The Practice of Diaspora: Literature, Translation and the Rise of Black Internationalism*. Cambridge, MA: Harvard University Press, 2003.

Ellison, Ralph. "Richard Wright's Blues." In *Shadow and Act*, 77–94. New York: Vintage Books, 1995.

Erkilla, Betsy. "Phillis Wheatley and the Black American Revolution." In *A Mixed Race: Ethnicity in Early America*, ed. Frank Shuffleton, 225–40. New York: Oxford University Press, 1993.

Farnsworth, Robert. *Melvin B. Tolson: Plain Talk and Poetic Prophecy*. Columbia: University of Missouri Press, 1984.

Fauset, Jessie. "The Gift of Laughter." In *The New Negro*, ed. Robert Hayden, 161–68. New York: Atheneum Press, 1968.

———. "Our Book Shelf." *Crisis* 23 (1925): 35.

Favor, J. Martin. *Authentic Blackness: The Folk in the New Negro Renaissance*. Durham, NC: Duke University Press, 1999.

Fetrow, Fred. *Robert Hayden*. Boston: Twayne Publishers, 1984.

Flasch, Joy. *Melvin B. Tolson*. New York: Twayne Publishers, 1972.

Foster, Frances Smith, ed. Introduction to *A Brighter Coming Day: A Frances Ellen Watkins Harper Reader*. New York: Feminist Press, 1990.

Gabbin, Joanne V. "Blooming in the Whirlwind: The Early Poetry of Gwendolyn Brooks." In *The Furious Flowering of African American Poetry*, ed. Joanne V. Gabbin, 252–73. Charlottesville: University of Virginia Press, 1999.

Gaines, Kevin Kelly. *Uplifting the Race: Black Leadership, Politics, and Culture in the Twentieth Century*. Chapel Hill: University of North Carolina Press, 1996.

Gates, Henry Louis, Jr. *Figures in Black: Words, Signs and the "Racial" Self*. New York: Oxford University Press, 1987.

———. *The Signifying Monkey: A Theory of African American Literary Criticism*. Oxford: Oxford University Press, 1988.

———. *The Trials of Phillis Wheatley: America's First Black Poet and Her Encounters with the Founding Fathers*. New York: Basic Civitas, 2003.

———, and Nellie McKay, general eds. *Norton Anthology of African American Literature*. New York: W. W. Norton and Company, 1997.

Gayle, Addison. "Cultural Strangulation: Black Literature and the White Aesthetic." In *The Black Aesthetic*, ed. Addison Gayle, 38–45. New York: Doubleday, 1972.

Gelpi, Albert. *A Coherent Splendor: The American Poetic Renaissance*. Cambridge: Cambridge University Press, 1987.

Gendron, Dennis. "Robert Hayden: A View of His Life and Development as a Poet." PhD diss., University of North Carolina at Chapel Hill, 1975.

Gilroy, Paul. *The Black Atlantic: Modernity and Double Consciousness*. Cambridge, MA: Harvard University Press, 1993.

Greenblatt, Stephen. *Renaissance Self-Fashioning: From More to Shakespeare*. Chicago: University of Chicago Press, 1980.

Grossberg, Lawrence, and Jennifer Daryl Slack. "An Introduction to Stuart Hall's Essay." *Critical Studies in Mass Communication* 2 (1985): 89.

Hall, Stuart. "Signification, Representation, Ideology: Althusser and the Post-Structuralist Debates." *Critical Studies in Mass Communication* 2 (1985): 91–113.

Hannaford, Ivan. *Race: The History of an Idea in the West.* Washington, DC: Woodrow Wilson Center Press, 1996.

Hansell, William H. "Three Artists in Melvin B. Tolson's Harlem Gallery." *Black American Literature Forum* 18, no. 3 (1984): 122–27.

————. "The Uncommon Commonplace in the Early Poems of Gwendolyn Brooks." *College Language Association Journal* 30, no. 3 (1987): 261–77.

Harper, Frances Ellen Watkins. *Complete Poems of Frances E. W. Harper,* ed. Maryemma Graham. New York: Oxford University Press, 1987.

Hatcher, John. *From the Auroral Darkness: The Life and Poetry of Robert Hayden.* Oxford: Ronald Publishing, 1984.

Hayden, Robert. *Angle of Ascent: New and Selected Poems.* New York: Liveright, 1975.

————. *Collected Prose,* ed. Frederick Glaysher. Ann Arbor: University of Michigan Press, 1984.

————. *Heart-Shape in the Dust.* Detroit: Falcon Press, 1940.

————, and Myron O'Higgins. *The Lion and the Archer.* Nashville, TN: Hemphill Press, 1948.

Henderson, Stephen. "Introduction: The Forms of Things Unknown." In *Understanding the New Black Poetry: Black Speech and Black Music as Poetic References.* New York: William Morrow and Company, Inc., 1973.

Hill, Patricia Liggins. "'Let Me Make the Songs for the People': A Study of Frances Watkins Harper's Poetry." *Black American Literature Forum* 15, no. 2 (Summer 1981): 60–65.

Howells, William Dean. Introduction to Dunbar, *Lyrics of Lowly Life.*

Huggins, Nathan. *Harlem Renaissance.* New York: Oxford University Press, 1973.

Hughes, Langston. *The Collected Poems of Langston Hughes,* vol. 1, ed. Arnold Rampersad. New York: Knopf, 2001.

————. "The Negro Artist and the Racial Mountain." In *Within the Circle: An Anthology of African American Literary Criticism from the Harlem Renaissance to the Present,* ed. Angelyn Mitchell, 55–59. Durham, NC: Duke University Press, 1994.

Hull, Gloria T. *Color, Sex, and Poetry: Three Women Writers of the Harlem Renaissance.* Bloomington: Indiana University Press, 1987.

Hutcheon, Linda. *A Theory of Parody: The Teachings of Twentieth Century Art Forms.* New York: Methuen, 1985.

Hutchinson, George. *The Harlem Renaissance in Black and White.* Cambridge, MA: Belknap Press of Harvard University Press, 1995.

Jackson, Angela. "The Night-Blooming Cereus." In *Robert Hayden: Essays on the Poetry,* ed. Laurence Goldstein and Robert Chrisman, 69–70. Ann Arbor: University of Michigan Press, 2001.

Jameson, Frederic. "Cognitive Mapping." In *Marxism and the Interpretation of Cul-*

ture, ed. Cary Nelson and Lawrence Grossberg, 347–57. Urbana: University of Illinois Press, 1988.

Jennings, Regina. "African Sun Imagery in the Poetry of Phillis Wheatley." *Pennsylvania English* 22, nos. 1–2 (2000): 68–76.

Johnson, Georgia Douglas. *Selected Works of Georgia Douglas Johnson,* ed. Claudia Tate. New York: G. K. Hall and Co., 1997.

Johnson, James Weldon. *The Book of American Negro Poetry.* New York: Harcourt Brace, 1922.

Jones, Meta. "Jazz Prosodies: Orality and Textuality." *Callaloo* 25, no. 1 (2002): 66–91.

Keeling, John. "Paul Laurence Dunbar and the Mask of Dialect." *Southern Literary Journal* 25, no. 2 (1993): 24–38.

Kent, George. "Aesthetic Values in the Poetry of Gwendolyn Brooks." In Mootry and Smith, *A Life Distilled,* 30–46.

Kunitz, Stanley. "Bronze by Gold." *Poetry* (April 1950): 53.

Kutzinski, Vera. "Changing Permanences: Historical and Literary Revisionism in Robert Hayden's 'Middle Passage.'" *Callaloo* 9, no. 1 (1986): 171–83.

Lee, Don L. "Gwendolyn Brooks: Beyond the Wordmaker—The Making of an African Poet." Preface to Brooks, *Report from Part One.*

Lewis, Ceri W. "The Historical Background of Early Welsh Verse." In *A Guide to Welsh Literature,* vol. 1, ed. A. O. H. Jarman and Gwilym Rees Hughes, 11–50. Swansea, UK: C. Davis, 1976.

Lewis, David Levering. *When Harlem Was in Vogue.* New York: Oxford University Press, 1989.

Locke, Alain. "The Concept of Race as Applied to Social Culture." In *The Critical Temper of Alain Locke: A Selection of His Essays on Art and Culture,* ed. Jeffery C. Stewart, 423–32. New York: Garland Publishing, Inc., 1983.

———. "The New Negro." In *Within the Circle: An Anthology of African American Literary Criticism From the Harlem Renaissance to the Present,* ed. Angelyn Mitchell, 21–31. Durham, NC: Duke University Press, 1994.

———. "Review of The Weary Blues, by Langston Hughes." *Palms* (October 1926): 24.

Manson, Michael. "Sterling Brown and the Vestiges of the Blues: The Role of Race in English Verse Structure." *MELUS* 21, no. 1 (Spring 1996): 21–40.

Melhem, D. H. *Gwendolyn Brooks: Poetry and the Heroic Voice.* Lexington: University of Kentucky Press, 1987.

Mootry, Maria K. "'The Step of Iron Feet': Creative Practice in the War Sonnets of Melvin B. Tolson and Gwendolyn Brooks." *Obsidian II: Black American Literature in Review* 2, no. 3 (1987): 69–87.

———, and Gary Smith, eds. *A Life Distilled: Gwendolyn Brooks, Her Poetry and Fiction.* Chicago: University of Chicago Press, 1987.

Morris, David B. *The Religious Sublime: Christian Poetry and Critical Tradition in 18th Century England.* Lexington: University of Kentucky Press, 1972.

Moryck, Brenda Ray. "A Point of View (An Opportunity Dinner Reaction)." *Opportunity* (August 1924): 248.

Nielsen, Aldon Lynn. *Black Chant: The Languages of African American Postmodernism.* New York: Cambridge University Press, 1997.

———. "Melvin B. Tolson and the Deterritorialization of Modernism." *African American Review* 26, no. 2 (1992): 241–55.

Nott, Walt. "'Uncultivated Barbarian to 'Poetical Genius': The Public Presence of Phillis Wheatley." *MELUS* 18, no. 3 (1993): 21–32.

Okeke-Ezigbo, Emeka. "Paul Laurence Dunbar: Straightening the Record." *College Language Association Journal* 24, no. 4 (1981): 481–96.

Pearce, Roy Harvey. *The Continuity of American Poetry.* Middletown, CT: Wesleyan University Press, 1987.

Perkins, David. General introduction to *English Romantic Writers.* New York: Harcourt Brace Jovanovich, 1967.

Pinson, Hermine. "The Aesthetic Evolution of Melvin B. Tolson: A Thematic Study of His Poetry." PhD diss., Rice University, 1991.

Post, Constance. "Image and Idea in the Poetry of Robert Hayden." *College Language Association Journal* 20 (1976): 164–75.

Redding, J. Saunders. *To Make a Poet Black.* Chapel Hill: University of North Carolina Press, 1939.

Redmond, Eugene. *Drumvoices: The Mission of African American Poetry: A Critical History.* Garden City, NY: Anchor Press, 1976.

Reid, Margaret Ann. *Black Protest Poetry: Polemics from the Harlem Renaissance and the Sixties.* New York: P. Lang, 2001.

Revell, Peter. *Paul Laurence Dunbar.* Boston: Twayne Publishers, 1979.

Richards, Phillip. "Phillis Wheatley and Literary Americanization." *American Quarterly* 44, no. 2 (June 1992): 163–91.

Richmond, M. A. *Bid the Vassal Soar: Interpretive Essays on the Life and Poetry of Phillis Wheatley and George Moses Horton.* Washington, DC: Howard University Press, 1974.

Rigsby, Gregory. "Form and Content in Phillis Wheatley's Elegies." *CLA Journal* 19, no. 2 (December 1975): 248–57.

Robinson, William H., ed. *Critical Essays on Phillis Wheatley.* Boston: G. K. Hall, 1982.

Russell, Mariann B. "Evolution of Style in the Poetry of Melvin B. Tolson." In *Black American Poets between Worlds, 1940–1960,* ed. R. Baxter Miller, 1–18. Knoxville: University of Tennessee Press, 1986.

Sanders, Mark. *Afro-Modernist Aesthetics and the Poetry of Sterling Brown.* Atlanta: University of Georgia Press, 1999.

Schopenhauer, Arthur. *The Works of Schopenhauer,* ed. Will Durant. New York: Ungar, 1955.

Shapiro, Karl. Preface to *Harlem Gallery,* by Melvin B. Tolson. New York: Twayne Publishers, 1965.

Sherman, Joan R. *The Black Bard of North Carolina: George Moses Horton and His Poetry.* Chapel Hill: University of North Carolina Press, 1997.

Shields, John C. "Phillis Wheatley's Subversive Pastoral." *Eighteenth Century Studies* 27, no. 4 (1994): 631–47.

Simmons, Ruth. Interview with Morley Safer. "Sharecropper's Daughter 18th President of Brown University." *60 Minutes,* March 4, 2001.

Smith, Cynthia J. "'To Maecenas': Phillis Wheatley's Invocation of an Idealized Reader." *Black American Literature Forum* 23, no. 3 (1989): 579–92.

Smith, Barbara Hernstein. *Contingencies of Value: Alternative Perspective for Critical Theory.* Cambridge, MA: Harvard University Press, 1988.

Smith, Gary. "Gwendolyn Brooks' 'Children of the Poor,' Metaphysical Poetry and the Inconditions of Love." *Obsidian II: Black Literature in Review* 1, nos. 1–2 (1986): 39–51.

———. "A Hamlet Rives Us: The Sonnets of Melvin B. Tolson." *College Language Association Journal* 29, no. 3 (1986): 261–75.

Sollors, Werner. Introduction to *The Invention of Ethnicity,* ed. Werner Sollors. New York: Oxford University Press, 1989.

Stanford, Ann Folwell. "An Epic with a Difference: Sexual Politics in Gwendolyn Brooks' 'The Anniad.'" *American Literature* 67, no. 2 (June 1995): 283–301.

———. "'Like Narrow Banners for Some Gathering War': Aesthetics and Gwendolyn Brooks' 'The Sundays of Satin-Legs Smith.'" *College Literature* 17, nos. 2–3 (1990): 162–82.

Story, Ralph. "Paul Laurence Dunbar: Master Player in a Fixed Game." *CLA Journal* 28, no. 1 (1983): 30–55.

Sundquist, Eric. *The Hammers of Creation: Folk Culture in Modern African American Fiction.* Athens: University of Georgia Press, 1992.

Tate, Allen. Preface to *Libretto for the Republic of Liberia.* New York: Twayne Publishers, 1953.

Tate, Claudia. "Anger So Flat: Gwendolyn Brooks' *Annie Allen.*" In Mootry and Smith, *A Life Distilled,* 140–50.

———, ed. "Gwendolyn Brooks." In *Black Women Writers at Work,* 39–48. New York: Continuum, 1983.

Thomas, Lorenzo. *Extraordinary Measures: Afro-Centric Modernism and Twentieth Century Poetry.* Tuscaloosa: University of Alabama Press, 2000.

Tolson, Melvin B. *Caviar and Cabbage: Selected Columns by Melvin B. Tolson from the Washington Tribune, 1937–1944,* ed. Robert Farnsworth. Columbia: University of Missouri Press, 1982.

———. *Harlem Gallery and Other Poems of Melvin B. Tolson,* ed. Raymond Nelson. Charlottesville: University of Virginia Press, 1999.

———. "The Harlem Group of Negro Writers." Master's thesis, Columbia University, 1940.

———. "Odyssey of a Manuscript." *New Letters* 48, no. 1 (1981): 1–22.

————. Papers of Melvin B. Tolson. Library of Congress, Washington, DC.

Tracy, Stephen. *Langston Hughes and the Blues.* Urbana: University of Illinois Press, 1988.

Trumpener, Katie. *Bardic Nationalism: The Romantic Novel and the British Empire.* Princeton, NJ: Princeton University Press, 1997.

Turco, Lewis. "*Angle of Ascent:* The Poetry of Robert Hayden." In *Robert Hayden: Essays on the Poetry,* ed. Laurence Goldstein and Robert Chrisman, 175–93. Ann Arbor: University of Michigan Press, 2001.

Turner, Darwin T. "Paul Laurence Dunbar: The Forgotten Symbol." *Journal of Negro History* 52, no. 1 (1967): 3–10.

Wagner, Jean. *Black Poets of the United States: From Paul Laurence Dunbar to Langston Hughes.* Urbana: University of Illinois Press, 1973.

Walker, Jeffery. *Bardic Ethos and the American Epic Poem.* Baton Rouge: Louisiana State University Press, 1989.

Washington, Mary Helen. "'The Darkened Eye Restored': Notes Toward a Literary History of Black Women." In *Within the Circle: An Anthology of African American Literary Criticism from the Harlem Renaissance to the Present,* ed. Angelyn Mitchell, 442–53. Durham, NC: Duke University Press, 1994.

Webster, Harvey Curtis. "Pity the Giants." *Nation* 195, no. 5 (1962): 96–97.

Wheatley, Phillis. *The Poems of Phillis Wheatley,* ed. Julian D. Mason Jr. 1966; Chapel Hill: University of North Carolina Press, 1989.

Whitman, Walt. "A Backward Glance o'er Travel'd Roads." In *Walt Whitman: Poetry and Prose,* 313–27. New York: Library of America, 1982.

Wilcox, Kirstin. "The Body into Print: Marketing Phillis Wheatley." *American Literature* 71, no. 1 (1999): 1–29.

Will, Barbara. *Gertrude Stein, Modernism, and the Problem of "Genius."* Edinburgh: Edinburgh University Press, 2000.

Willard, Carla. "Phillis Wheatley's Turns of Praise: Heroic Entrapment and the Paradox of Revolution." *American Literature* 67, no. 2 (1995): 233–56.

Williams, Kenny J. "The World of Satin-Legs, Mrs. Sallie, and the Blackstone Rangers: The Restricted Chicago of Gwendolyn Brooks." In Mootry and Smith, *A Life Distilled,* 47–70.

Williams, Pontheolla. *Robert Hayden: A Critical Analysis of His Poetry.* Urbana: University of Illinois Press, 1987.

Williams, Wilburn. "The Covenant of Timelessness with Time: Symbolism and History in Robert Hayden's *Angle of Ascent.*" *Massachusetts Review* 18 (1977): 731–49.

————. "The Desolate Servitude of Language: A Reading of Melvin B. Tolson." PhD diss., Yale University, 1979.

Zafar, Rafia. *We Wear the Mask: African Americans Write American Literature, 1760–1870.* New York: Columbia University Press, 1997.

Index

absolutism, in criticism, 7, 159, 161, 202. *See also* authenticity

Afro-modernism, 86, 120–21, 124

agency: 1, 4–6, 11–12, 193–94, 196–97, 226, 234; in abolitionist poetry, 21–24, 48–49; and ethnicity, 52, 79–80, 94; and gender, 43–44, 47, 118, 121–25; as imagination, 81–83, 93, 111, 118, 121–25, 128, 143, 155, 223; and modernism, 118, 133–34, 137, 214; and parody, 60–65; in poetics 4–6, 116–17, 122, 236–38, 254; in poststructuralist thought, 9; in romanticism, 82–83; as self-fashioning, 21–24, 29–31, 158–59, 258

"Akhenaten" (Hayden), 180–81, 193

Americanism: in abolitionist poetry, 24–36; in Paul Laurence Dunbar's work, 66–80; in the Harlem Renaissance, 83–87, 100–101, 128

"And shall I prime my children, pray, to pray?" (Brooks), 151

Angle of Ascent (Hayden), 160, 163, 169, 178–96, 255

"Anniad, The" (Brooks), 145–50

Annie Allen (Brooks), 118, 121, 140–52

"Antebellum Sermon, An" (Dunbar), 64–65

assimilation, 5, 10, 16, 163, 190, 191, 197, 200–201, 226; and gender, 43–44, 47–48; and ideological struggle, 87–89, 181; of national values, 71; and poetic mastery, 22; as poetic theme, 193; and politics of fulfillment, 73; as resistance, 5, 10, 21, 36, 79, 193–94, 255, 259; as self-defeating practice, 21, 54, 86, 119, 255; of traditional poetics, 30–33, 67, 200, 202, 226

Auden, W. H., 160, 169

authenticity: and binary logic, 214; as a construction, 94, 163; as critical priority, 7–8, 53, 239; and exclusion, 115; and identity, 9, 56, 60; and vernacular culture, 2, 48, 53, 123, 201

bard: in Celtic culture, 12–13; as poetic ideal, 12–15. *See also* bardic genius

bardic genius, 12–18, 255; in abolitionist poetry, 20–22, 36–37; for Gwendolyn Brooks, 120–25, 133–35, 150–55; for Paul Laurence Dunbar, 48, 50, 53–54, 70–75, 77–80; in the Harlem Renaissance, 83–87; for Robert Hayden, 157–58, 160–64, 174–76, 187–90; for Melvin B. Tolson, 201–4, 214–16, 246, 251–52